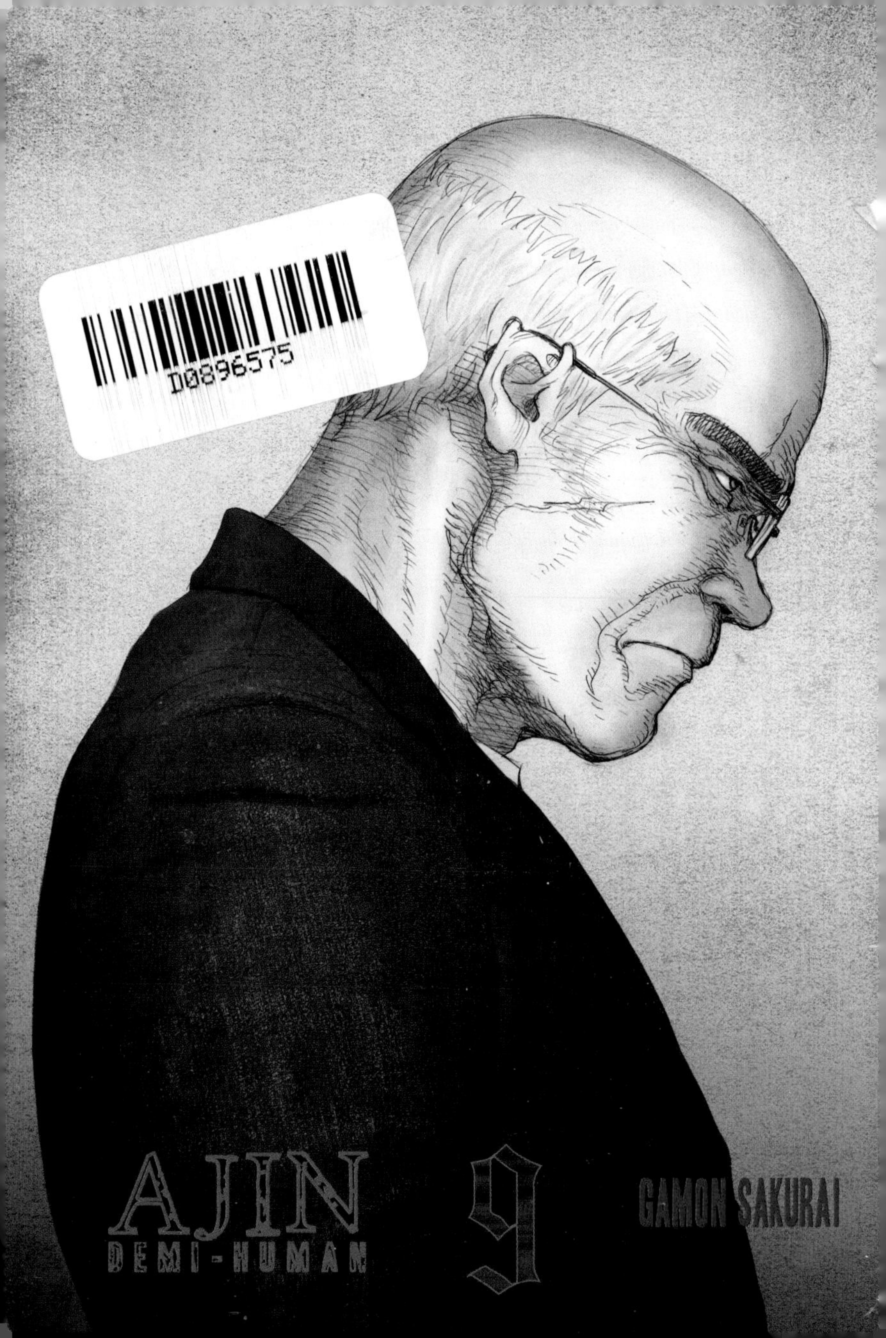
AJIN
DEMI-HUMAN
9
GAMON SAKURAI

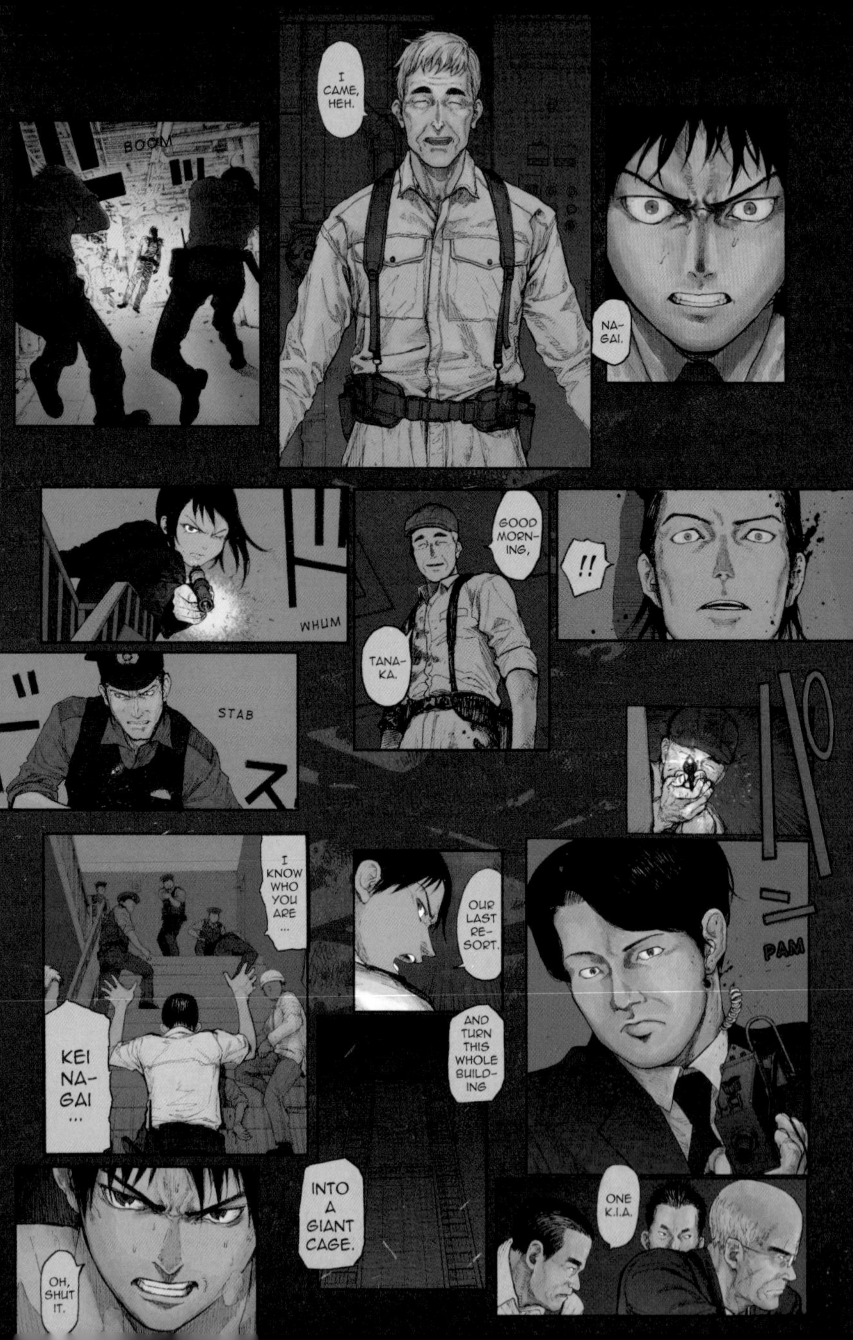
NA-GAI.
I CAME, HEH.
BOOM
!!
GOOD MORNING,
TANAKA.
WHUM
STAB
PAM
OUR LAST RESORT.
AND TURN THIS WHOLE BUILDING
I KNOW WHO YOU ARE ...
KEI NAGAI ...
ONE K.I.A.
INTO A GIANT CAGE.
OH, SHUT IT.

DRAMATIS PERSONAE

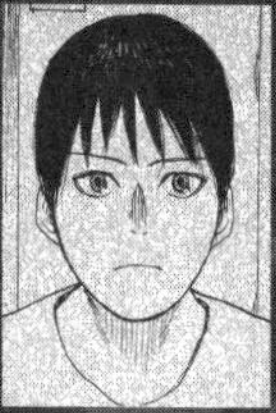

KEI NAGAI

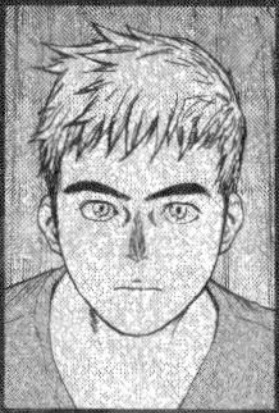

KO NAKANO

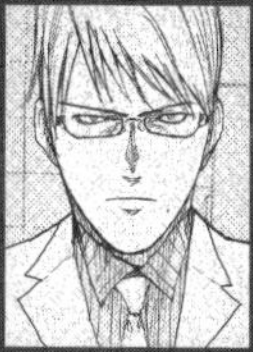

YUU TOSAKI

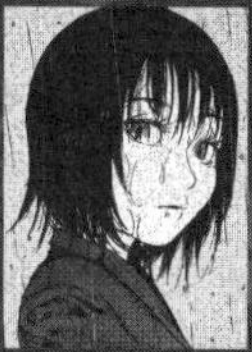

IZUMI SHIMOMURA

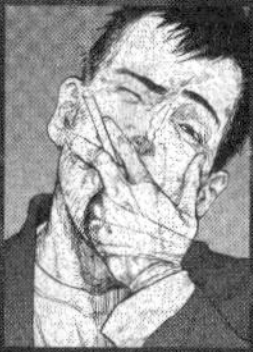

DR. IKUYA OGURA

THE FOUR BLACK SUITS

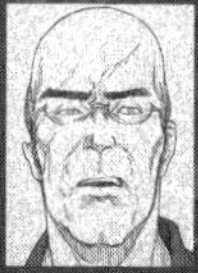

HIRASAWA

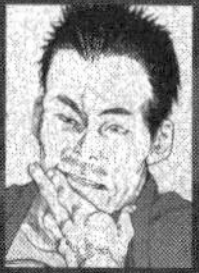

MANABE

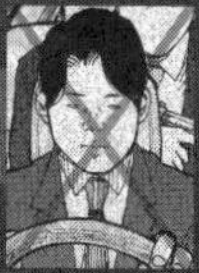

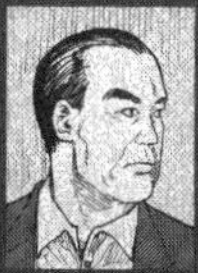

FORGE SAFETY

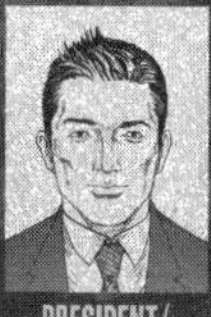

PRESIDENT/ KEIICHI KAI

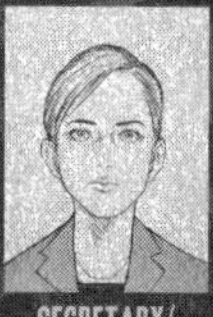

SECRETARY/ NAOMI LI

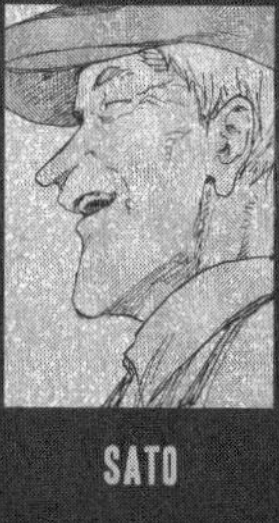

SATO

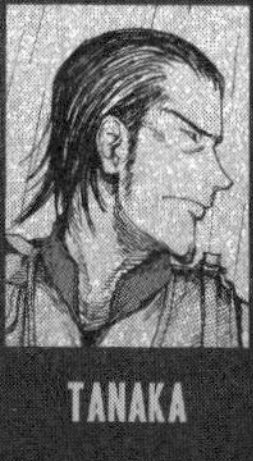

TANAKA

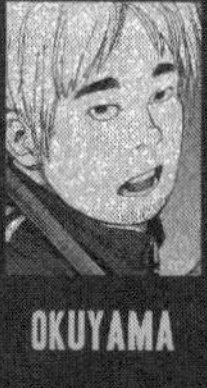

OKUYAMA

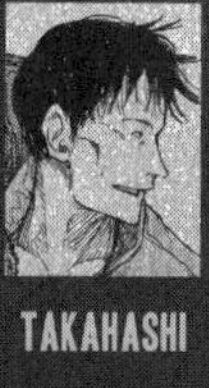

TAKAHASHI

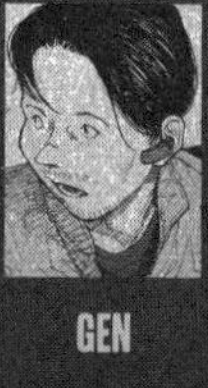

GEN

File 39: Battlefield Hardline ②

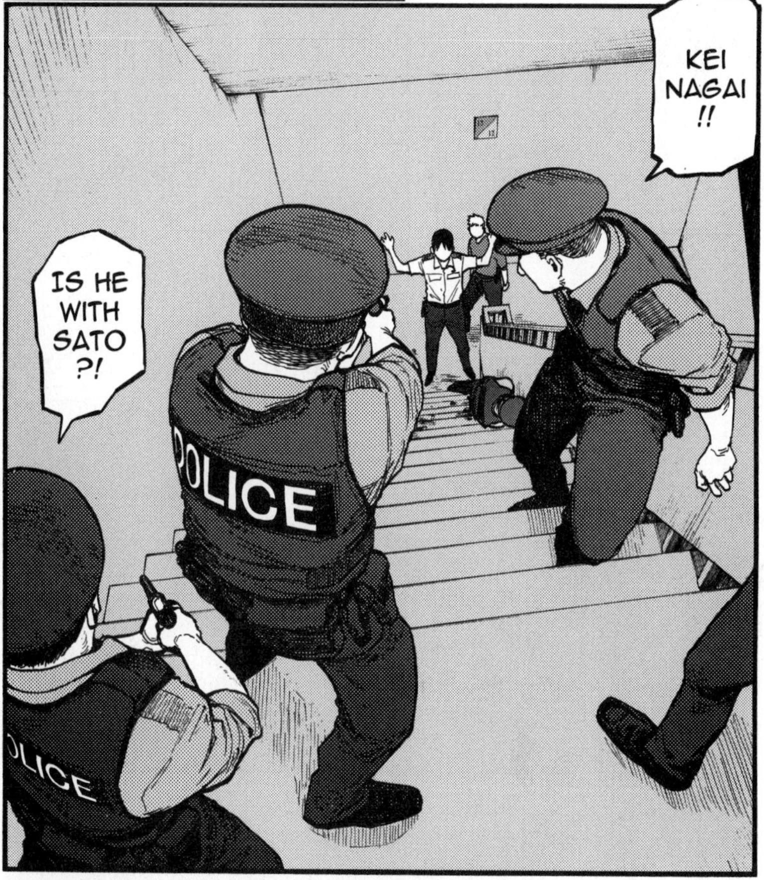
KEI NAGAI !!
IS HE WITH SATO ?!
POLICE
POLICE

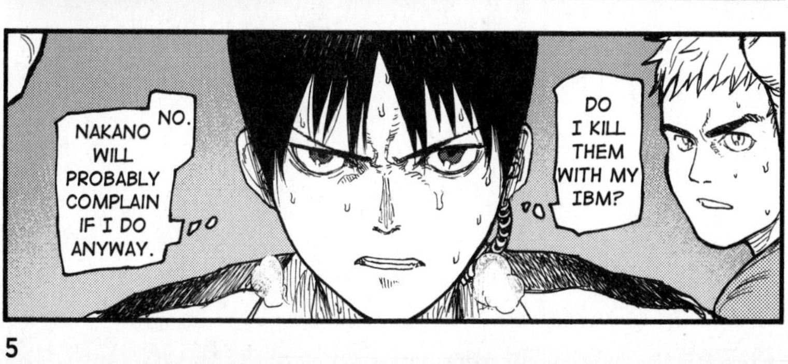
DO I KILL THEM WITH MY IBM?
NO. NAKANO WILL PROBABLY COMPLAIN IF I DO ANYWAY.

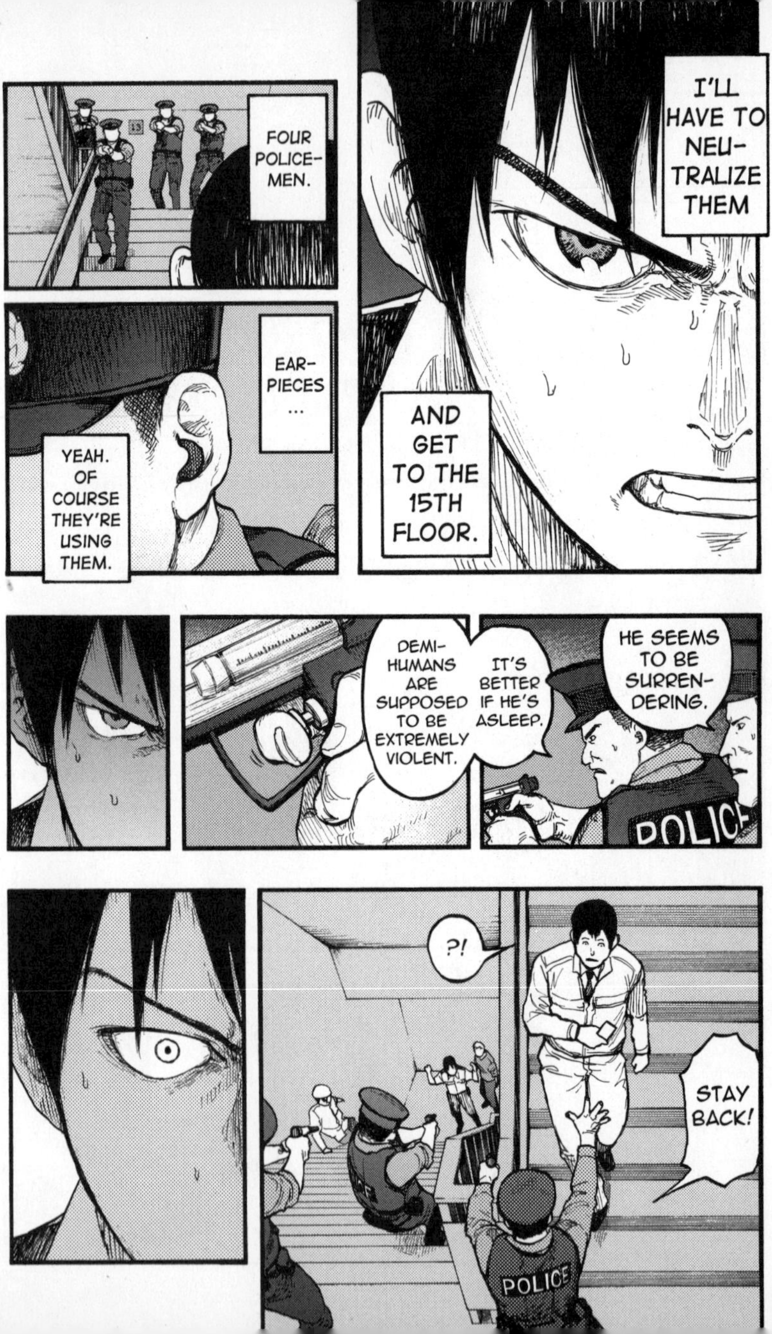
I'LL HAVE TO NEU-TRALIZE THEM
AND GET TO THE 15TH FLOOR.
FOUR POLICE-MEN.
EAR-PIECES ...
YEAH. OF COURSE THEY'RE USING THEM.
HE SEEMS TO BE SURREN-DERING.
IT'S BETTER IF HE'S ASLEEP.
DEMI-HUMANS ARE SUPPOSED TO BE EXTREMELY VIOLENT.
?!
STAY BACK!
POLICE

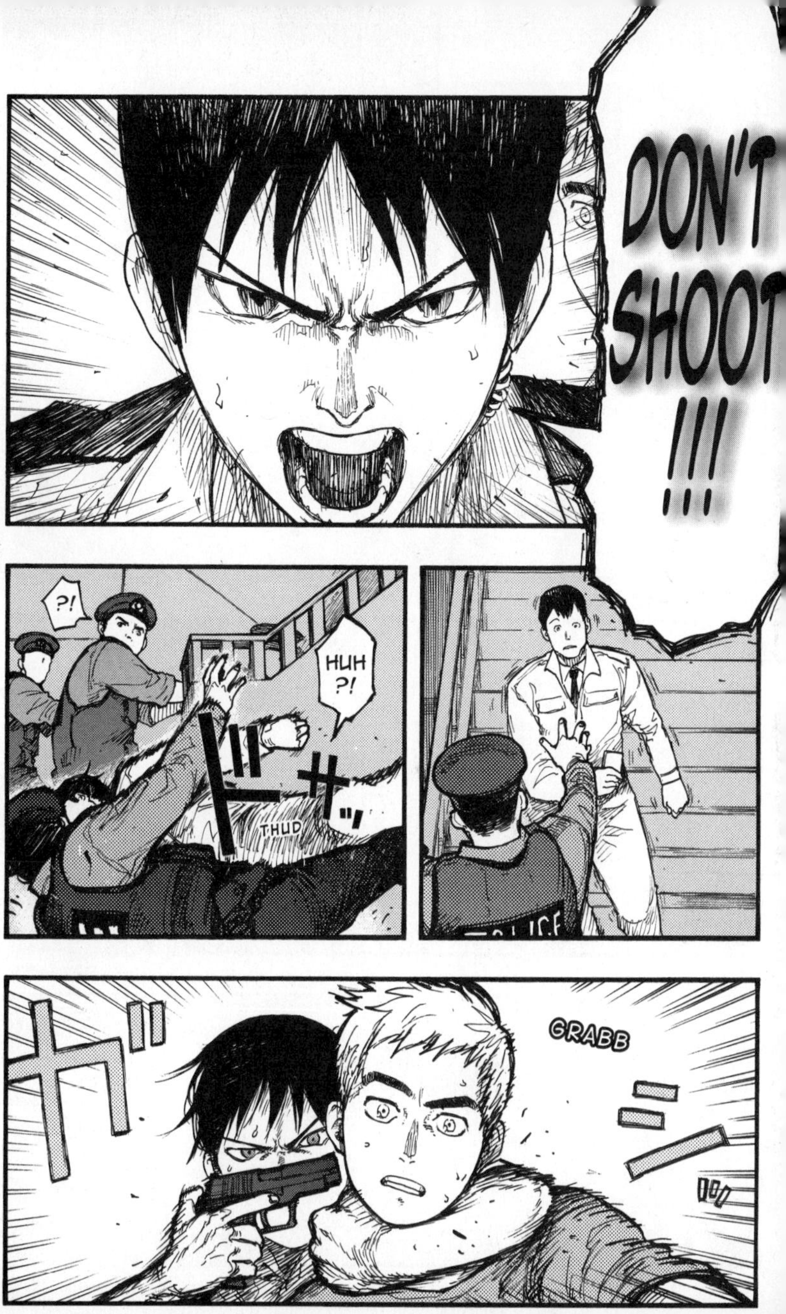
DON'T SHOOT !!!
HUH ?!
?!
THUD
GRABB

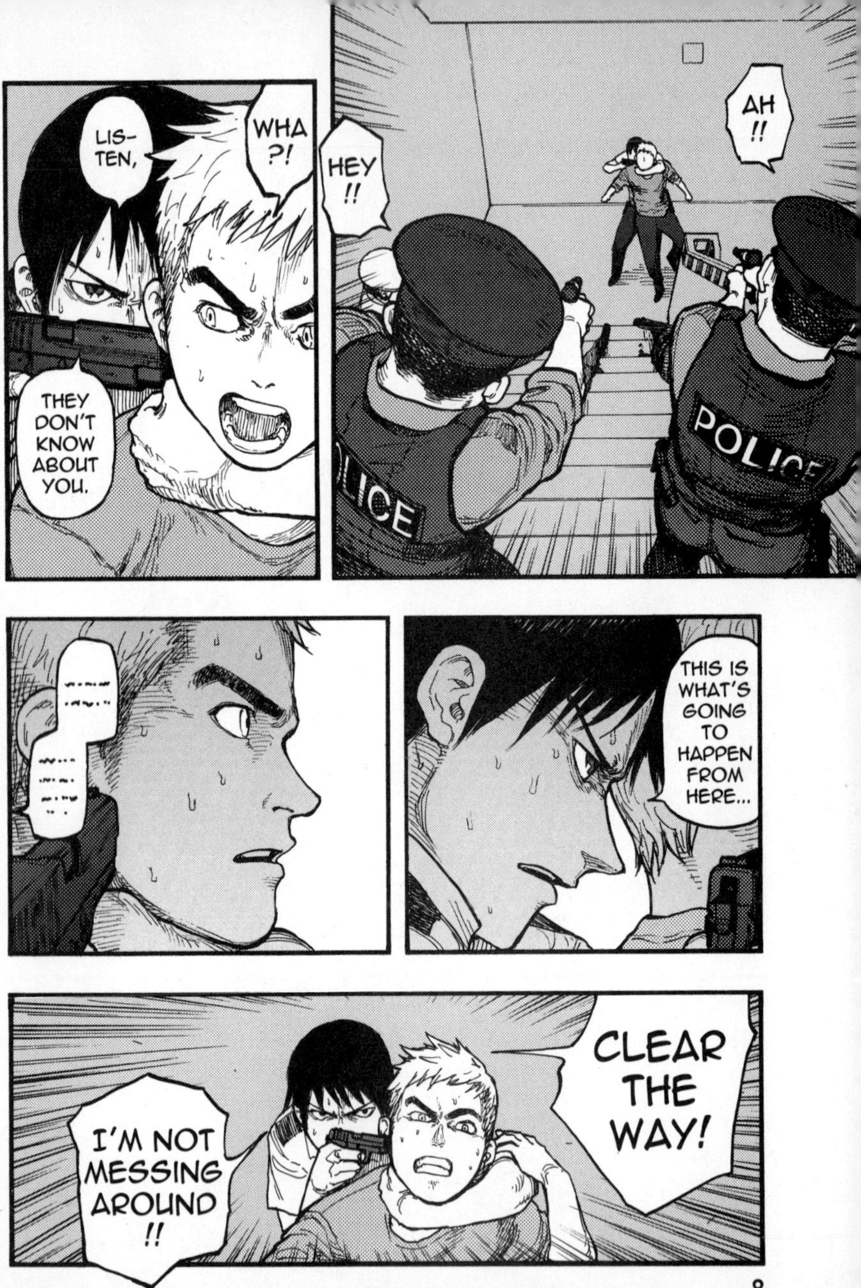
AH !!
HEY !!
WHA ?!
LIS- TEN,
THEY DON'T KNOW ABOUT YOU.
POLICE
POLICE
THIS IS WHAT'S GOING TO HAPPEN FROM HERE...
CLEAR THE WAY!
I'M NOT MESSING AROUND !!

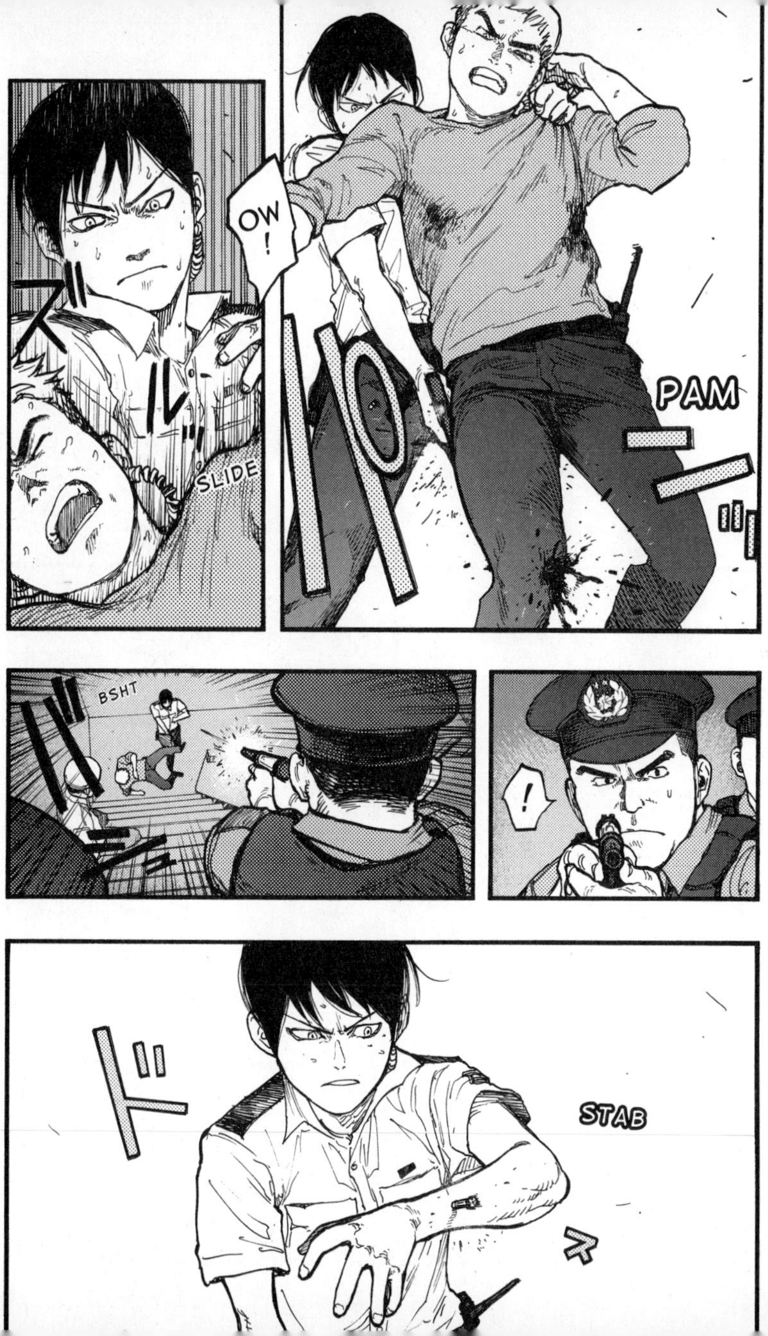
OW!
PAM
SLIDE
!
BSHT
STAB

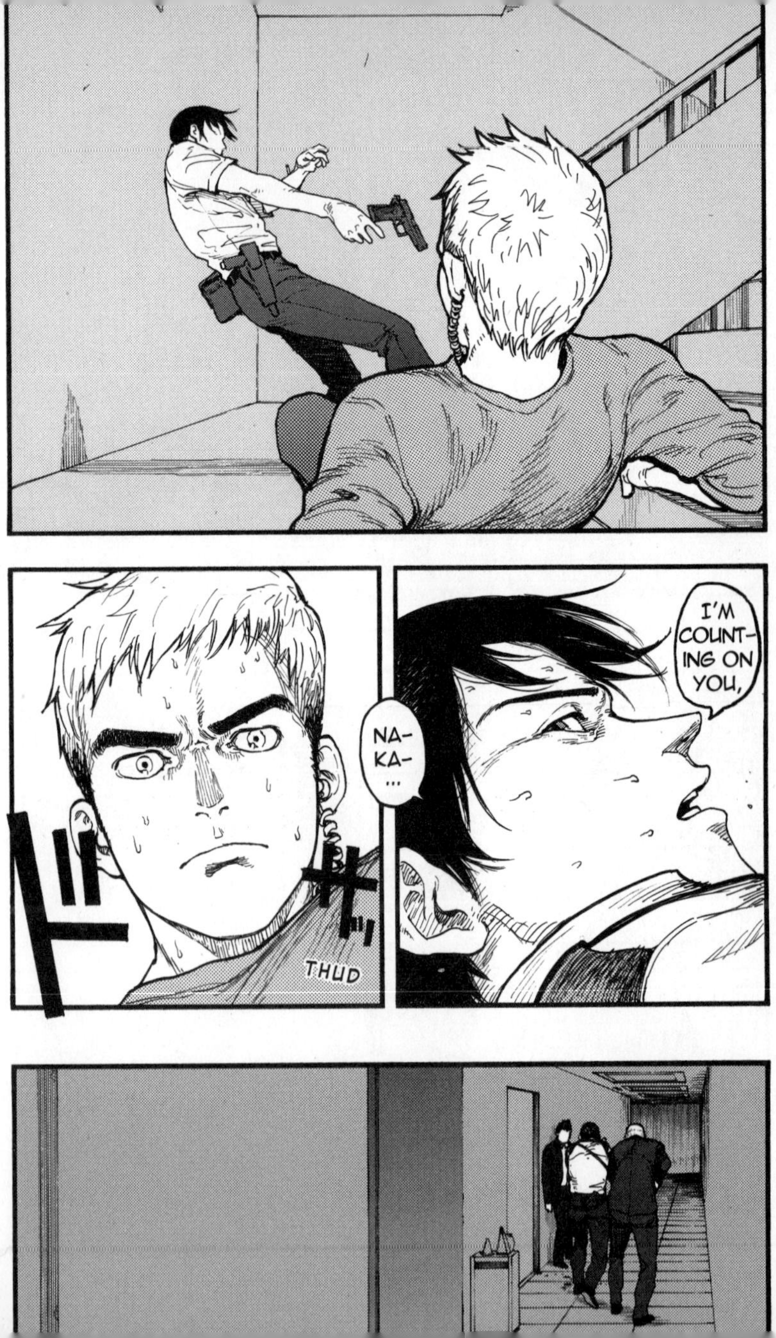
I'M COUNTING ON YOU,
NA-KA-...
THUD

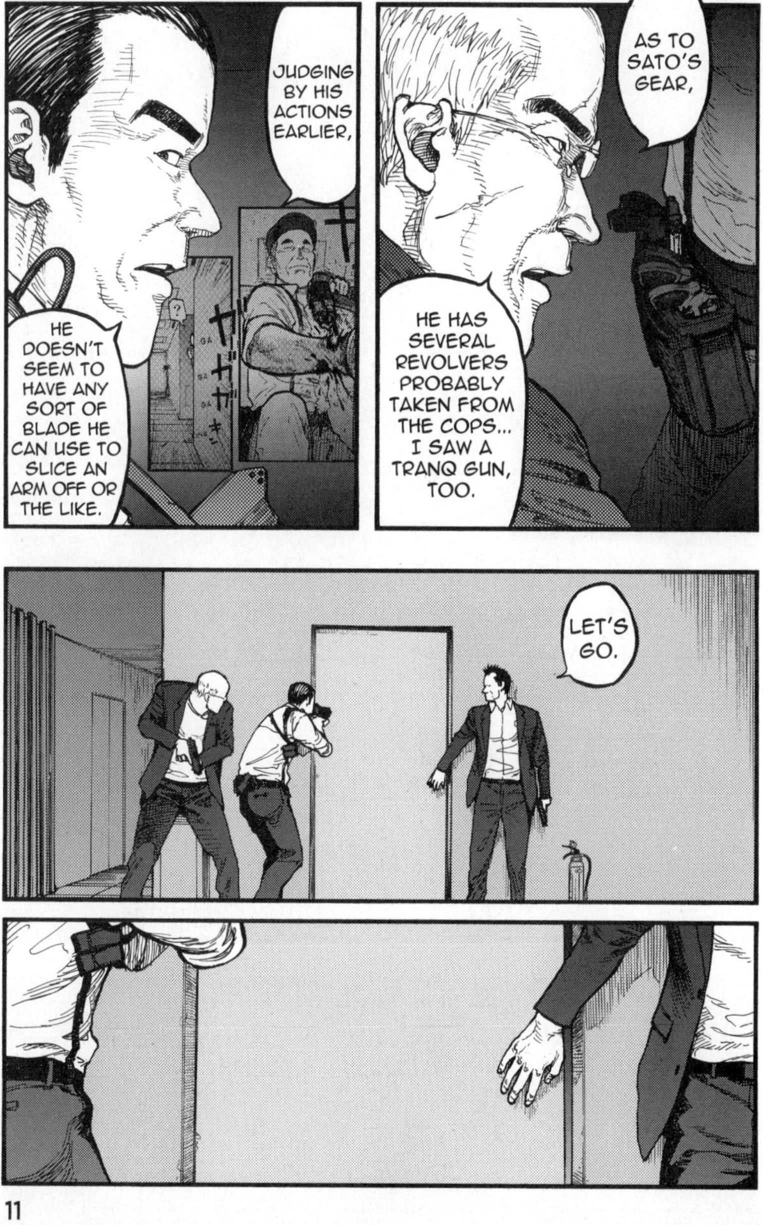
AS TO SATO'S GEAR,
HE HAS SEVERAL REVOLVERS PROBABLY TAKEN FROM THE COPS... I SAW A TRANQ GUN, TOO.
JUDGING BY HIS ACTIONS EARLIER,
HE DOESN'T SEEM TO HAVE ANY SORT OF BLADE HE CAN USE TO SLICE AN ARM OFF OR THE LIKE.
LET'S GO.

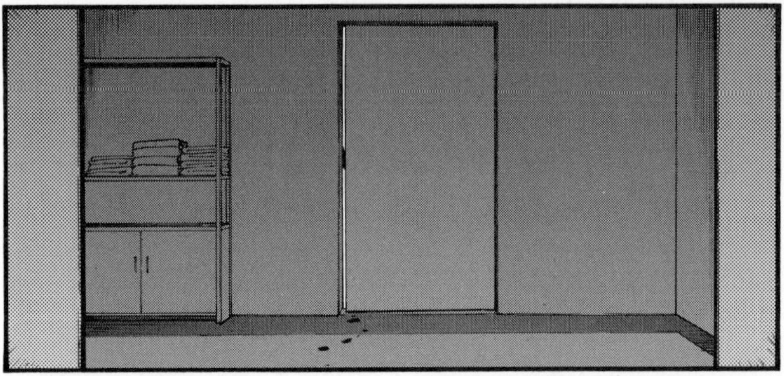
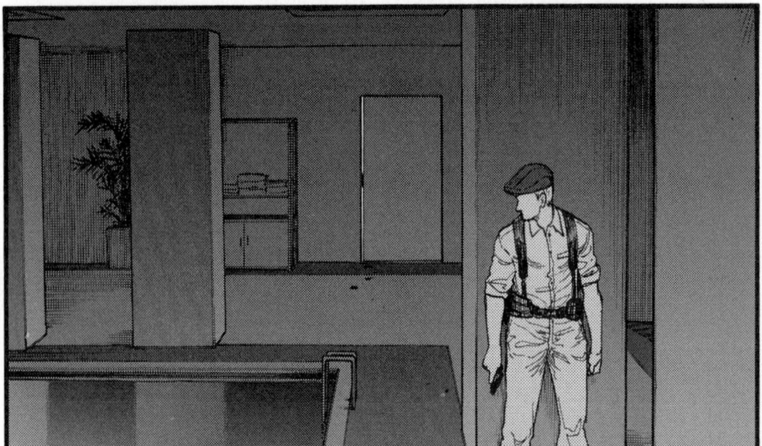
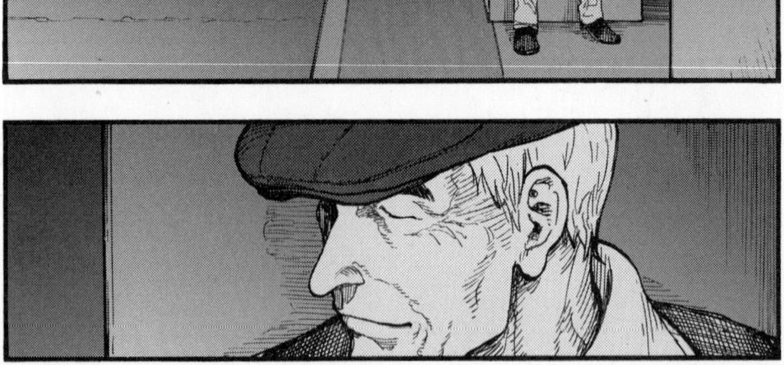

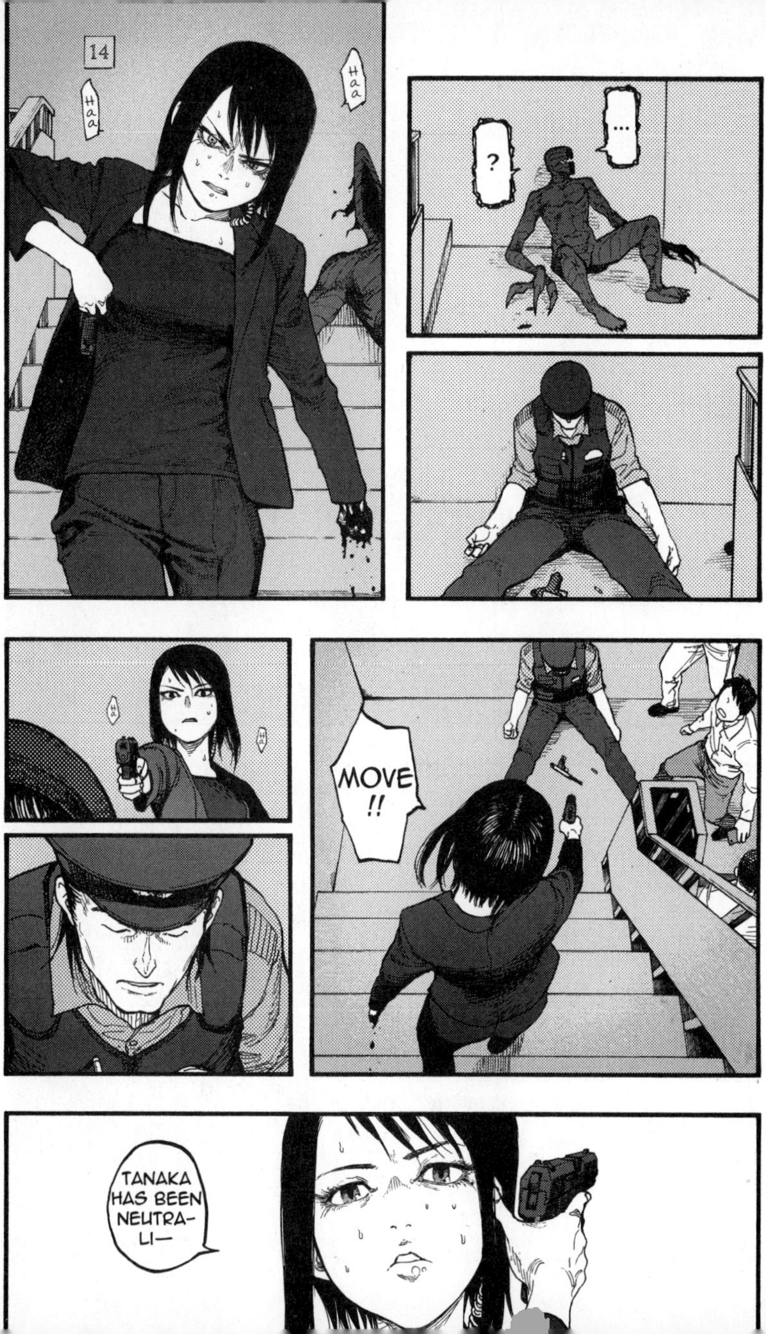
…
?
Haa
Haa
14
MOVE !!
Ha
Ha
TANAKA HAS BEEN NEUTRA-LI—

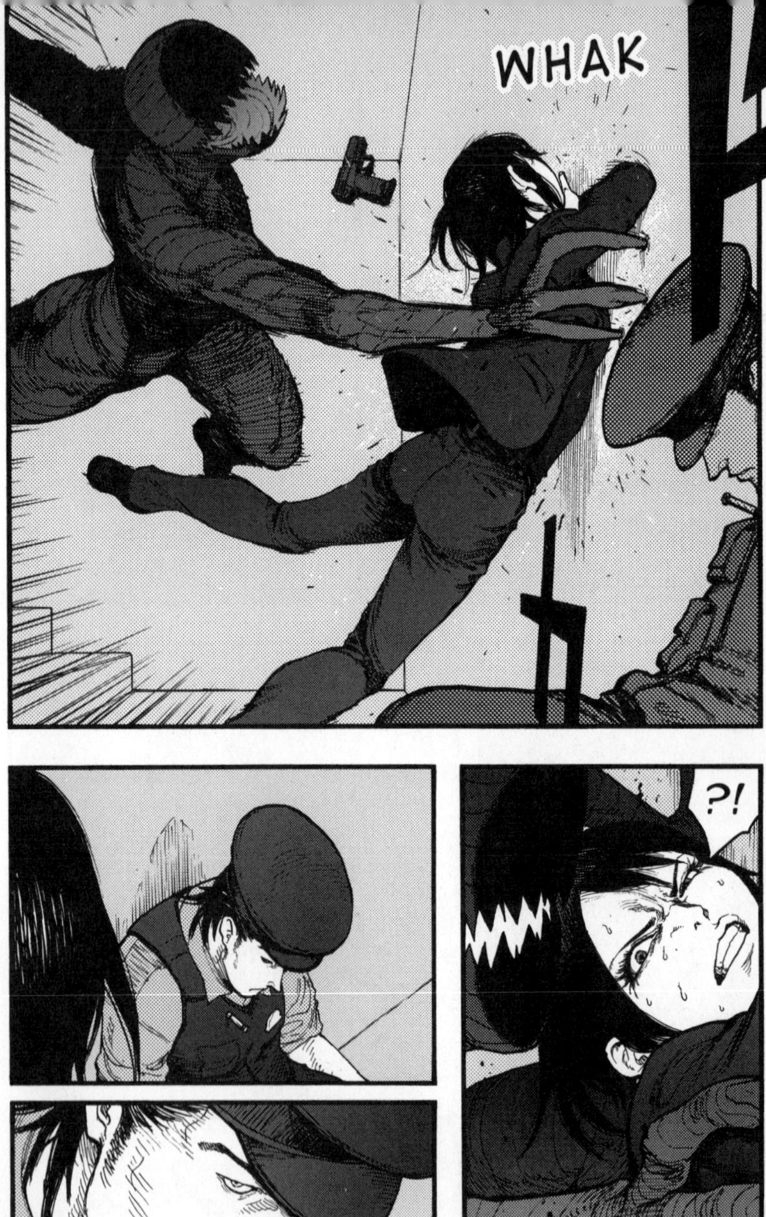
WHAK
?!

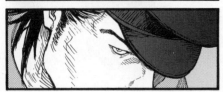

HIS BULLET-PROOF VEST...

IT WAS TOO THICK...

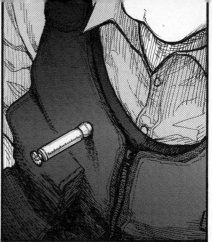

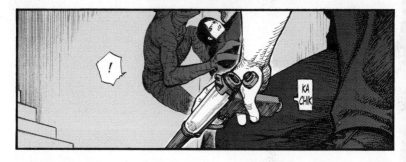

!

KA CHIK

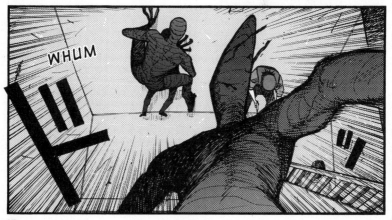

WHUM

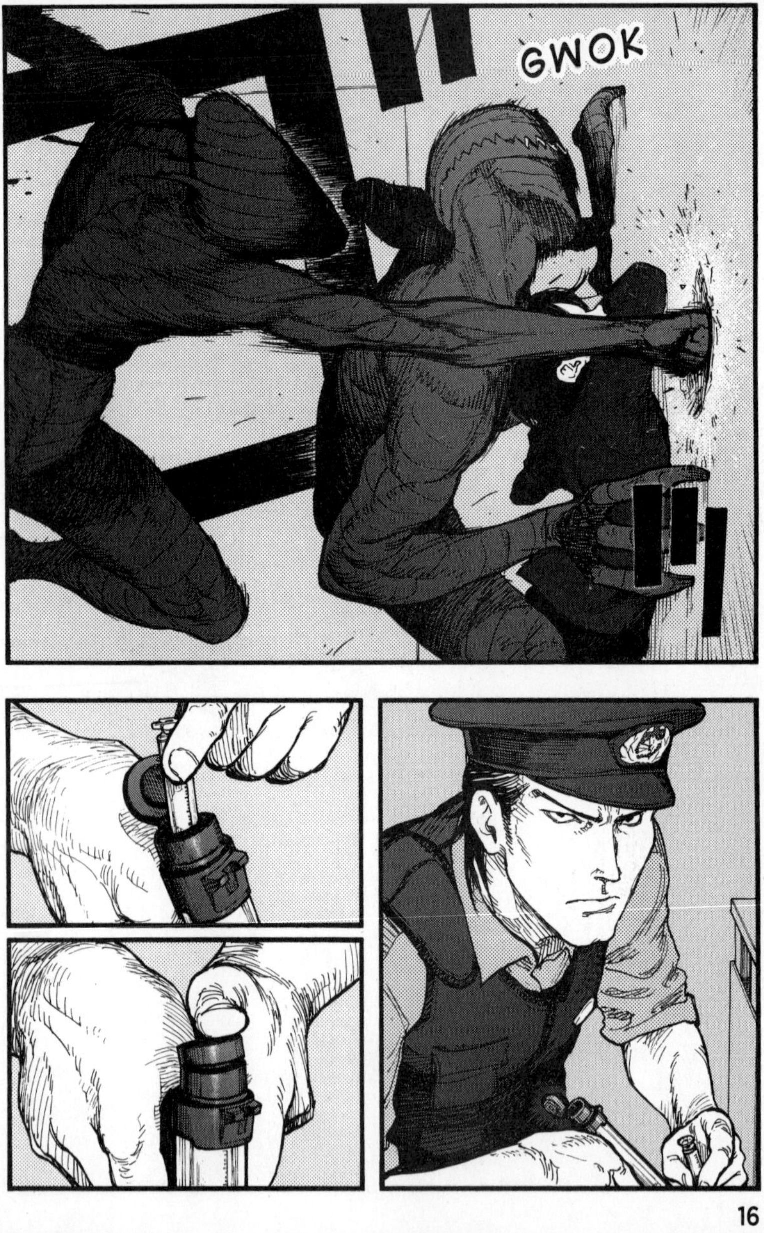
GWOK

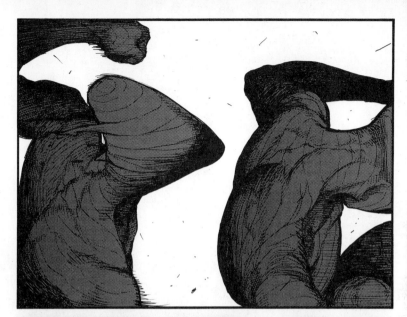

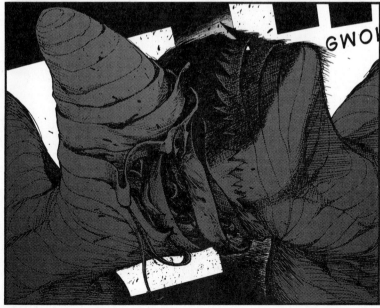

GWO

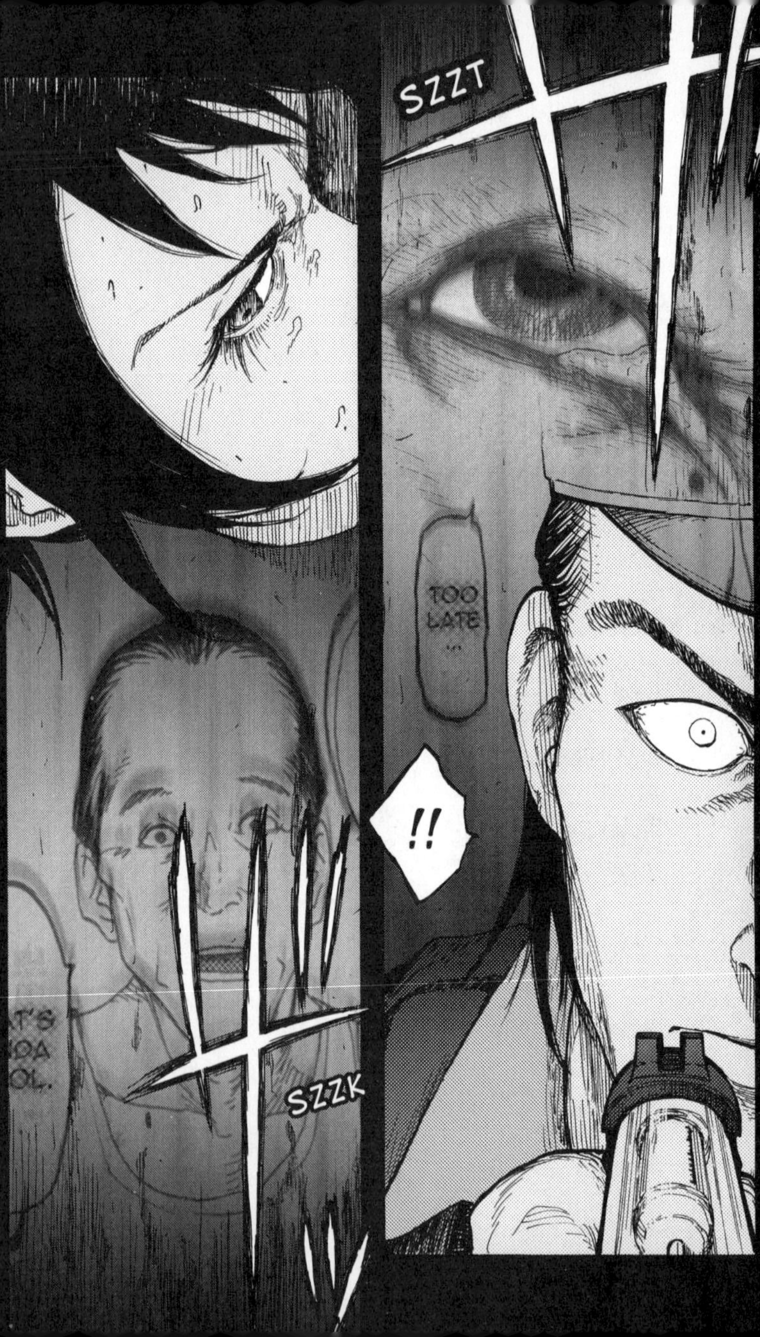
SZZT
TOO LATE ...
!!
SZZK

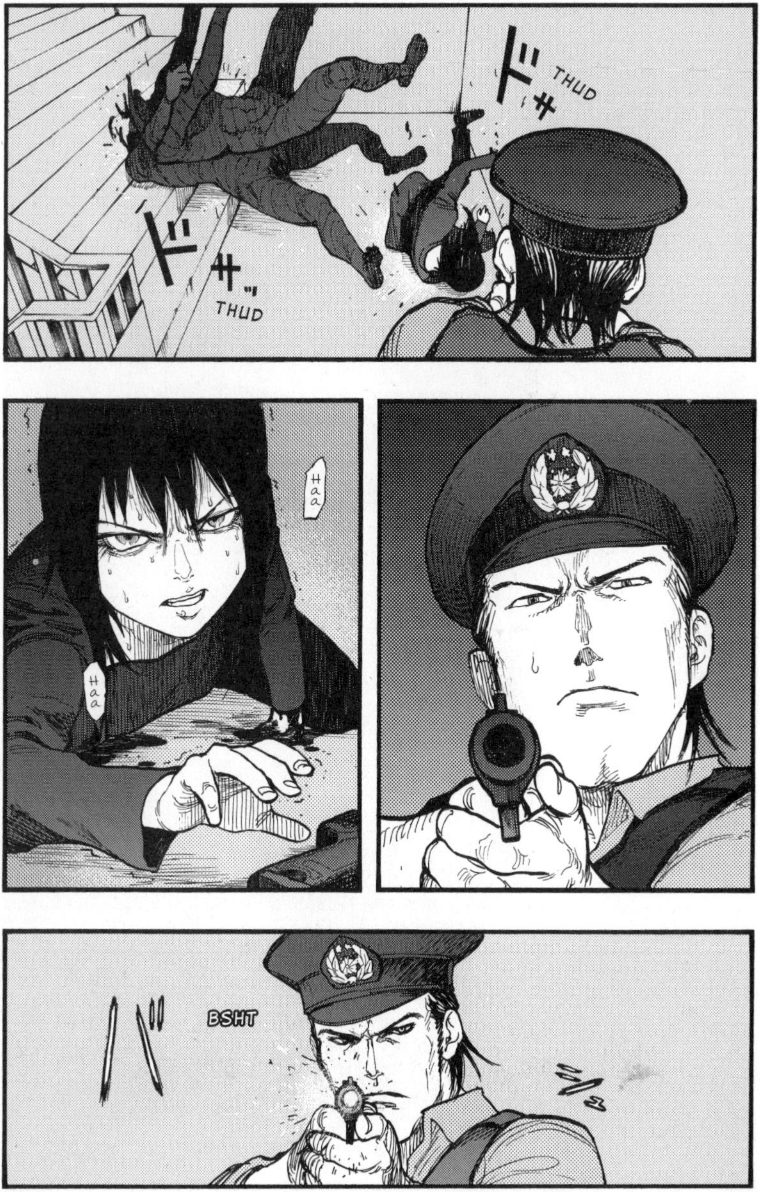
ドサ
THUD
ドサッ
THUD
Haa
Haa
バッ
BSHT

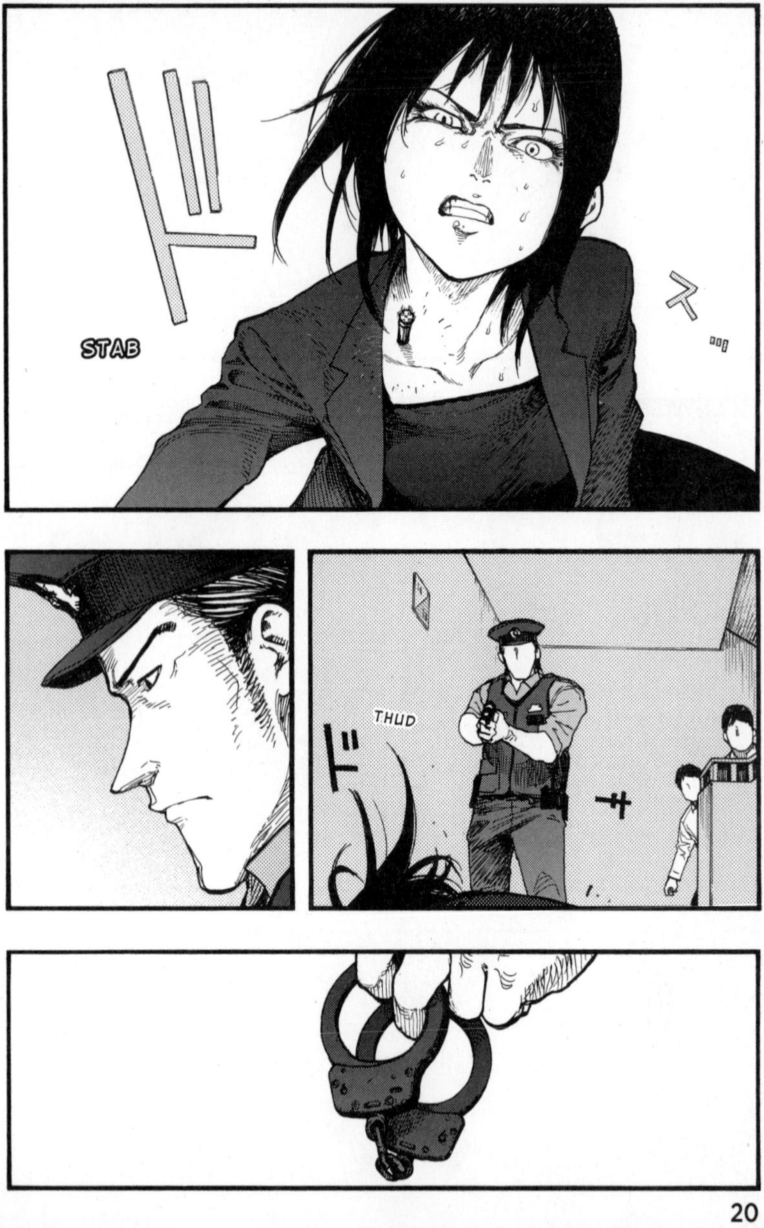
STAB
THUD

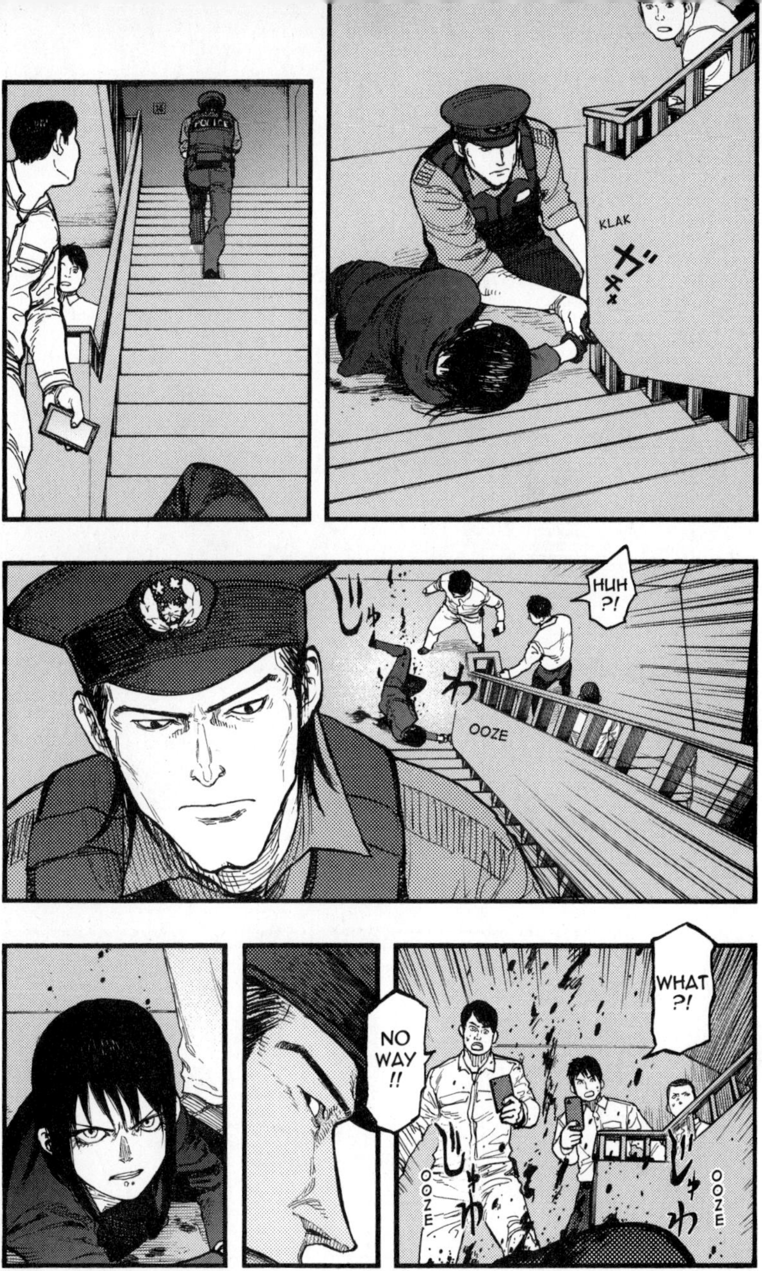
KLAK
HUH?!
OOZE
WHAT?!
NO WAY!!
OOZE
OOZE

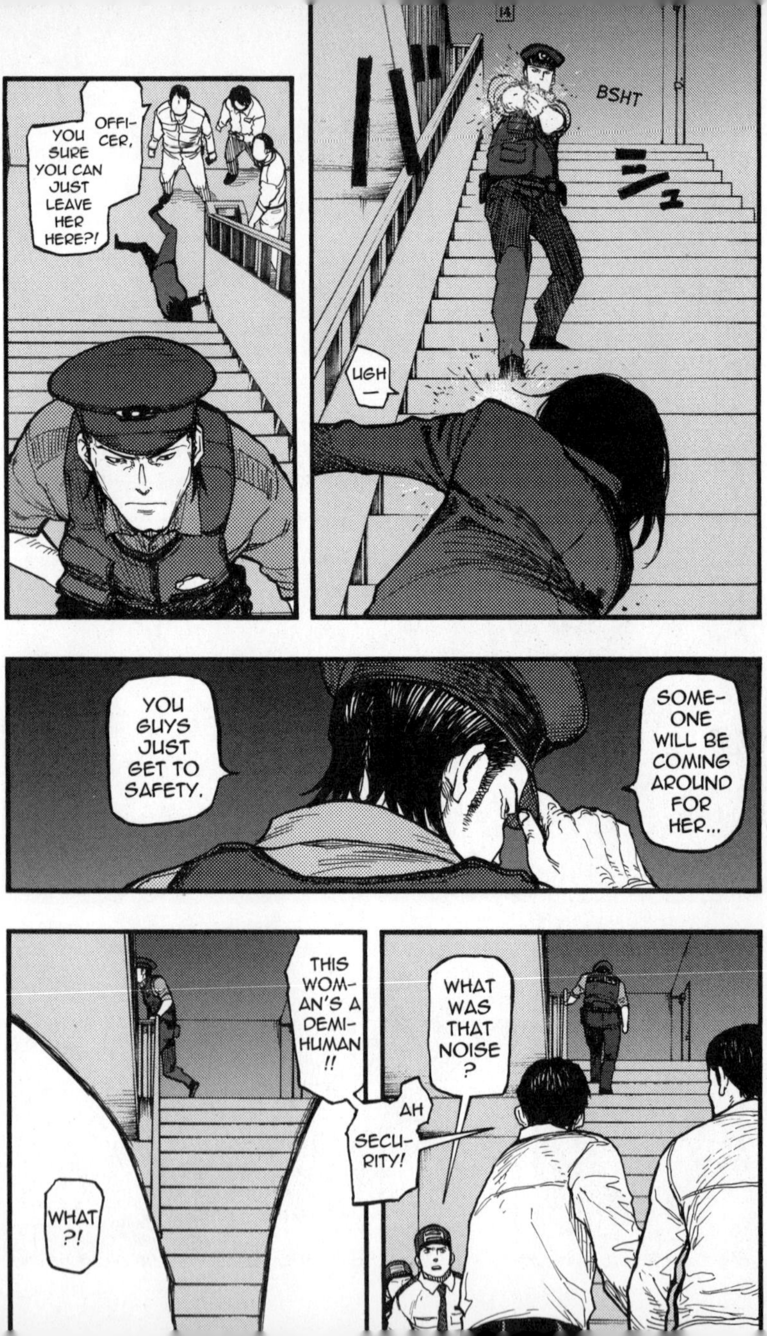
BSHT
シュ
UGH —
OFFICER, YOU SURE YOU CAN JUST LEAVE HER HERE?!
SOMEONE WILL BE COMING AROUND FOR HER...
YOU GUYS JUST GET TO SAFETY.
WHAT WAS THAT NOISE?
AH SECURITY!
THIS WOMAN'S A DEMIHUMAN!!
WHAT?!

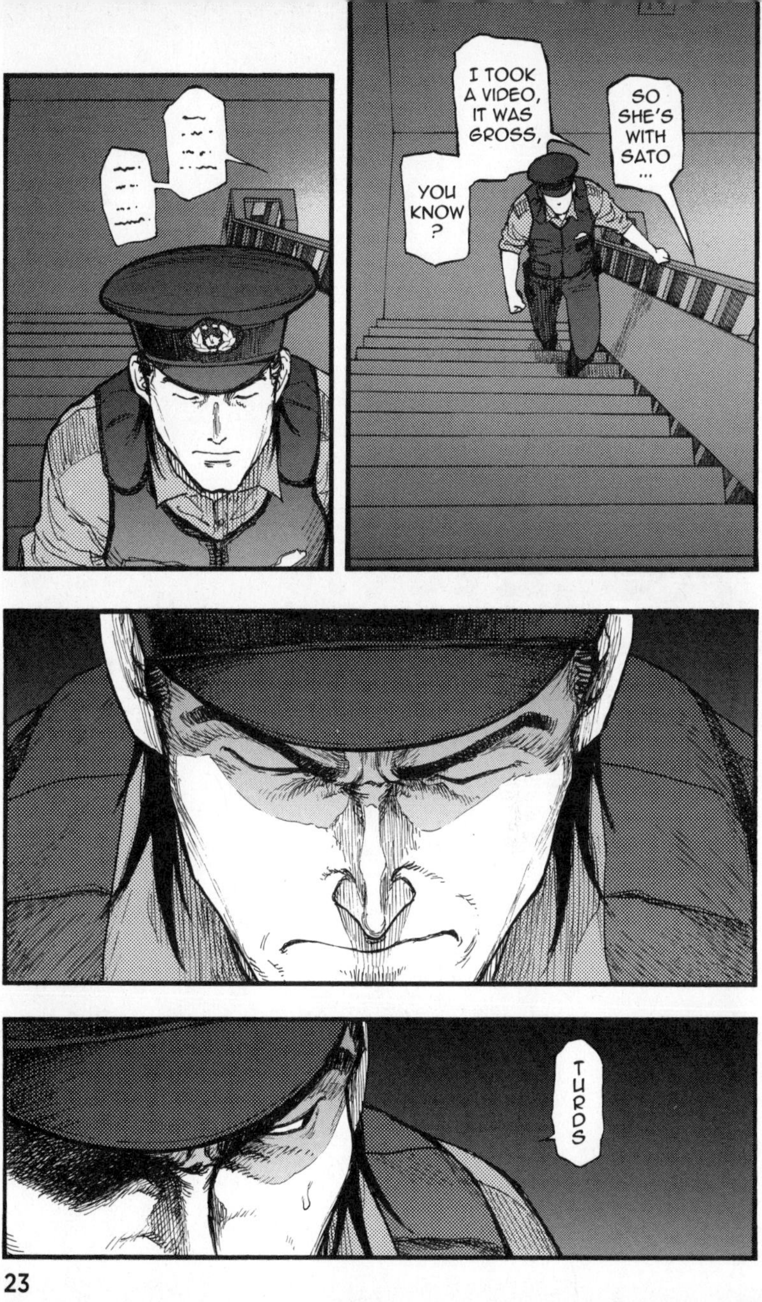
I TOOK A VIDEO, IT WAS GROSS,
YOU KNOW ?
SO SHE'S WITH SATO ...
TURDS

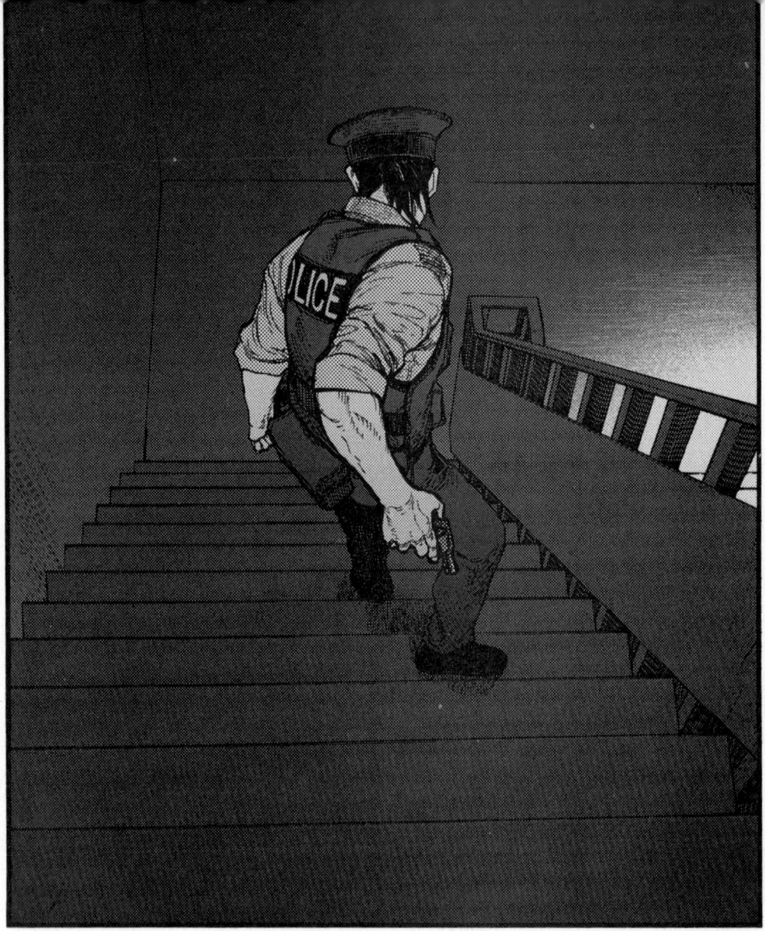
LICE

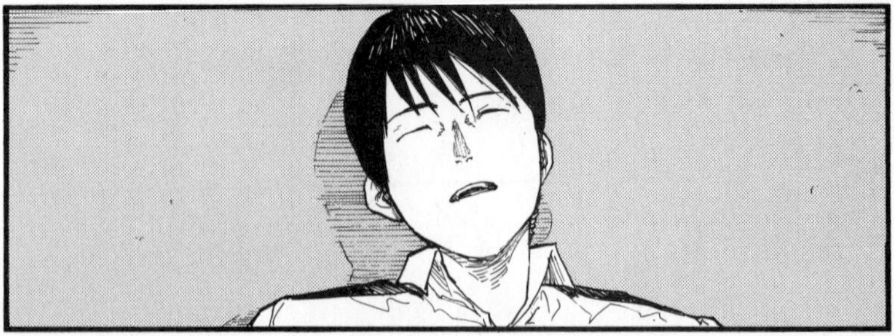

The Seattle Public Library

Central Library
www.spl.org

Checked Out On: 9/13/2023 18:14

XXXXXXXXXXX2185

Item Title	Due Date
0010091975960	10/4/2023
Ajin : demi-human. 9	

# of Items: 1

Balance Due: $14.00

Renew items at www.spl.org/MyAccount
or 206-386-4190

Sign up for due date reminders
at www.spl.org/notifications

You're free to be you at the Library.
Express who you are and choose what
you want to read, listen to or learn.

www.spl.org/FreeTo

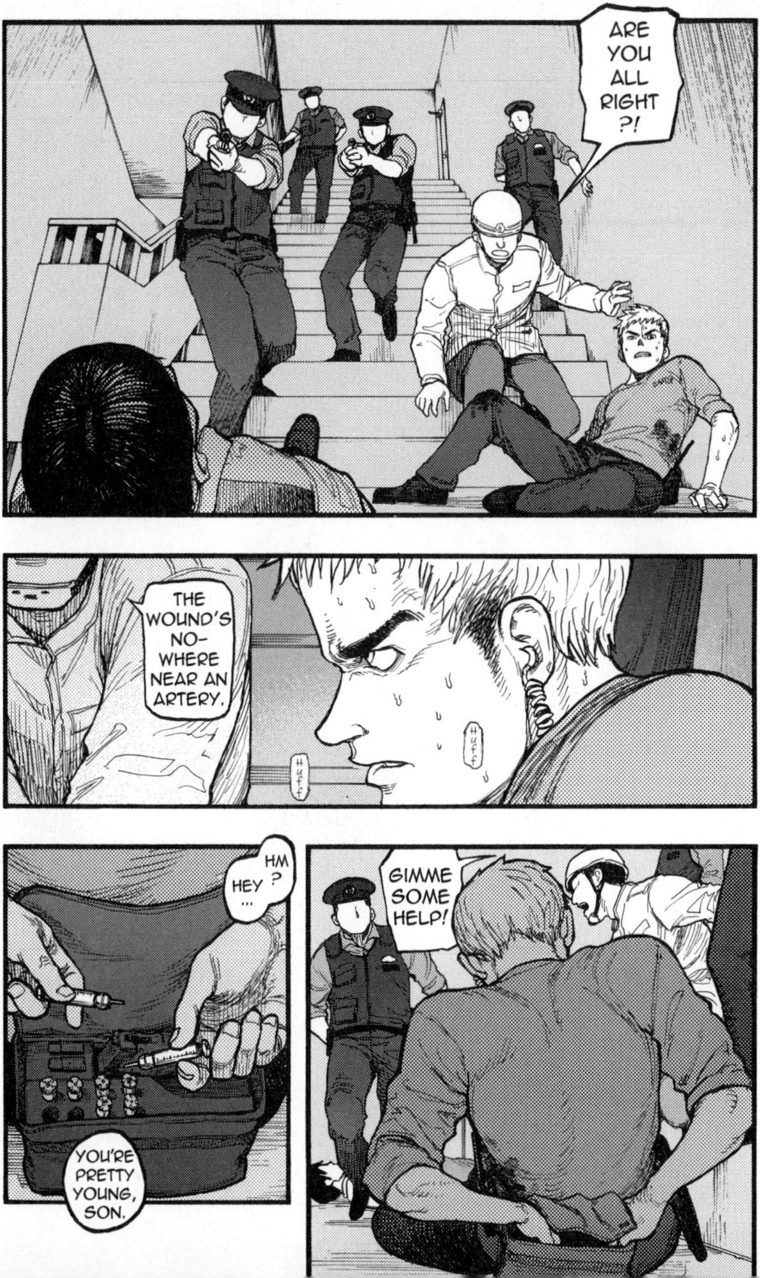
ARE YOU ALL RIGHT ?!
THE WOUND'S NO-WHERE NEAR AN ARTERY.
Huff
Huff
GIMME SOME HELP!
HM ?
HEY ...
YOU'RE PRETTY YOUNG, SON.

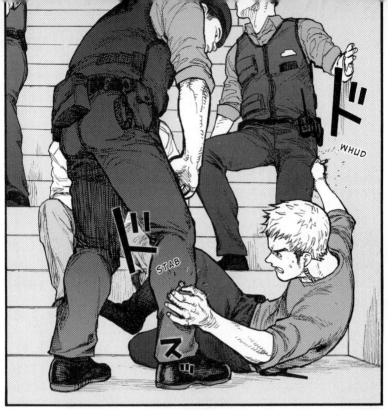

ド
WHUD

ド
STAB

ス

SLUMP

SLUMP

ガ
ク

HUH ?!

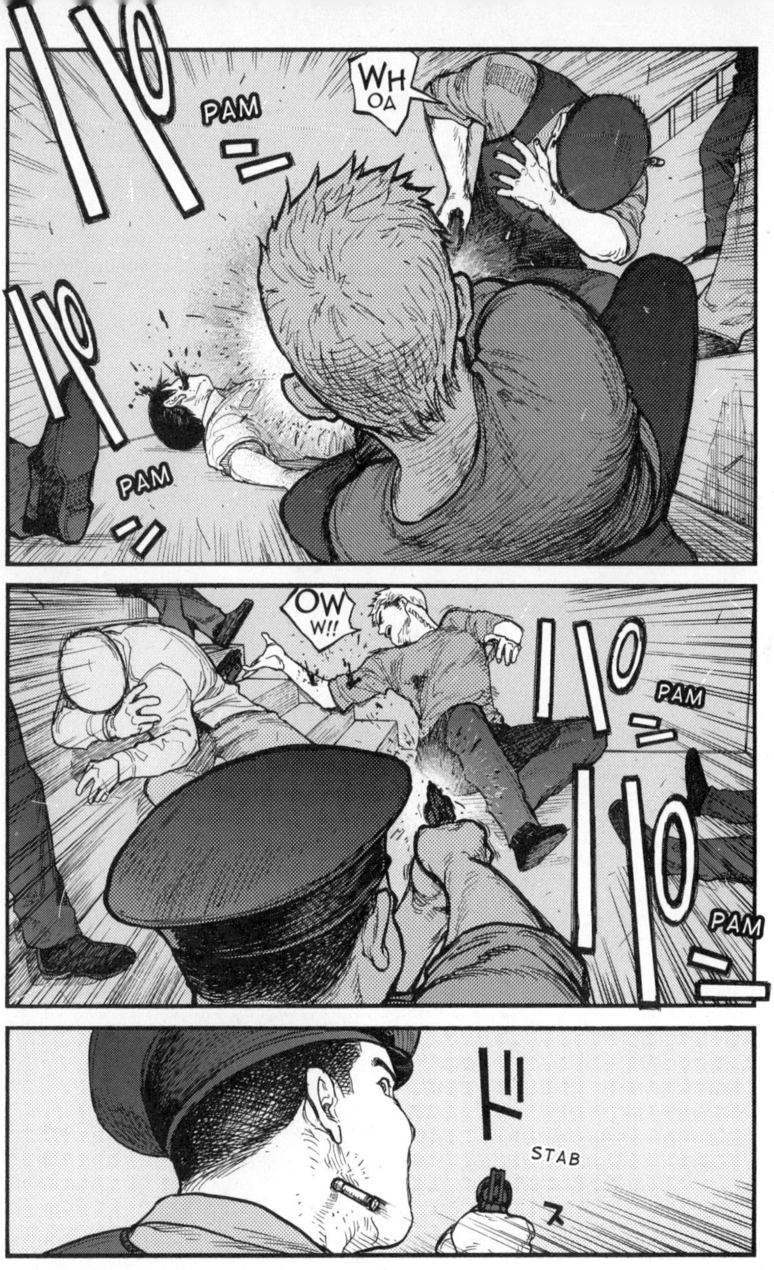
WHOA
PAM
PAM
OWW!!
PAM
PAM
STAB

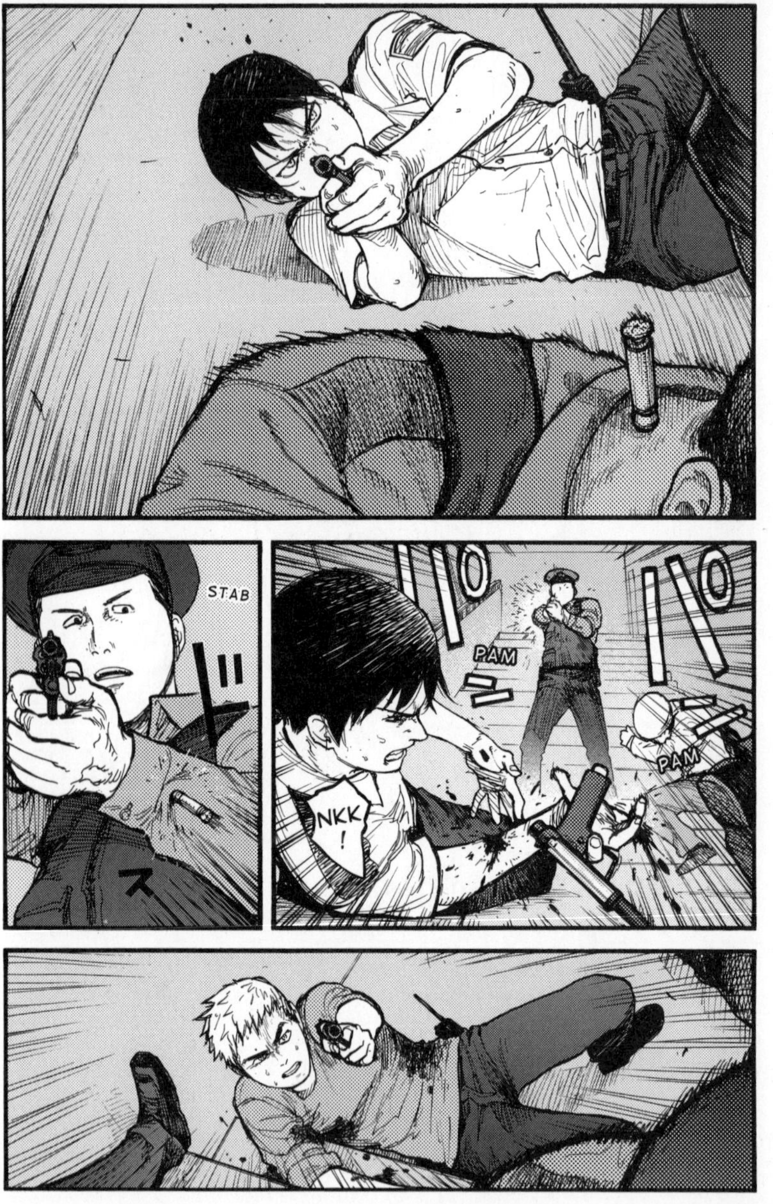
PAM
PAM
NKK!
STAB

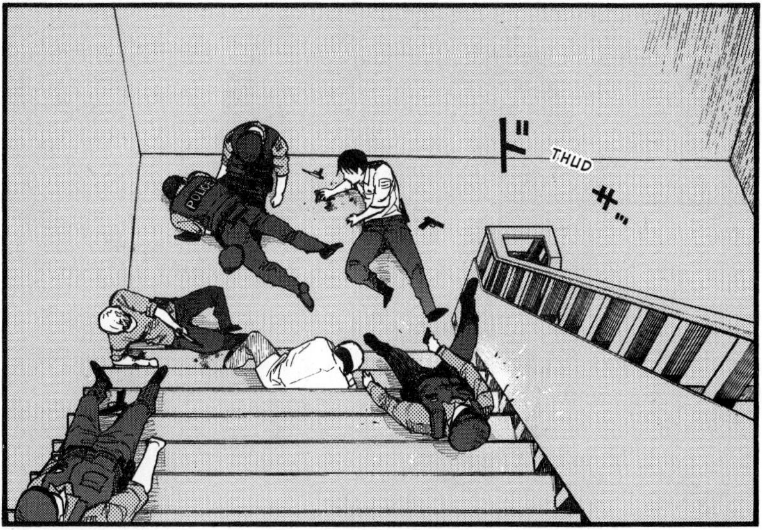
ド
THUD
ザッ
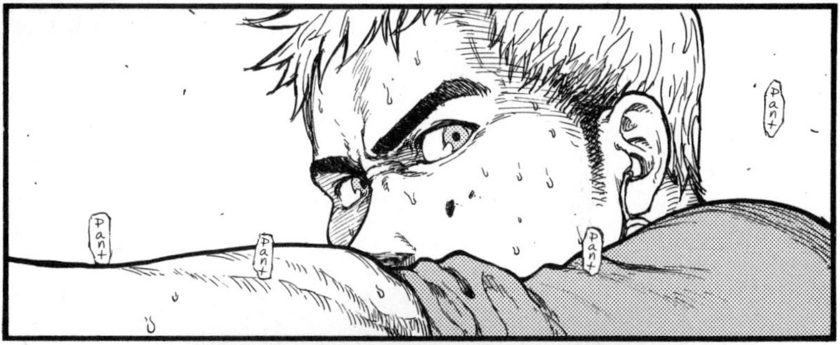
Pant
Pant
Pant
Pant
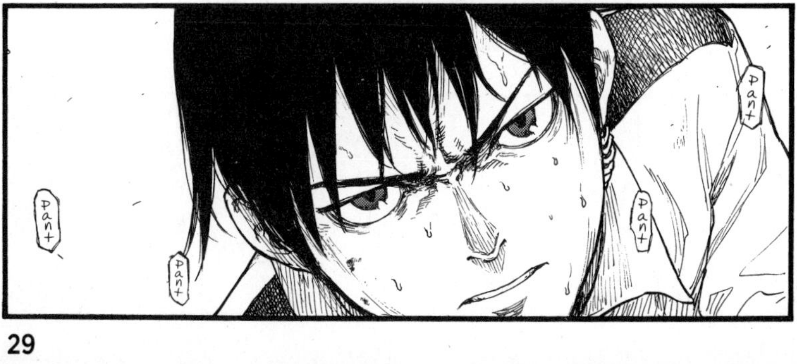
Pant
Pant
Pant
Pant

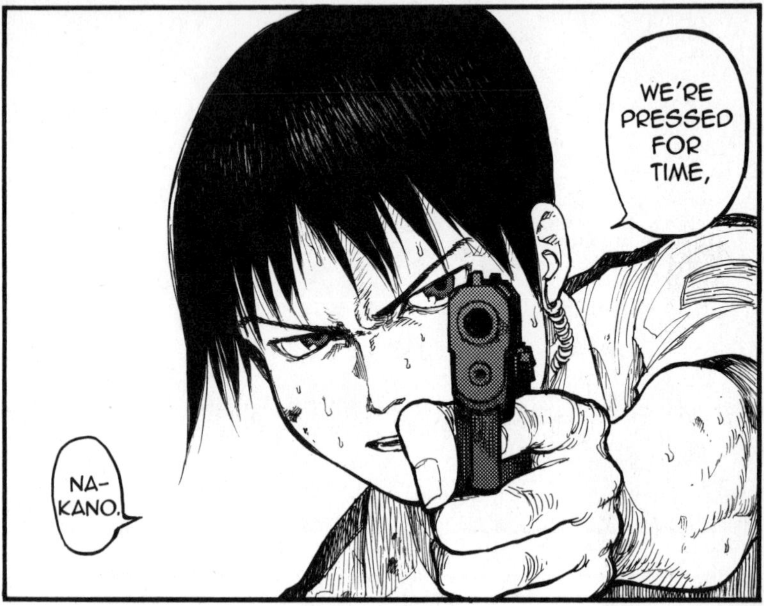
WE'RE PRESSED FOR TIME,
NA-KANO.

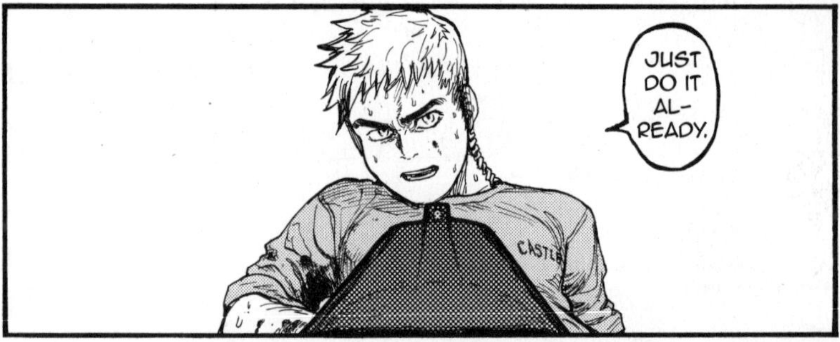
JUST DO IT AL-READY.
CASTLE

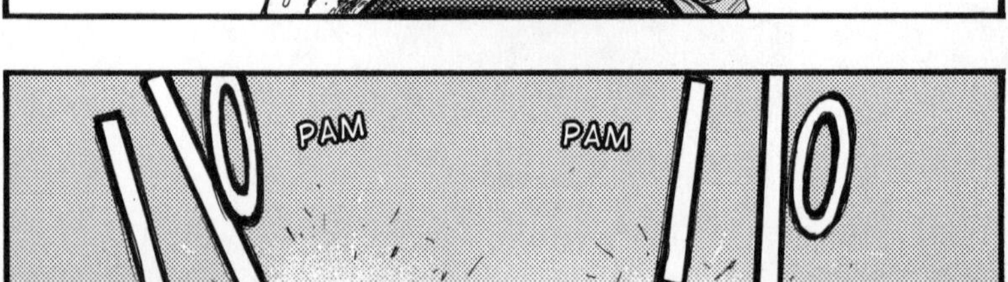
PAM
PAM

File:39 End

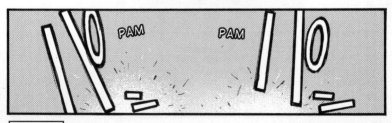

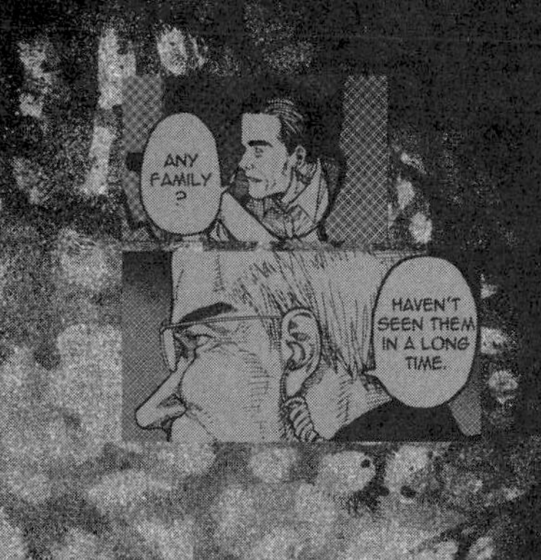
ANY FAMILY ?
HAVEN'T SEEN THEM IN A LONG TIME.

File 40: Battlefield Hardline ③

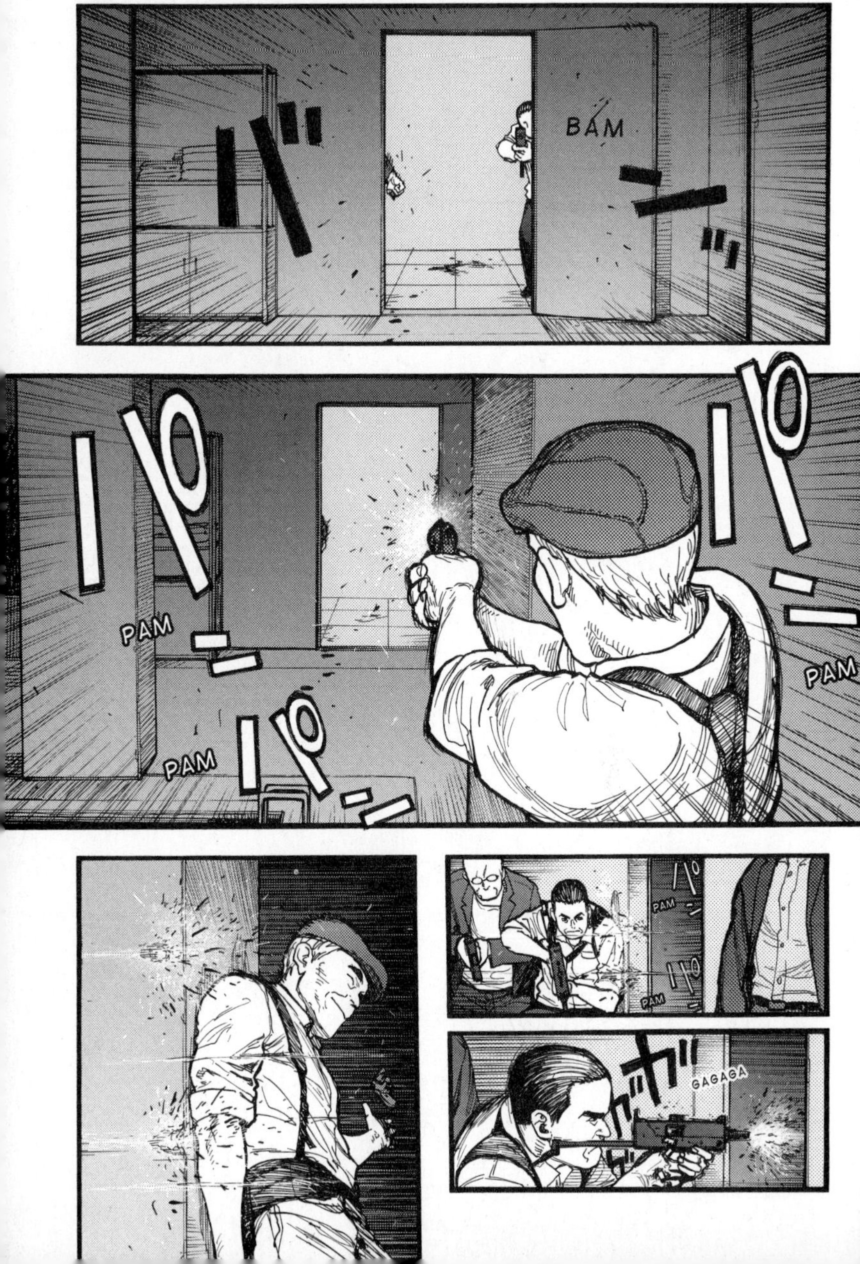
BAM
PAM
PAM
PAM
PAM
PAM
GAGAGA

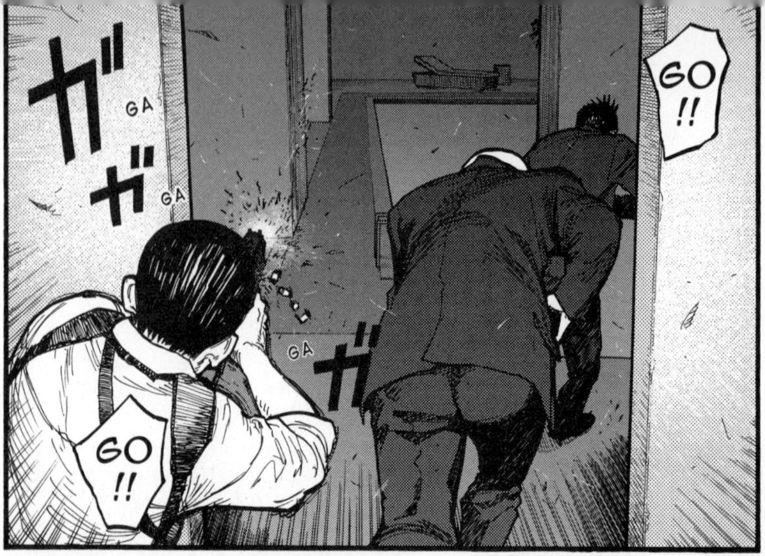
GO !!
ガ
GA
ガ
GA
GA
ガ
GO !!

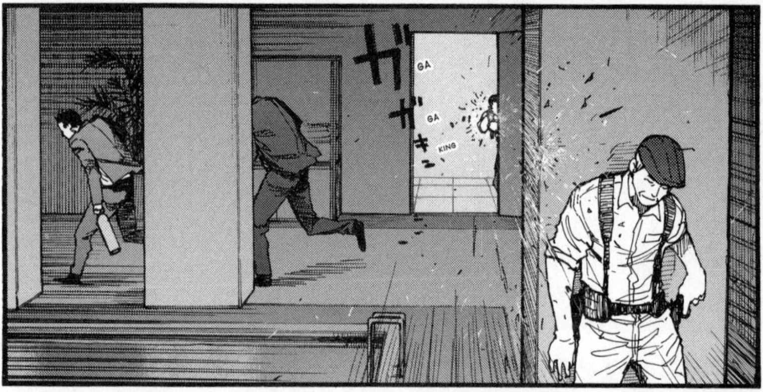
ガ
GA
ガ
GA
キュ
KING

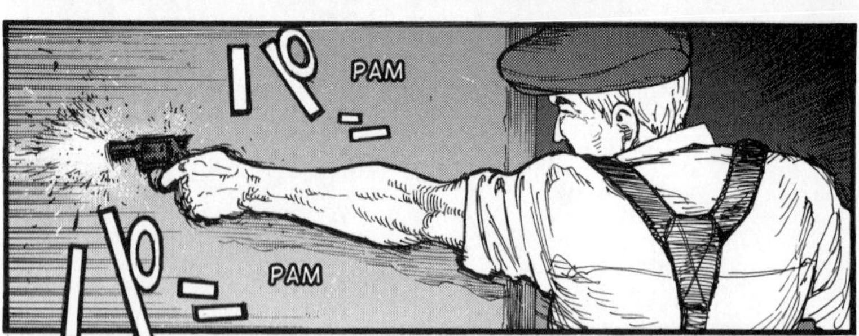
パ
PAM
パ
PAM

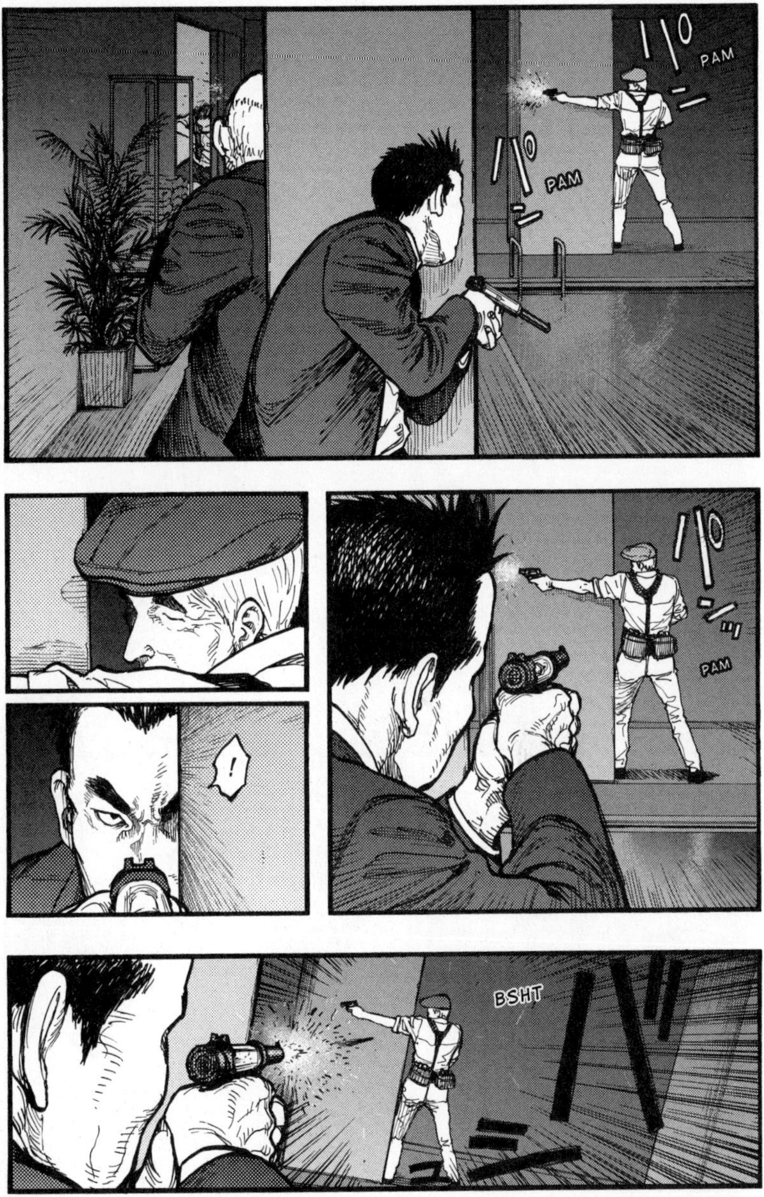
PAM
PAM
PAM
!
BSHT

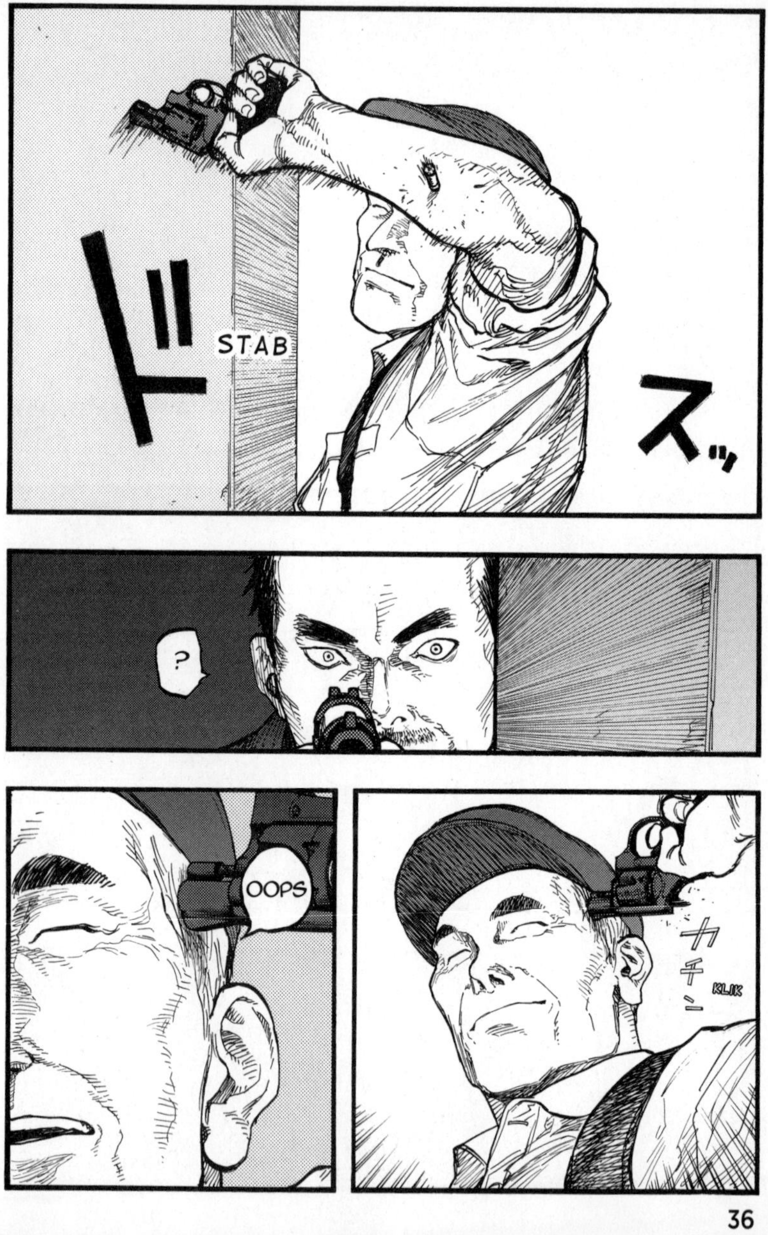
スッ
ドッ
STAB
?
カチン
KLIK
OOPS

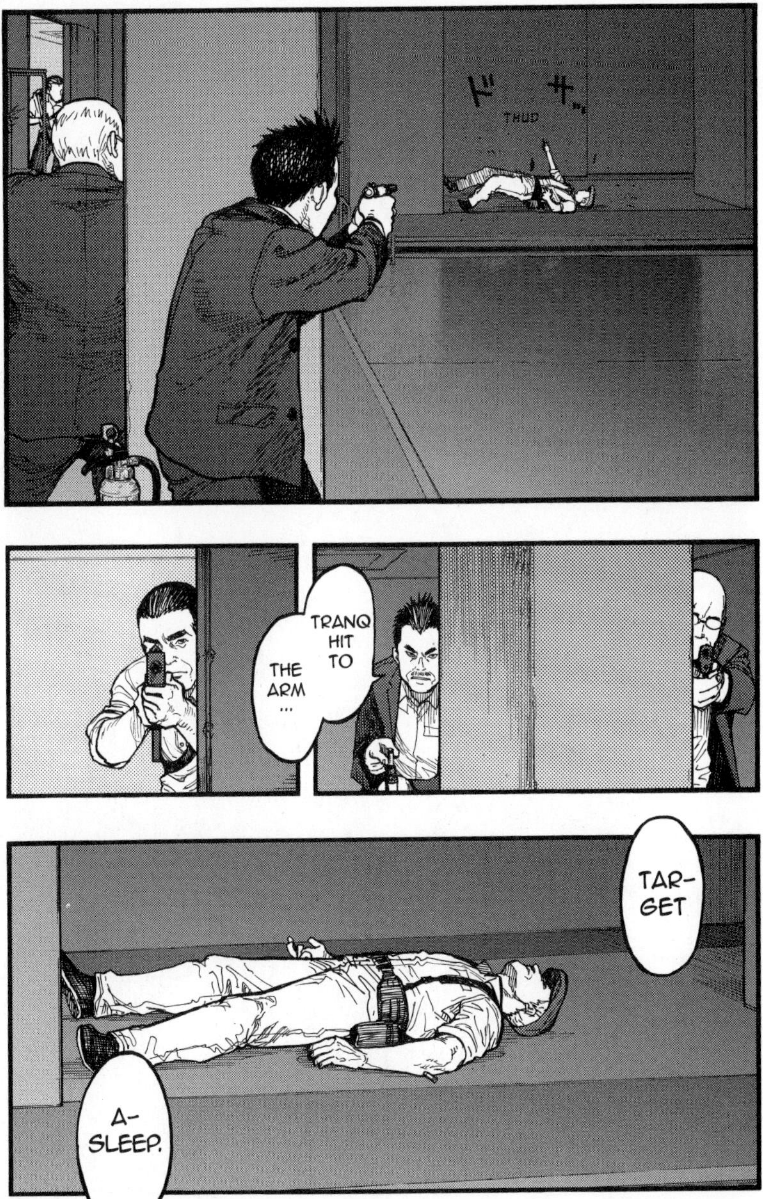
ドサッ
THUD
TRANQ HIT TO THE ARM ...
TARGET
ASLEEP.

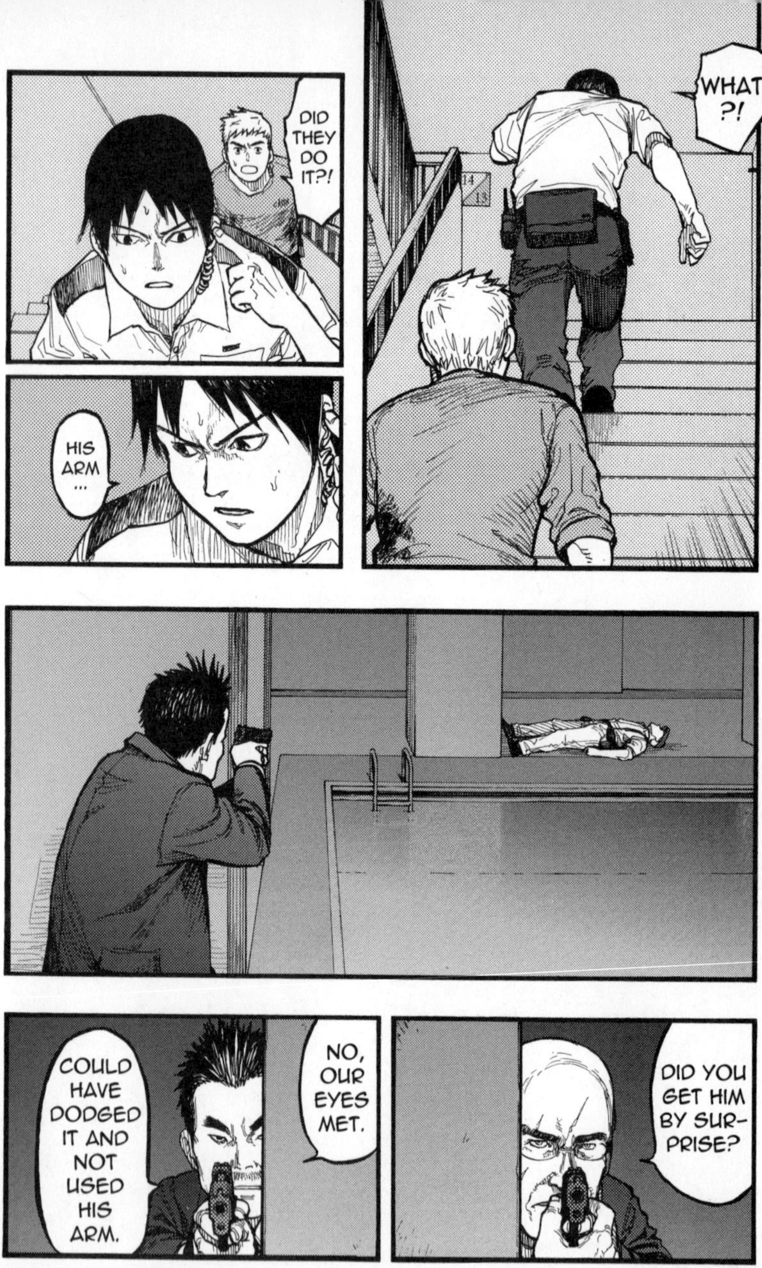
WHAT ?!
DID THEY DO IT?!
HIS ARM ...
DID YOU GET HIM BY SUR-PRISE?
NO, OUR EYES MET.
COULD HAVE DODGED IT AND NOT USED HIS ARM.

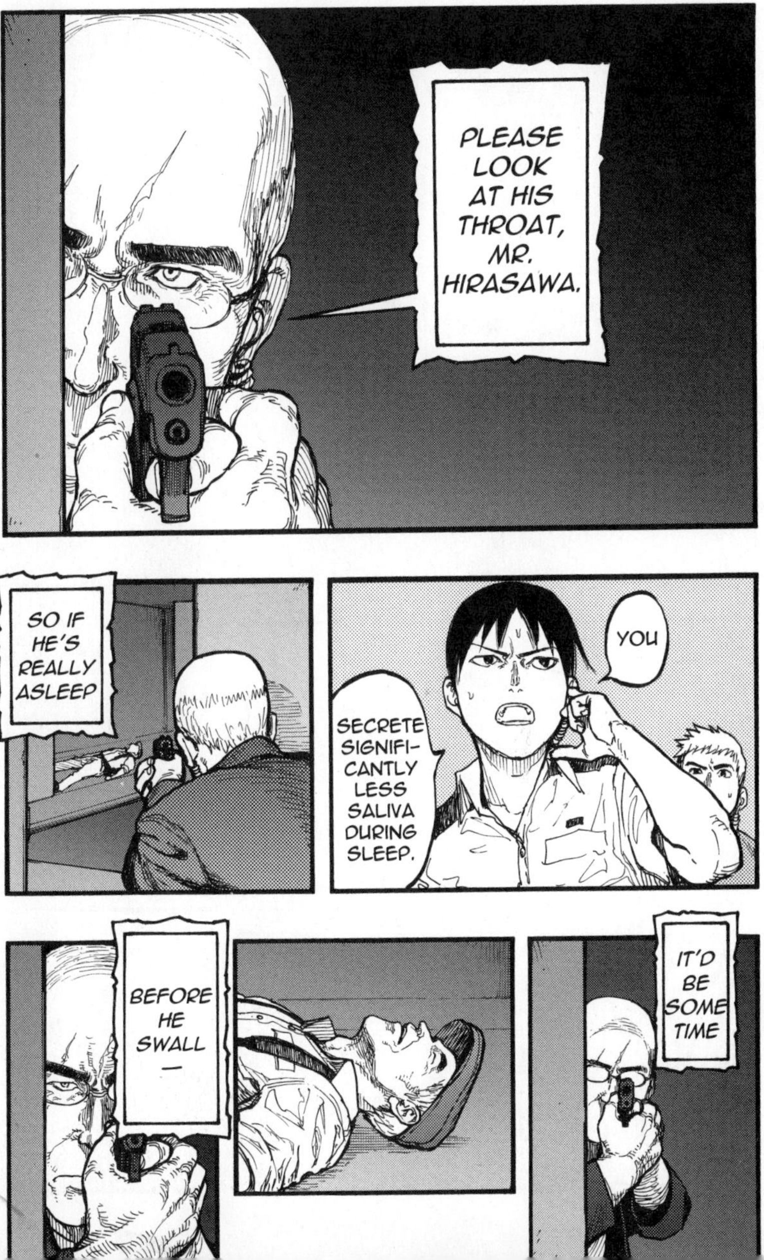
PLEASE LOOK AT HIS THROAT, MR. HIRASAWA.
YOU
SECRETE SIGNIFI-CANTLY LESS SALIVA DURING SLEEP.
SO IF HE'S REALLY ASLEEP
IT'D BE SOME TIME
BEFORE HE SWALL —

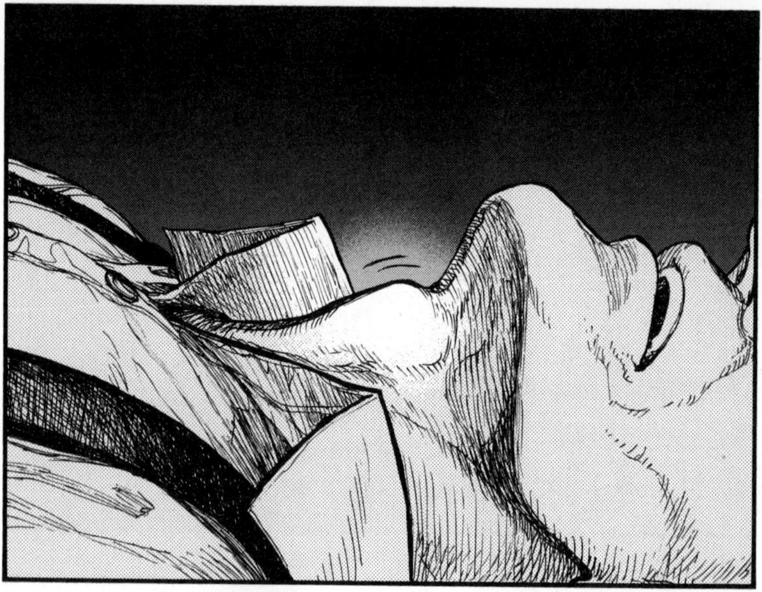

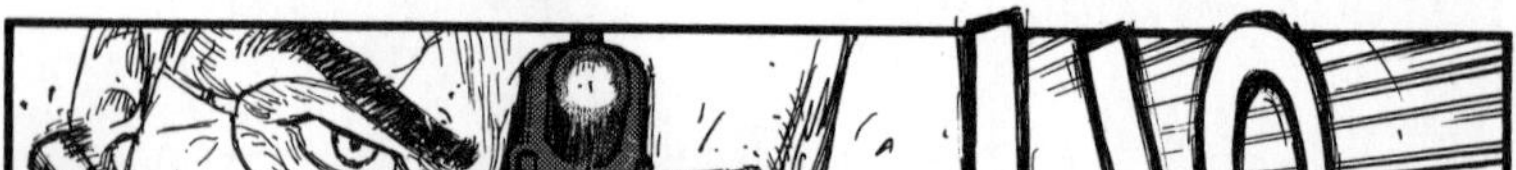
PAM

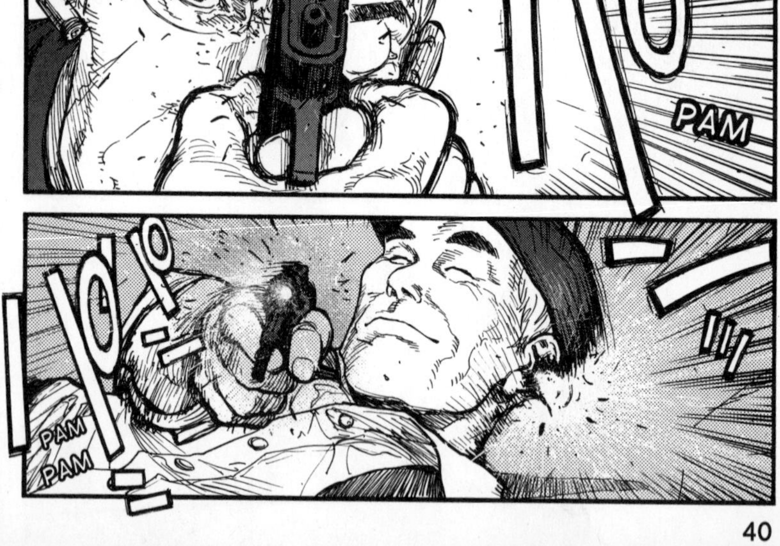
PAM
PAM

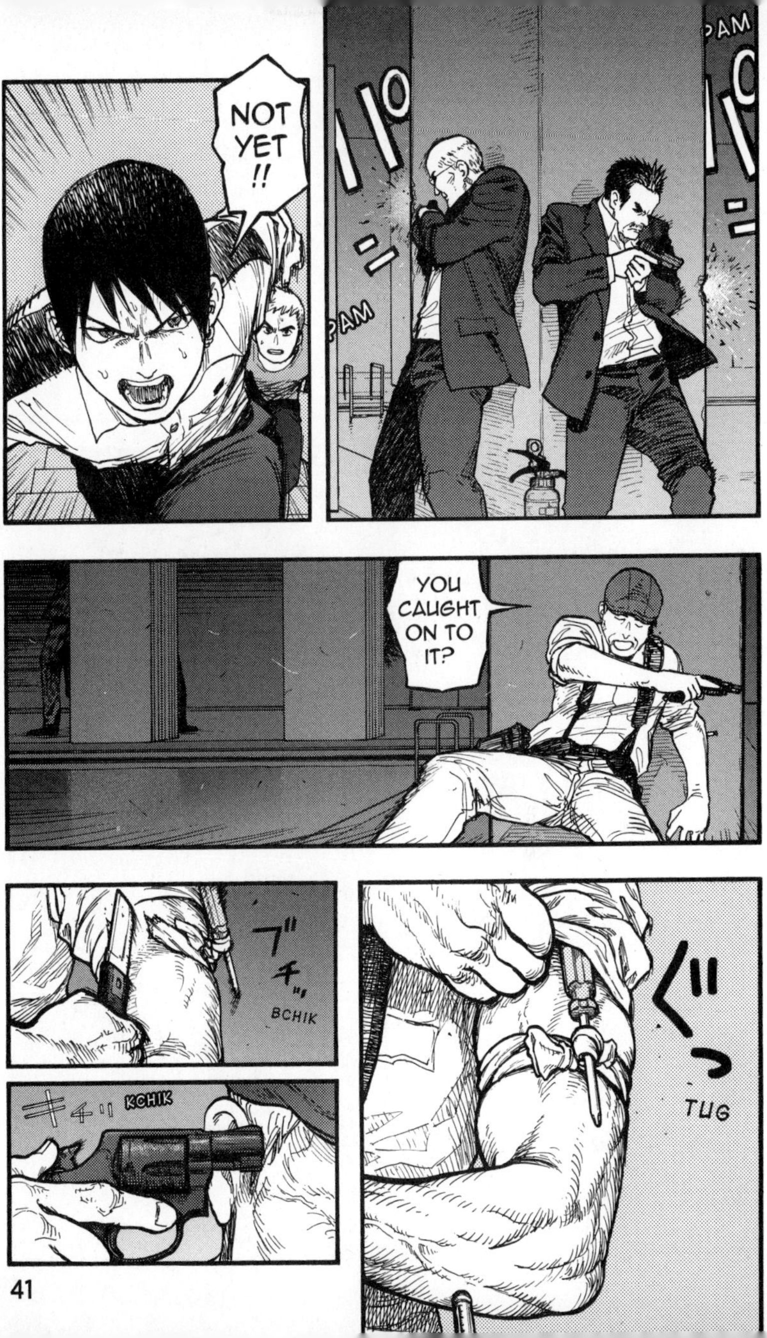
PAM
PAM
NOT YET !!
YOU CAUGHT ON TO IT?
TUG
BCHIK
KCHIK

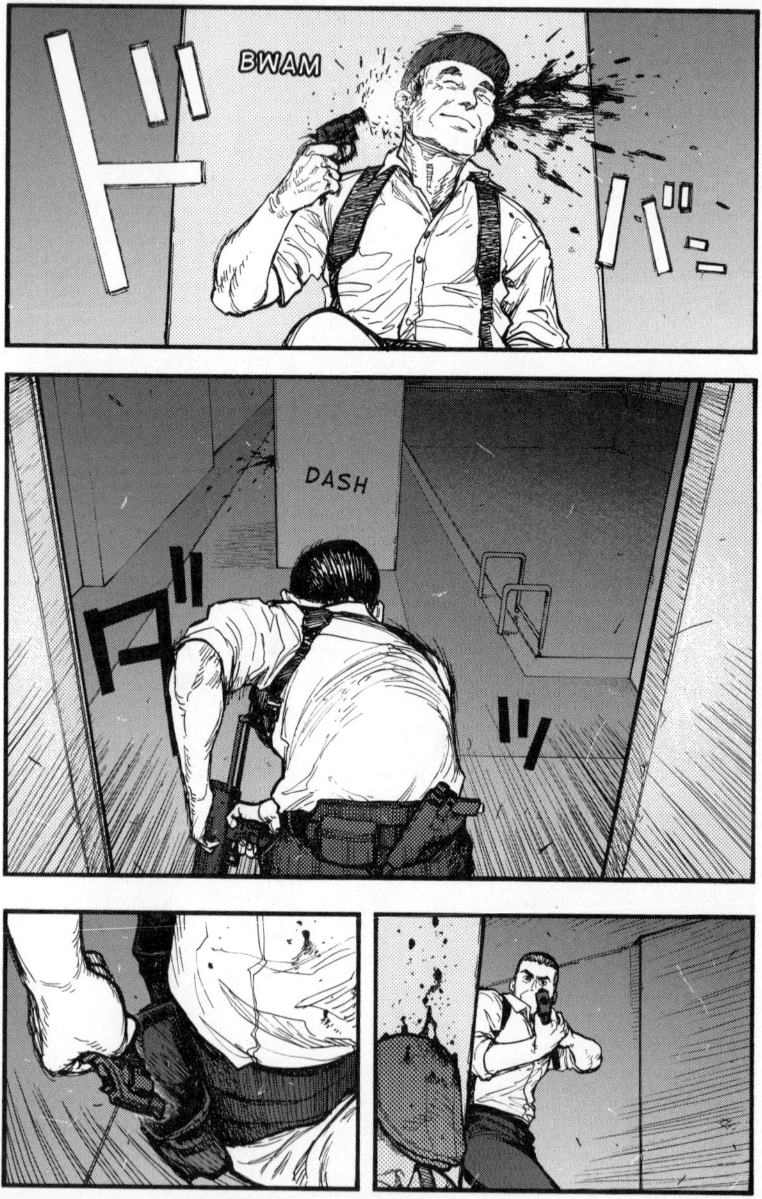
BWAM
DASH

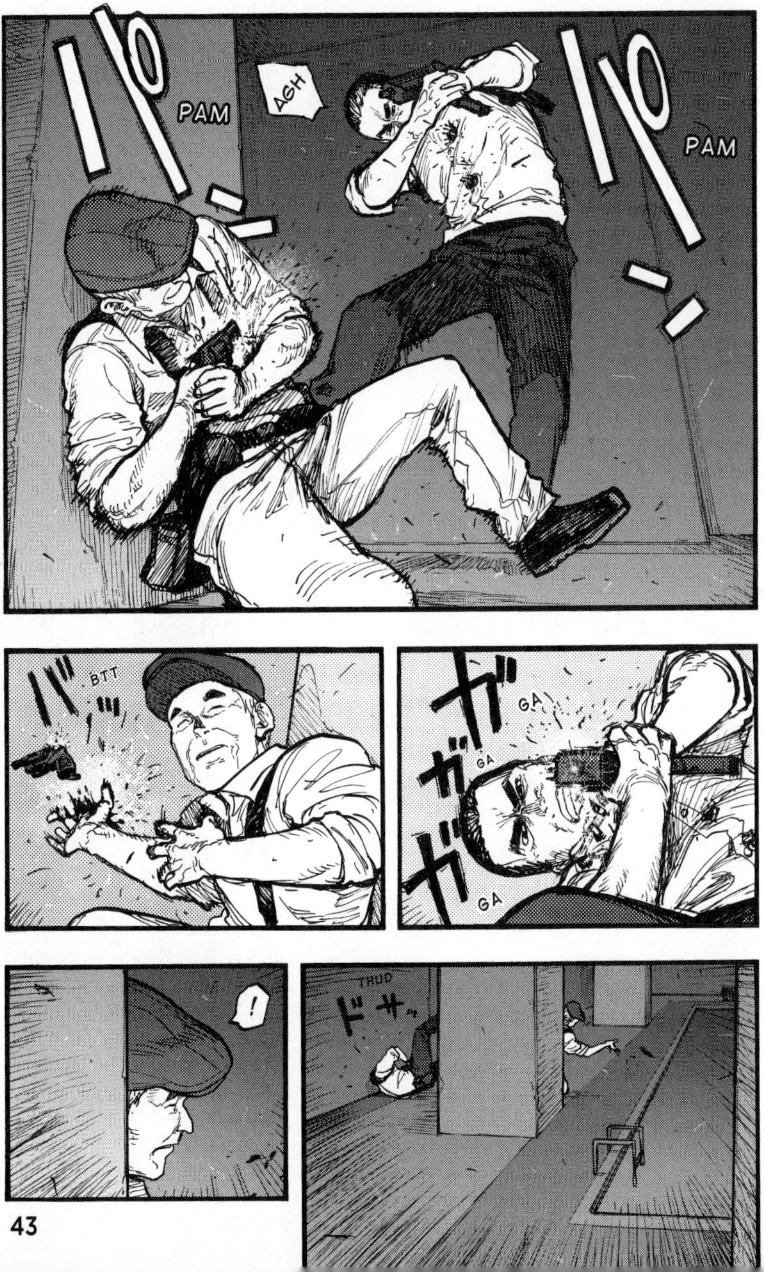
PAM
AGH
PAM
BTT
GA
GA
GA
!
THUD

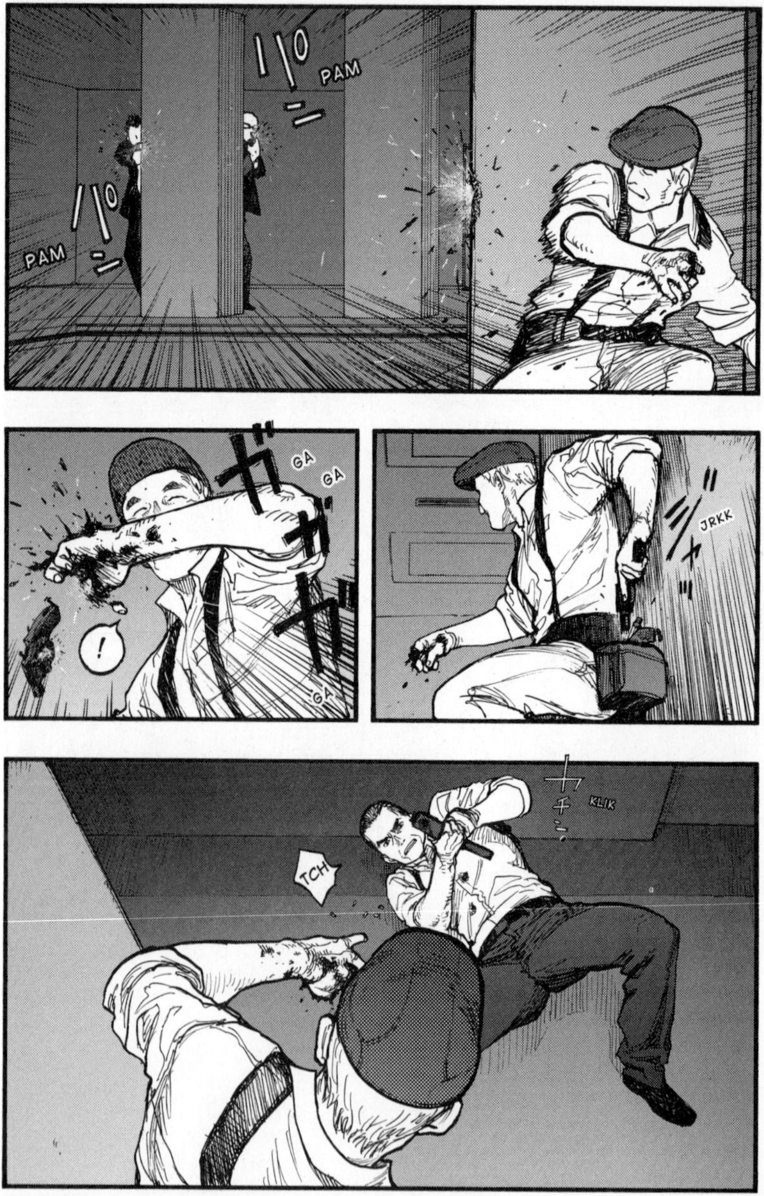
PAM
PAM
JRKK
GA
GA
!
GA
KLIK
TCH

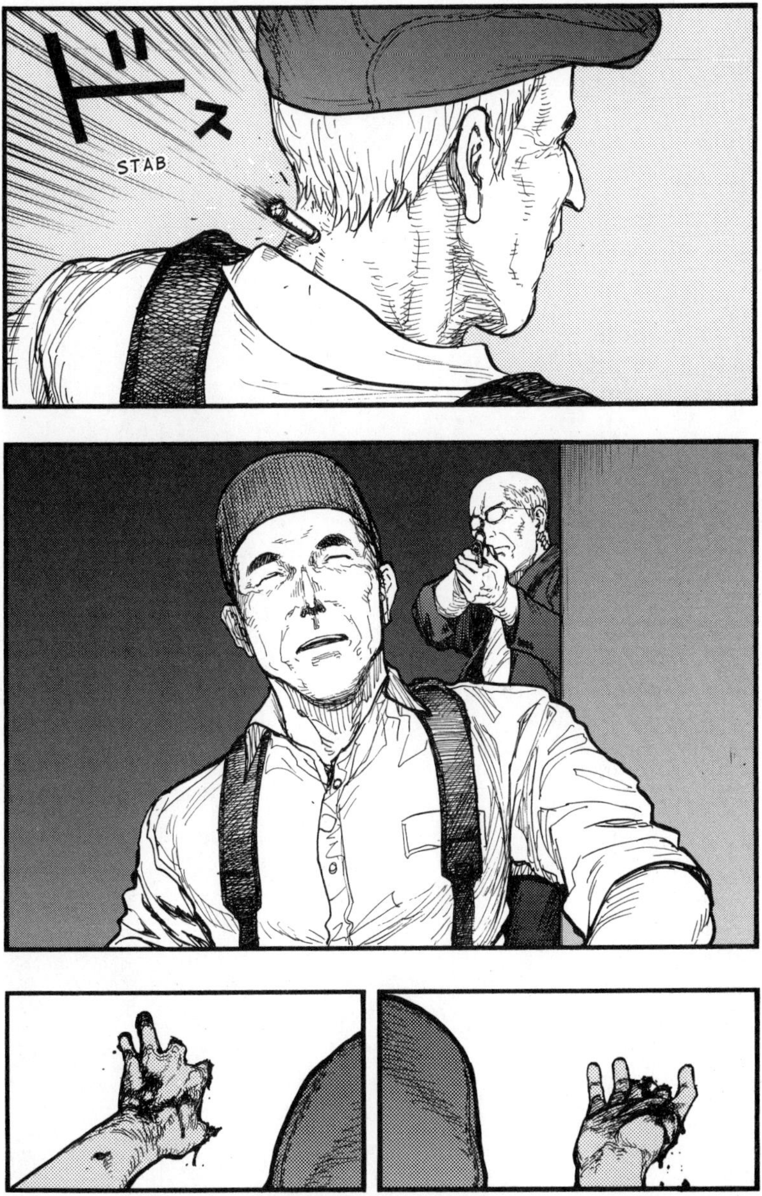
ドス
STAB

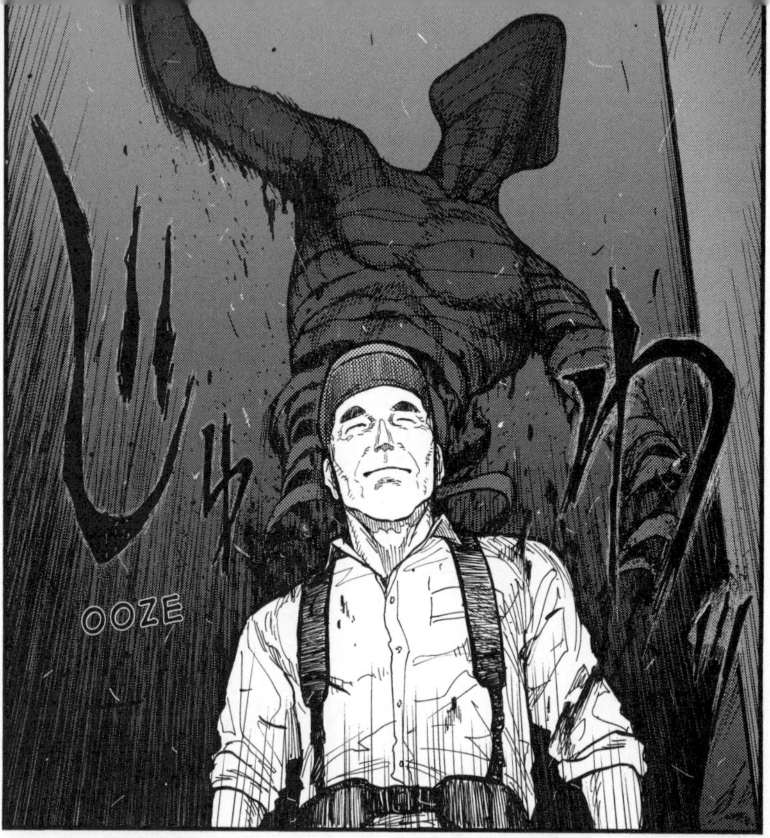
OOZE

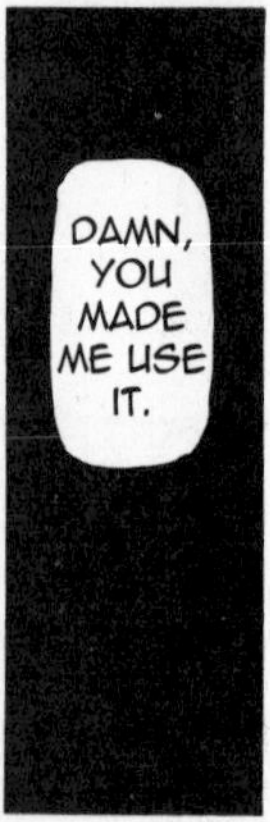
DAMN, YOU MADE ME USE IT.

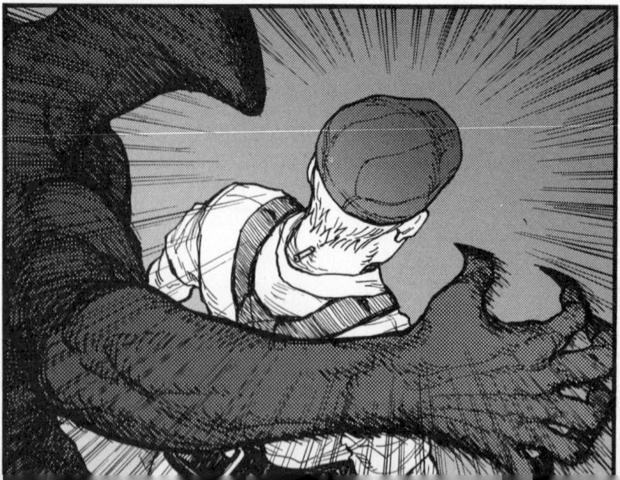

BTT

FWUSHHH

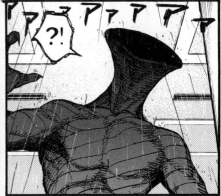

?!

POWER
RE-
STORED.

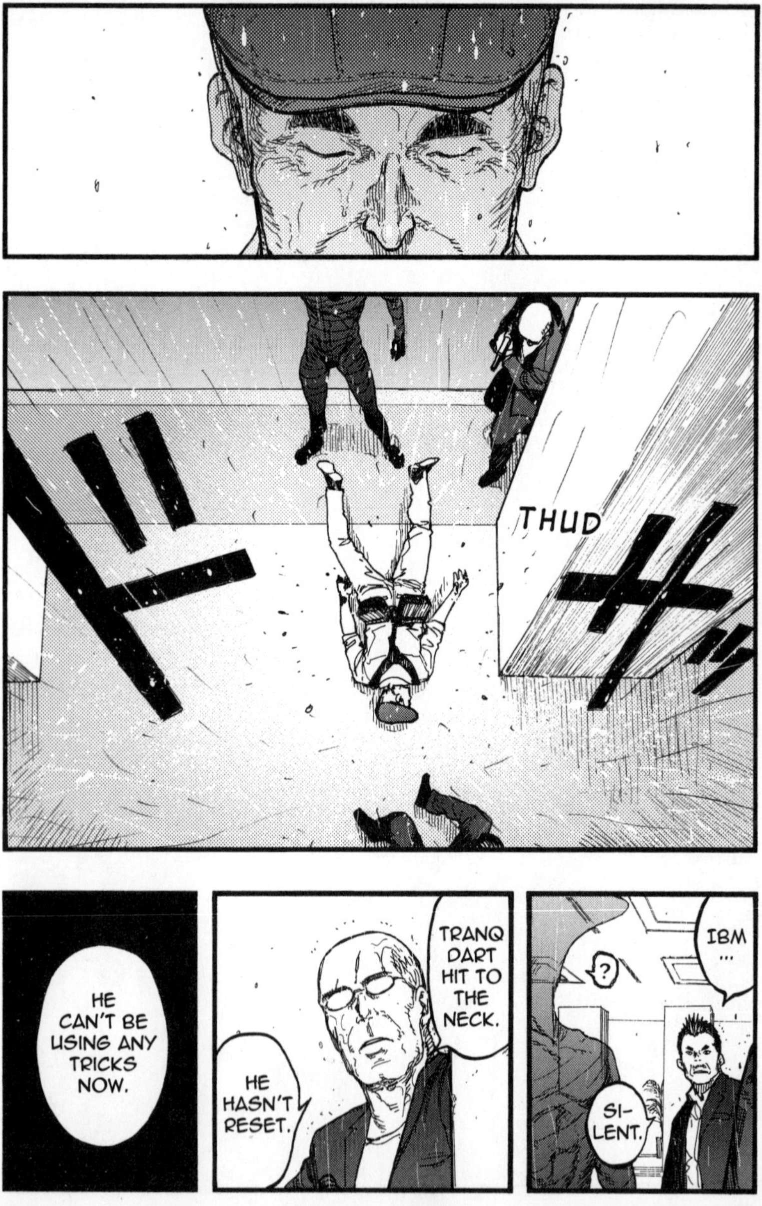
THUD
IBM ...
?
SI-LENT.
TRANQ DART HIT TO THE NECK.
HE HASN'T RESET.
HE CAN'T BE USING ANY TRICKS NOW.

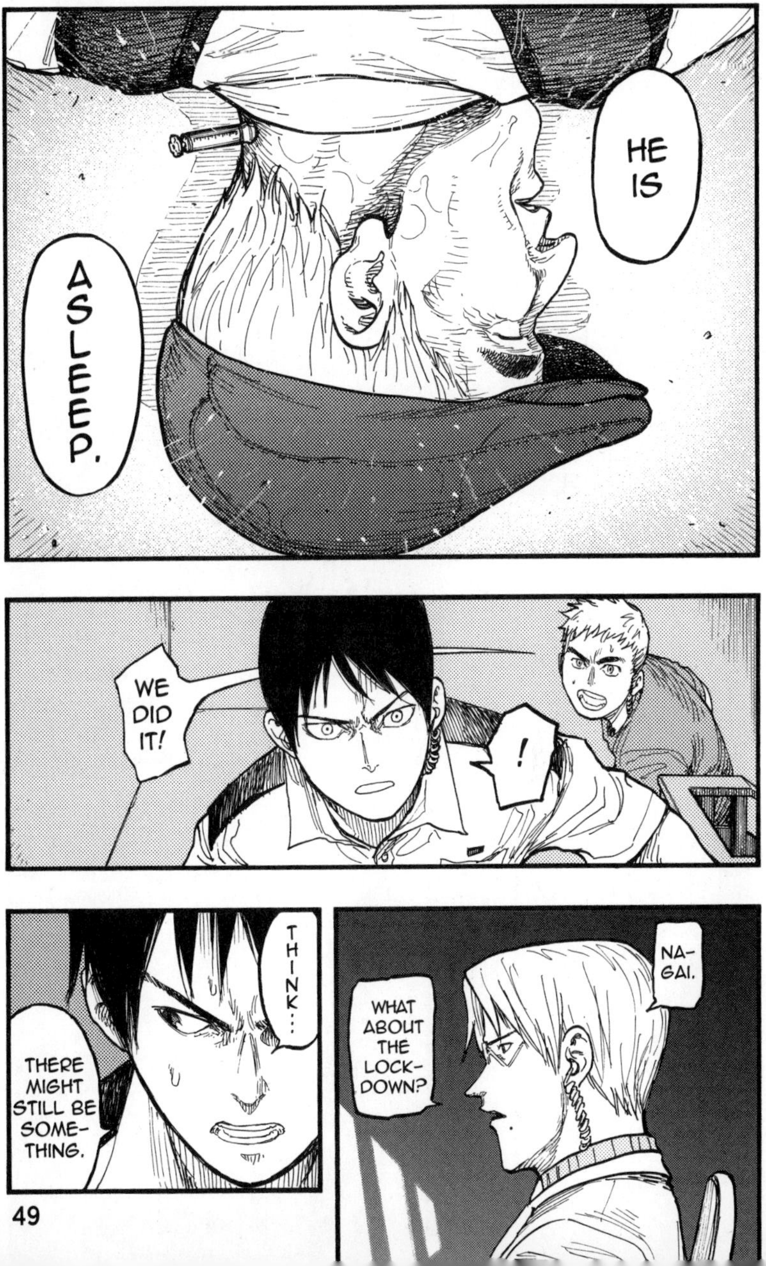
HE IS
ASLEEP.
WE DID IT!
!
NA-GAI.
WHAT ABOUT THE LOCK-DOWN?
THINK...
THERE MIGHT STILL BE SOME-THING.

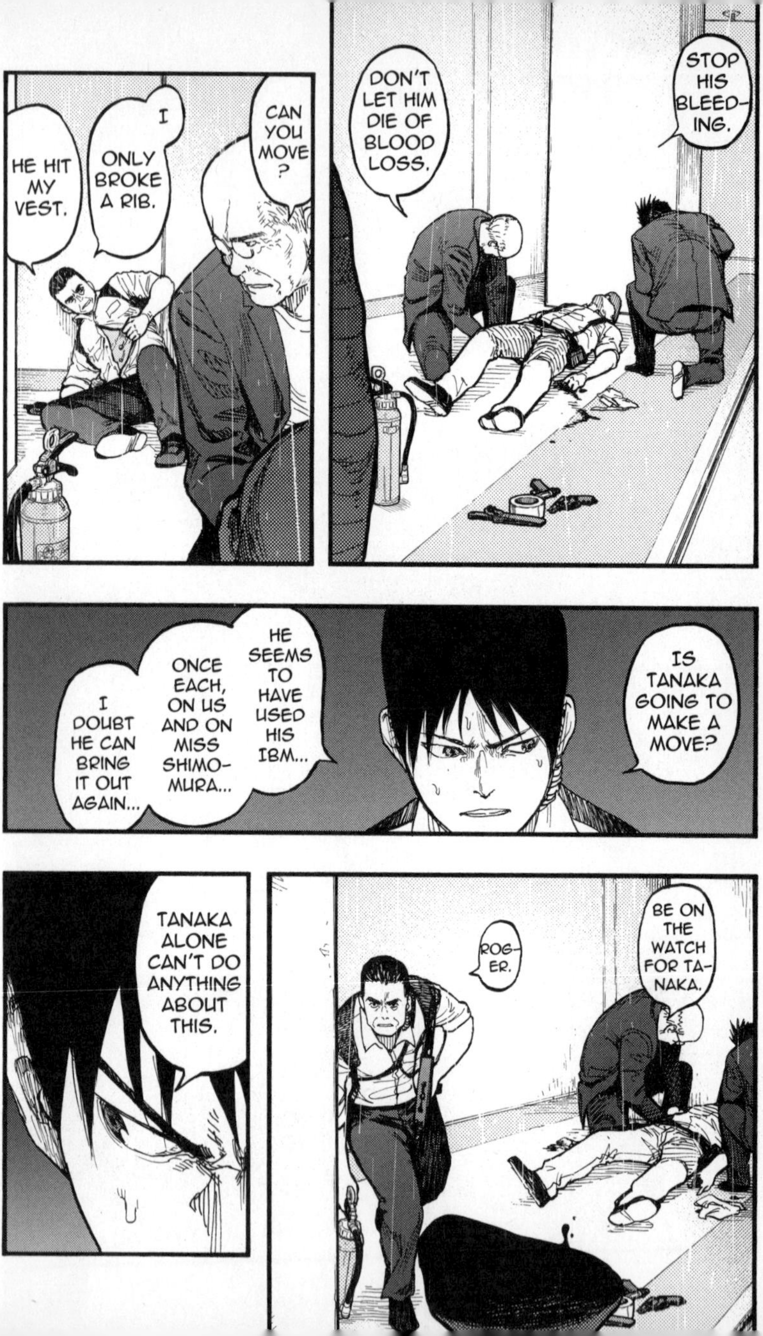
STOP HIS BLEEDING.
DON'T LET HIM DIE OF BLOOD LOSS.
CAN YOU MOVE?
I ONLY BROKE A RIB.
HE HIT MY VEST.
IS TANAKA GOING TO MAKE A MOVE?
HE SEEMS TO HAVE USED HIS IBM...
ONCE EACH, ON US AND ON MISS SHIMOMURA...
I DOUBT HE CAN BRING IT OUT AGAIN...
BE ON THE WATCH FOR TANAKA.
ROGER.
TANAKA ALONE CAN'T DO ANYTHING ABOUT THIS.

WHAT ELSE MIGHT THERE BE?

WHAT ELSE...

!

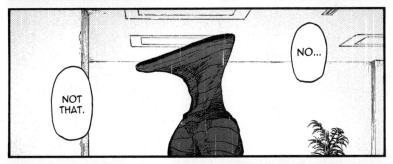

NO...

NOT THAT.

ONLY MINE CAN.

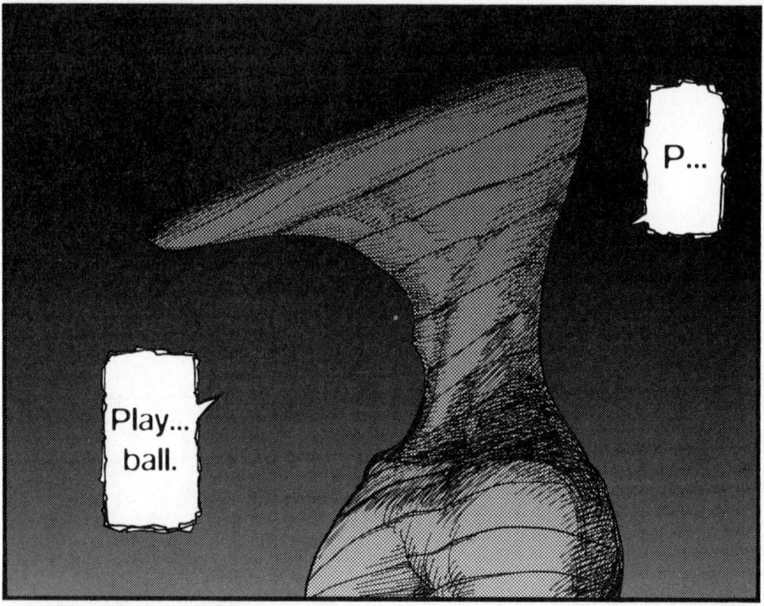
P...
Play... ball.
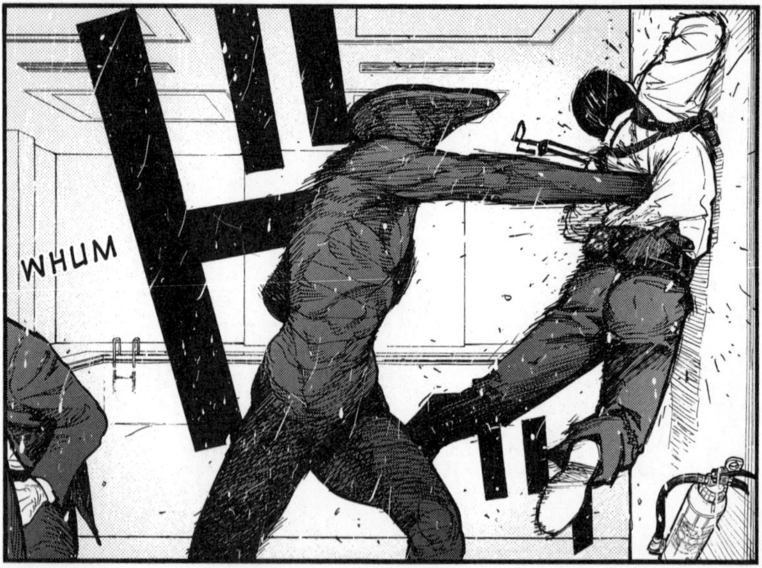
WHUM

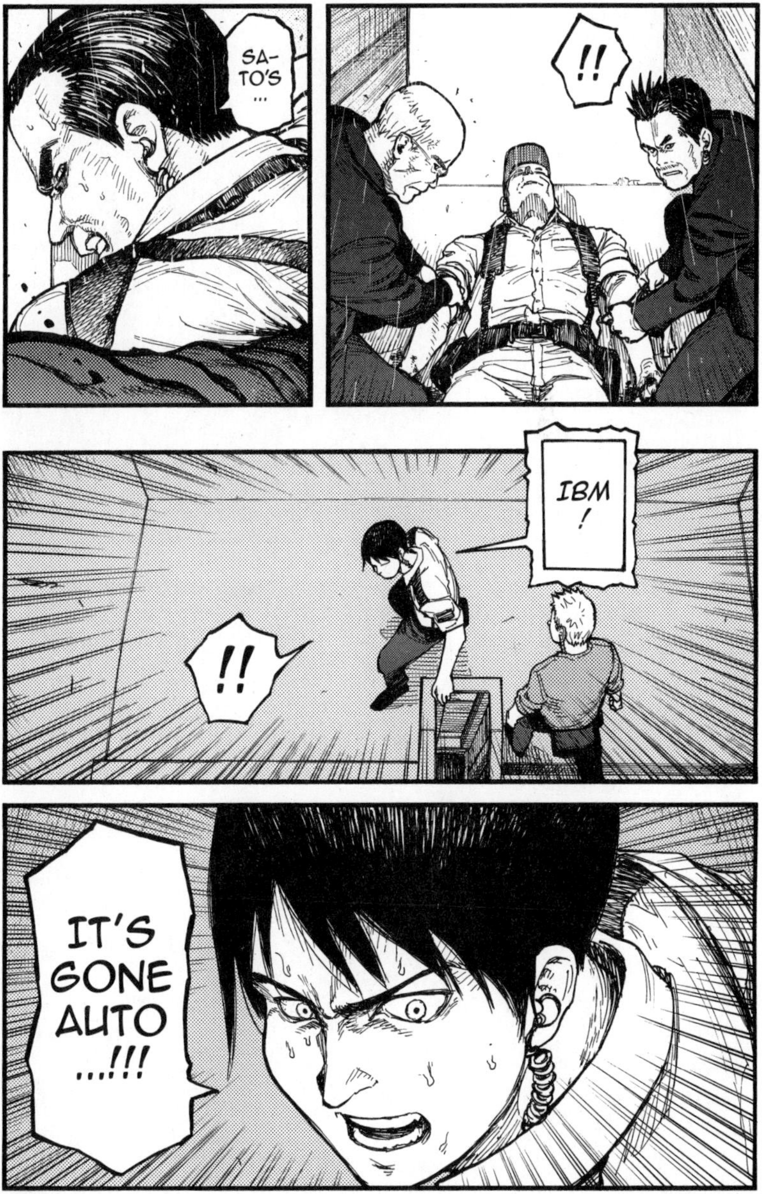
!!
SA-TO'S ...
IBM !
!!
IT'S GONE AUTO ...!!!

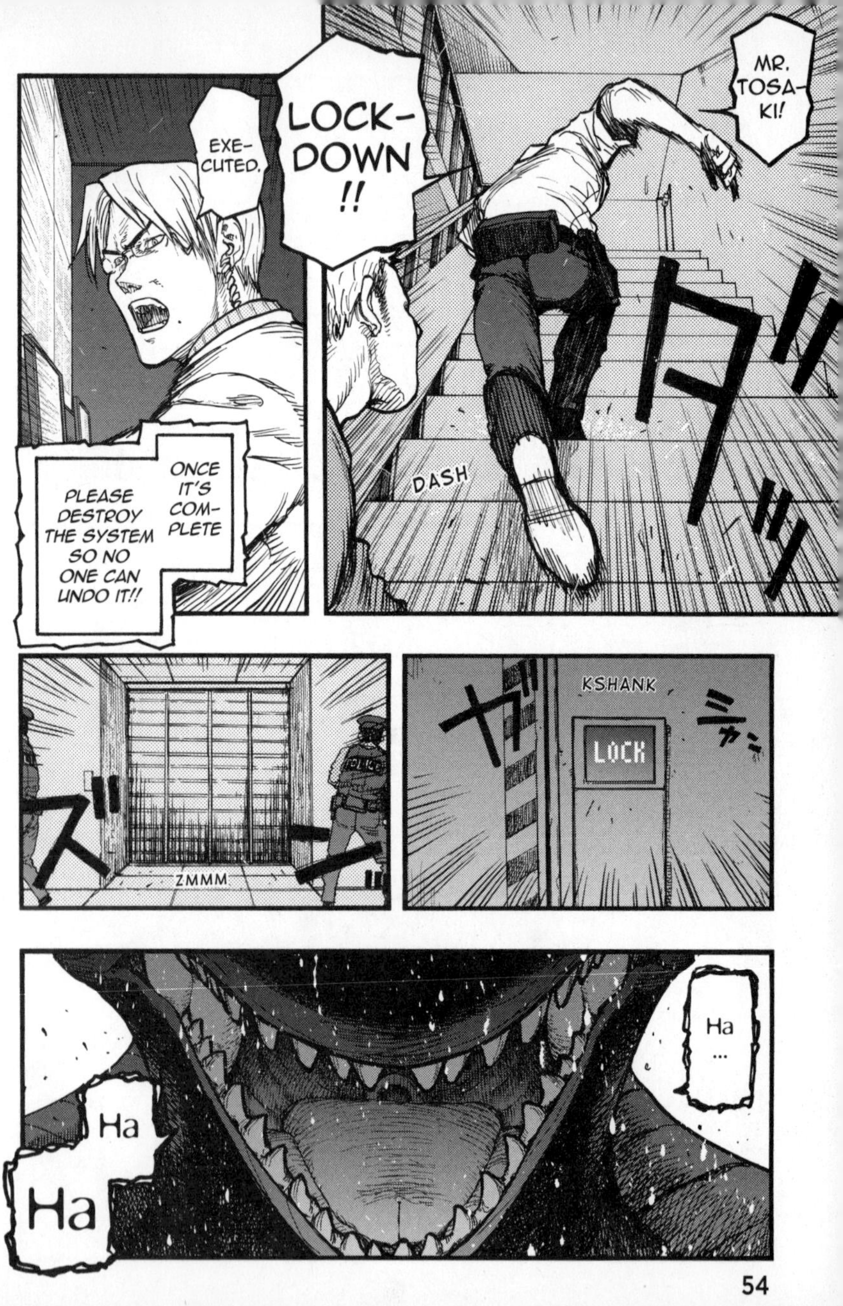
MR. TOSA-KI!
DASH
LOCK-DOWN !!
EXE-CUTED.
ONCE IT'S COM-PLETE
PLEASE DESTROY THE SYSTEM SO NO ONE CAN UNDO IT!!
KSHANK
LOCK
ZMMM
Ha ...
Ha
Ha

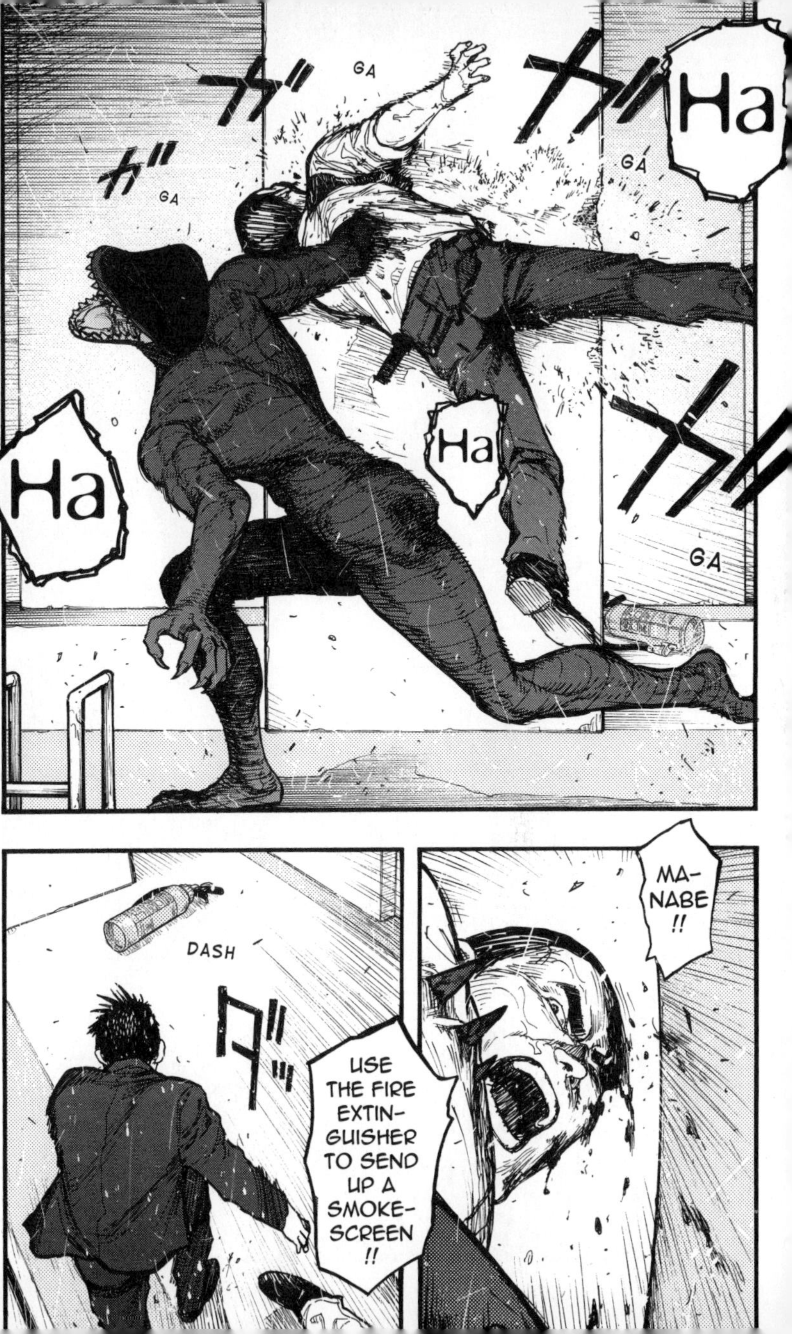
Ha
GA
GA
Ha
GA
GA
Ha
GA
MA-NABE !!
USE THE FIRE EXTINGUISHER TO SEND UP A SMOKESCREEN !!
DASH

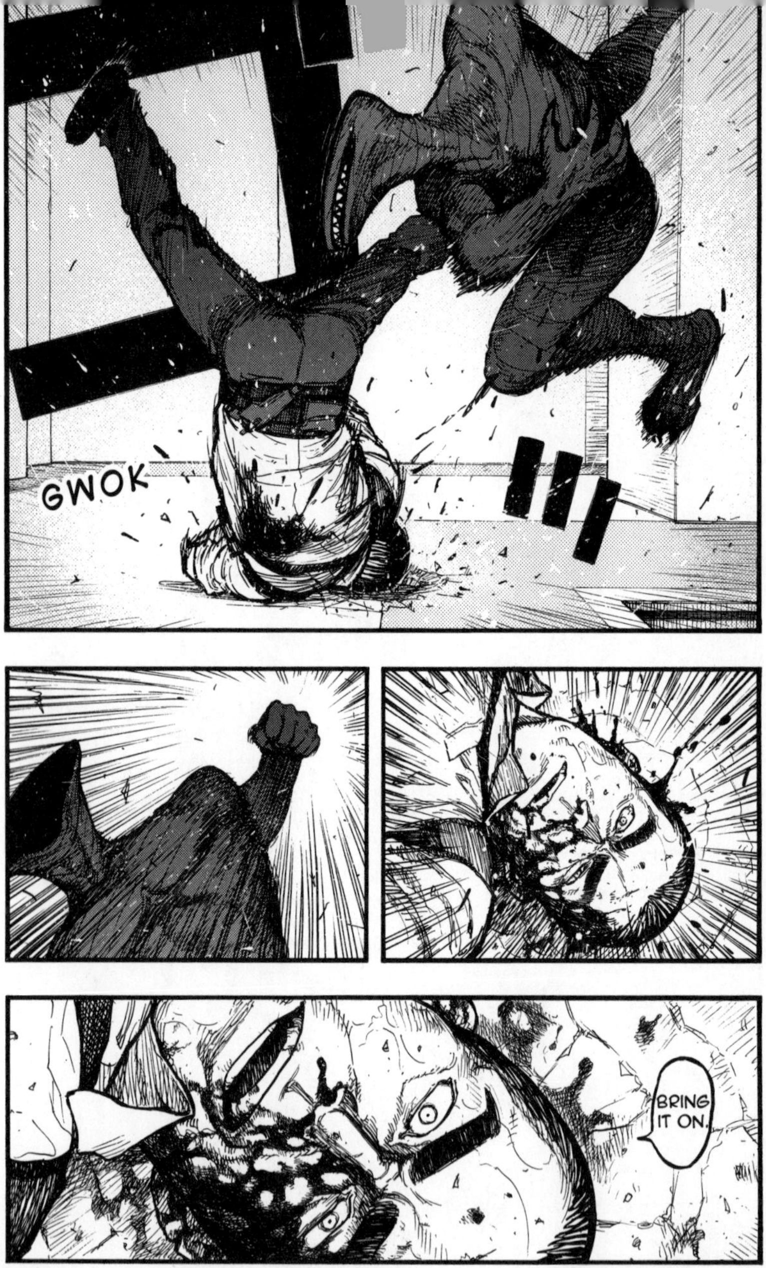
GWOK
BRING IT ON.

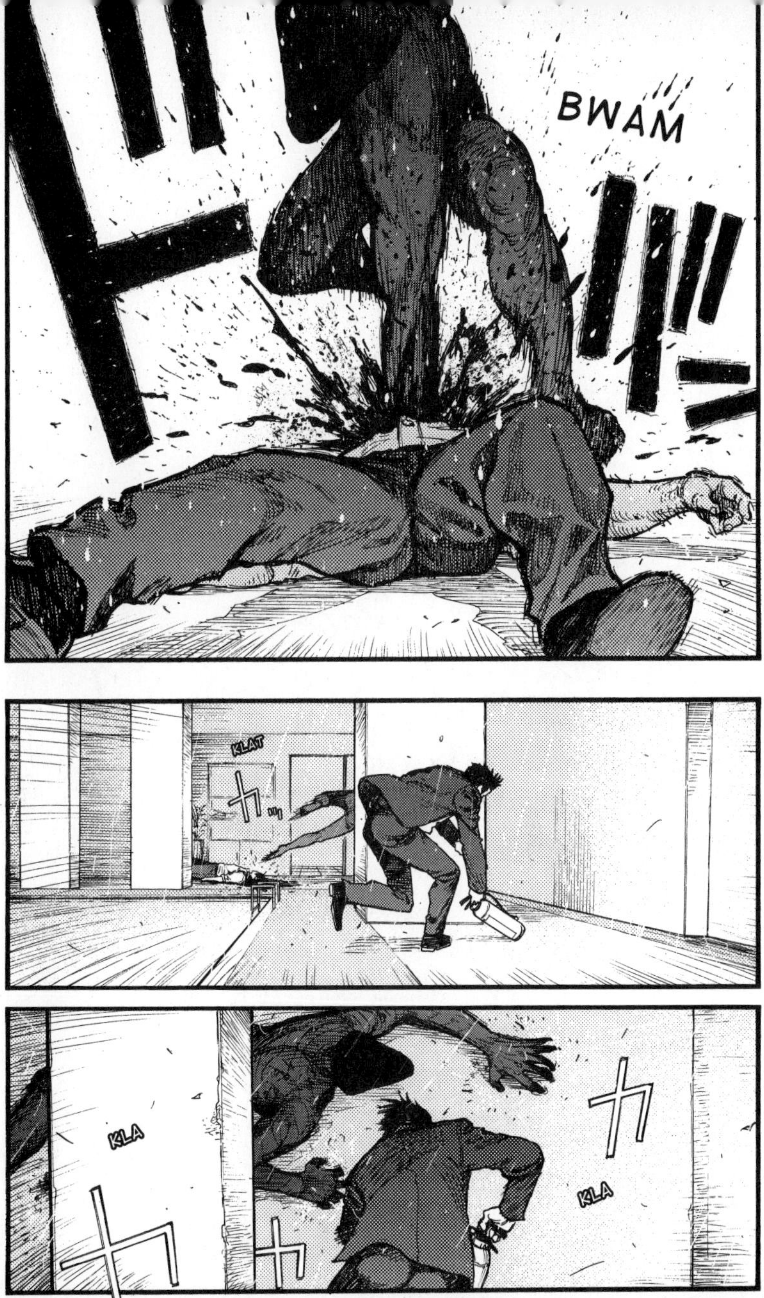
BWAM
KLAT
KLA
KLA

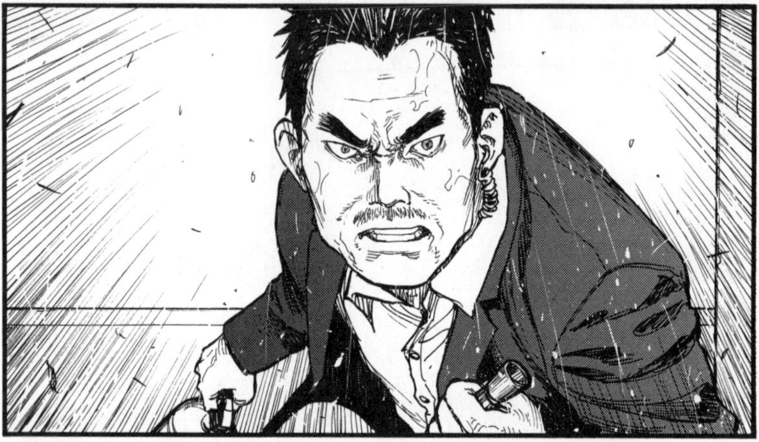

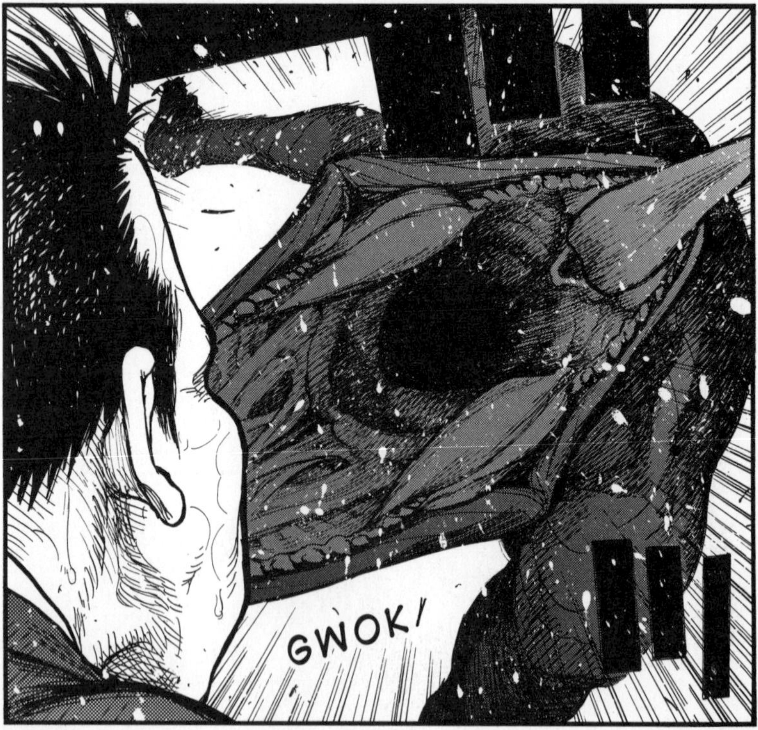
GWOK!

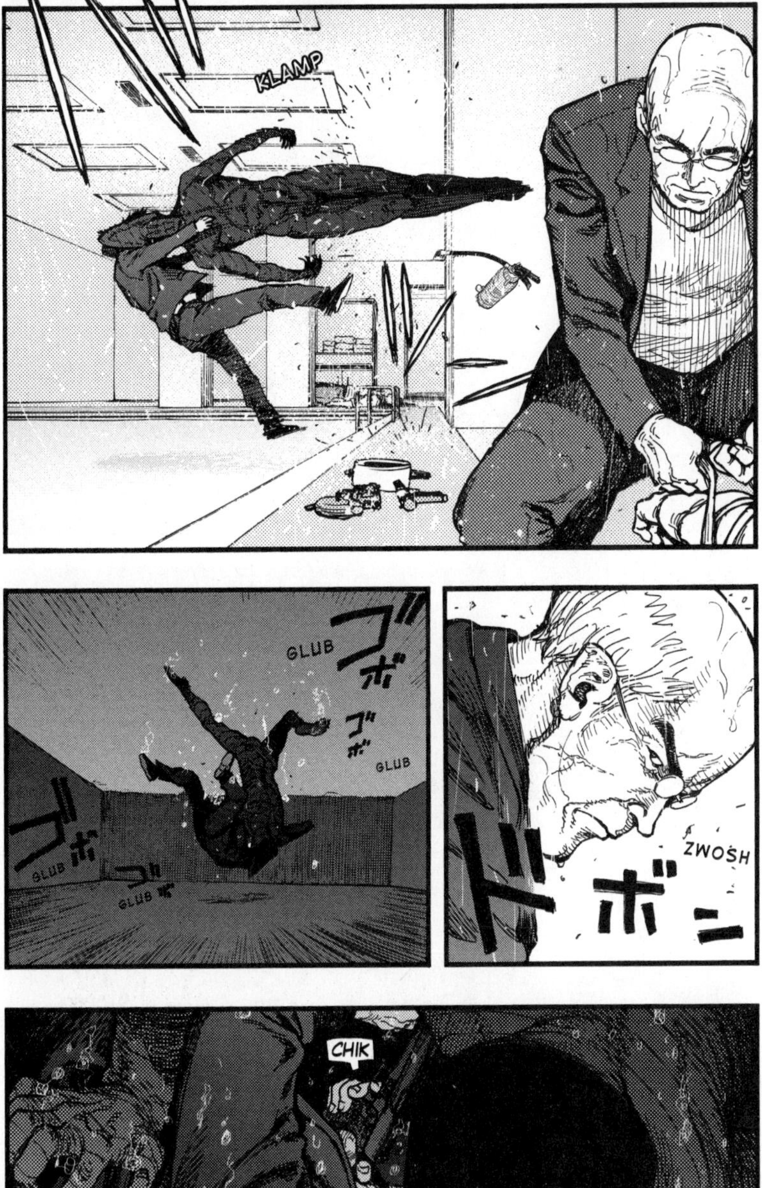
KLAMP
ZWOSH
ドボン
GLUB
ゴボ
ゴボ
GLUB
ゴボ
GLUB
ゴボ
GLUB
CHIK

DWOM
DWOM
DWOM...
ギュッ
SQUIK

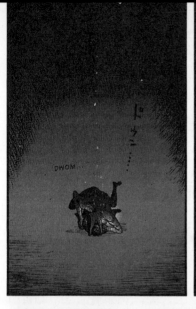

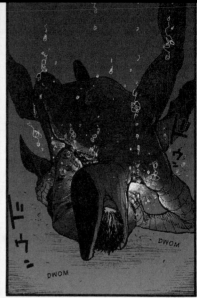

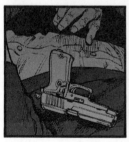

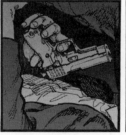

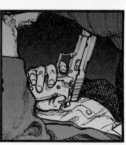

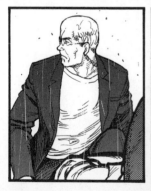

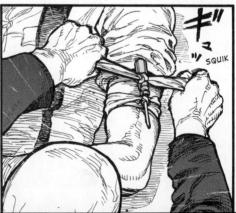

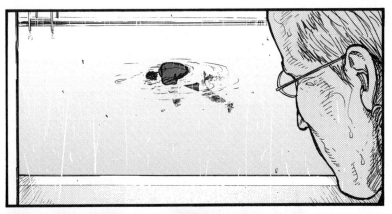

SPLASH

!

ZMM ズ

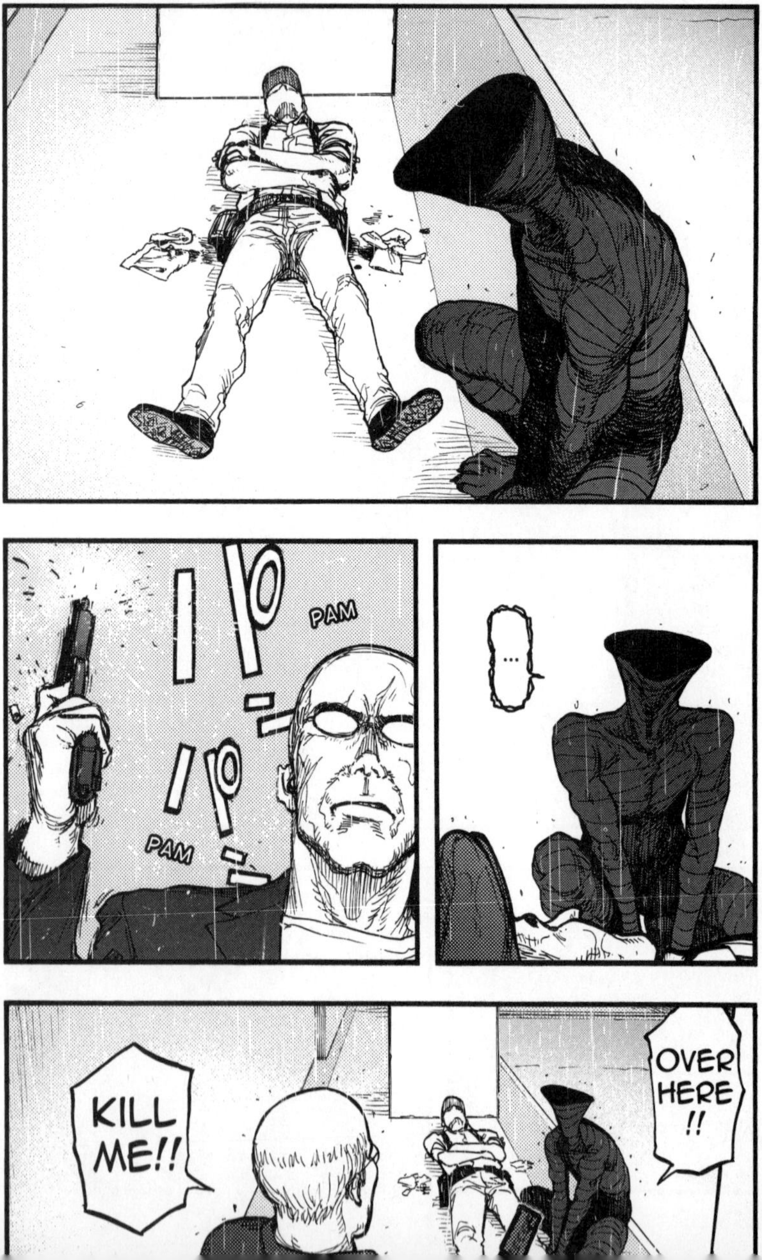
...
PAM
PAM
OVER HERE!!
KILL ME!!

WHAT'S WRONG WITH YOU ?!

CRUM BLE

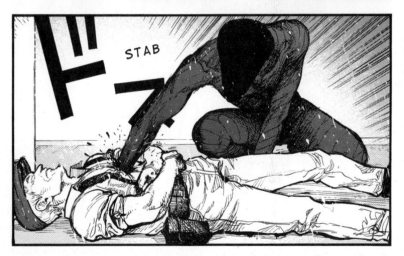

STAB

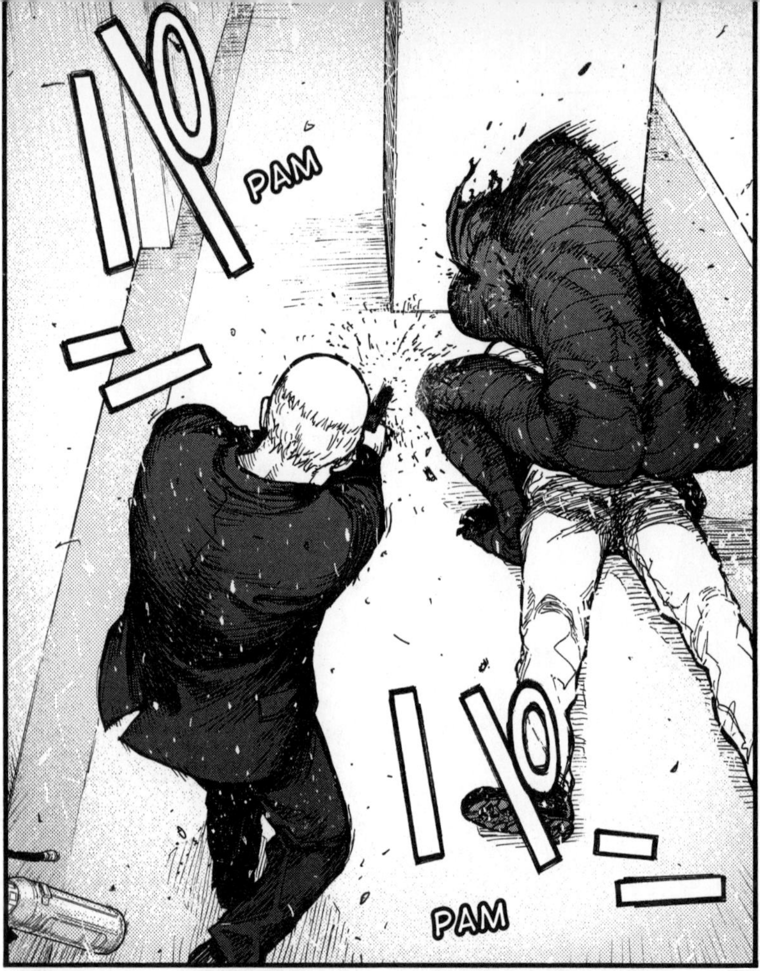
PAM
PAM
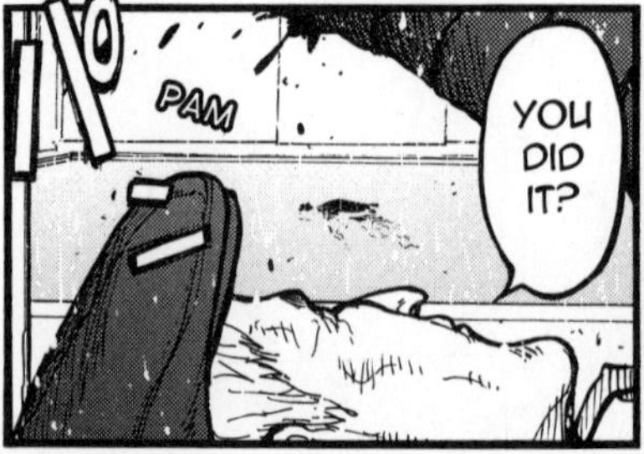
PAM
YOU DID IT?
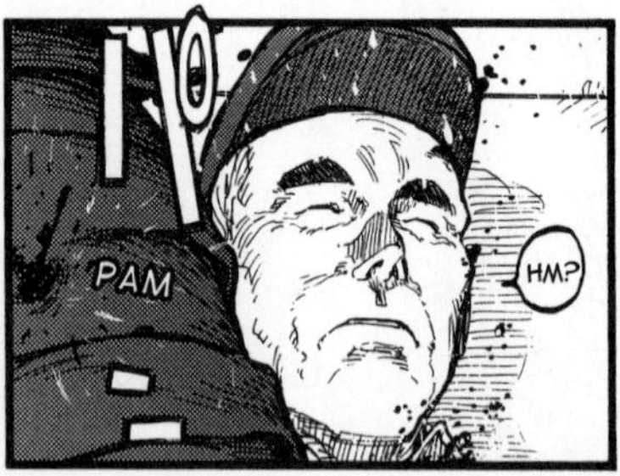
PAM
HM?

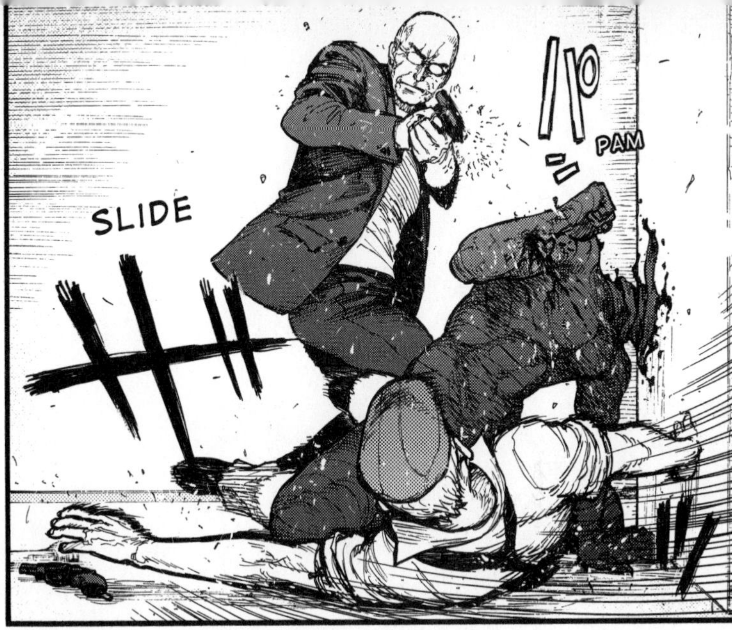
PAM
SLIDE
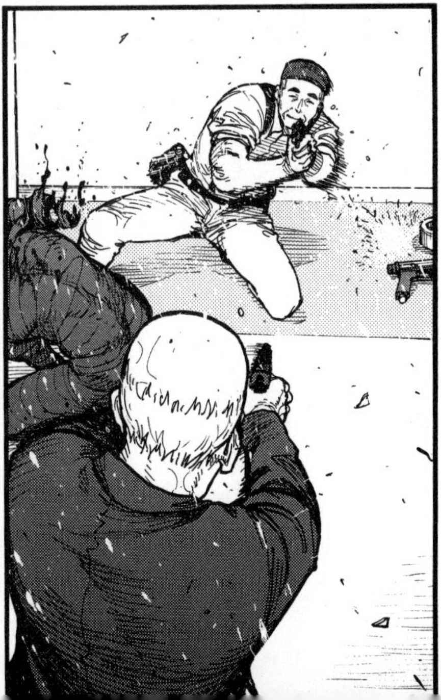
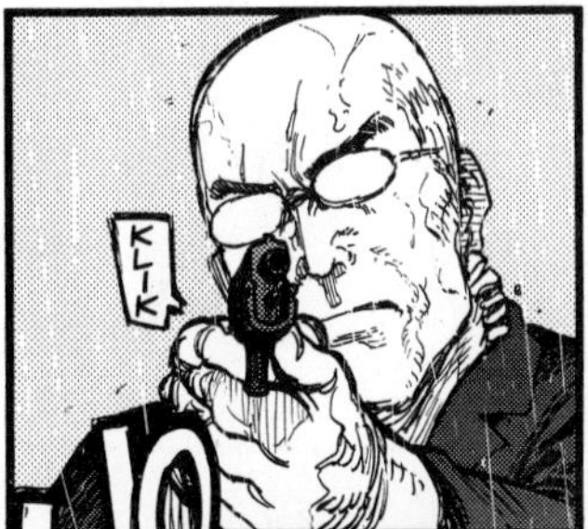
KLIK
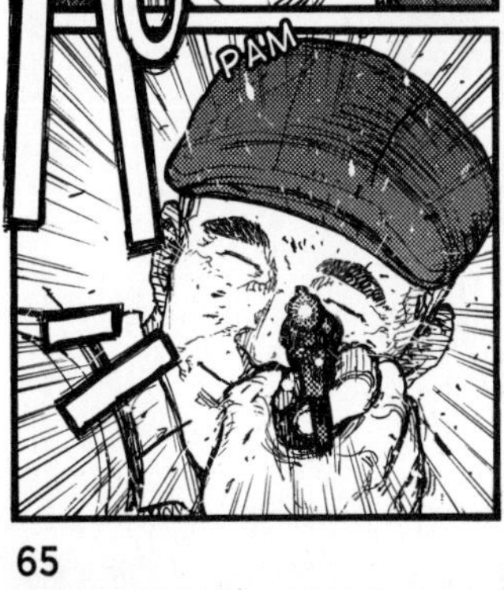
PAM

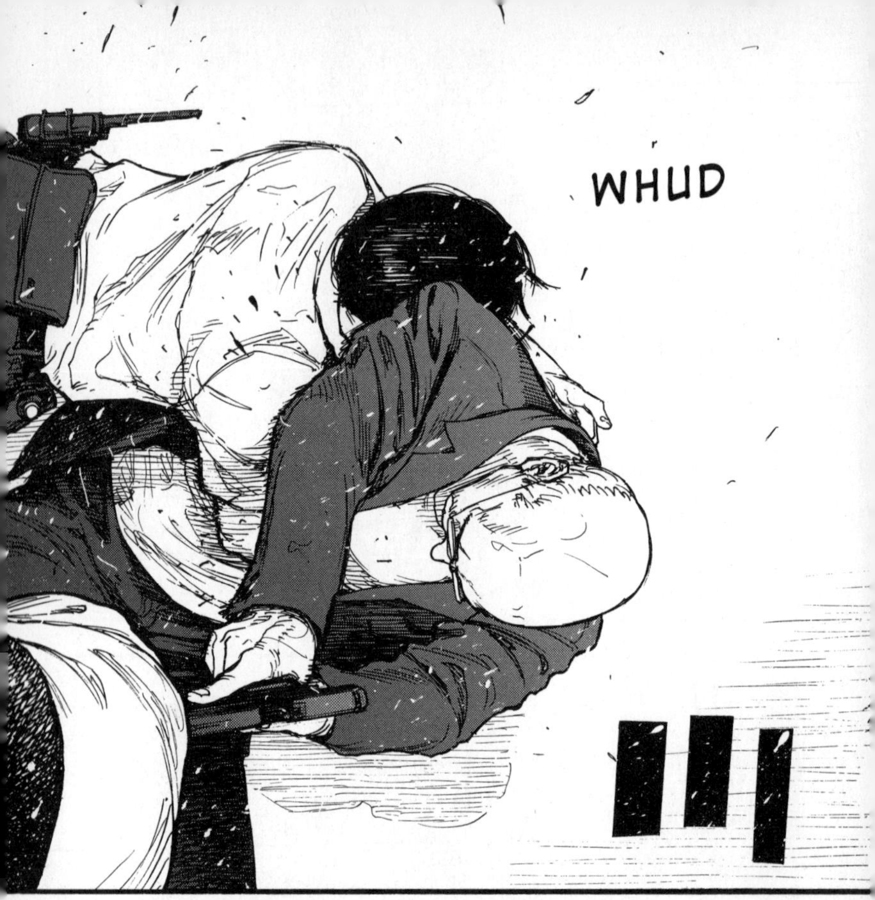
WHUD

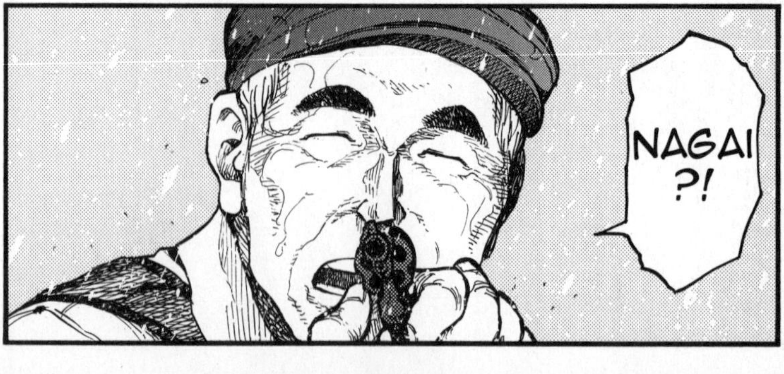
NAGAI ?!

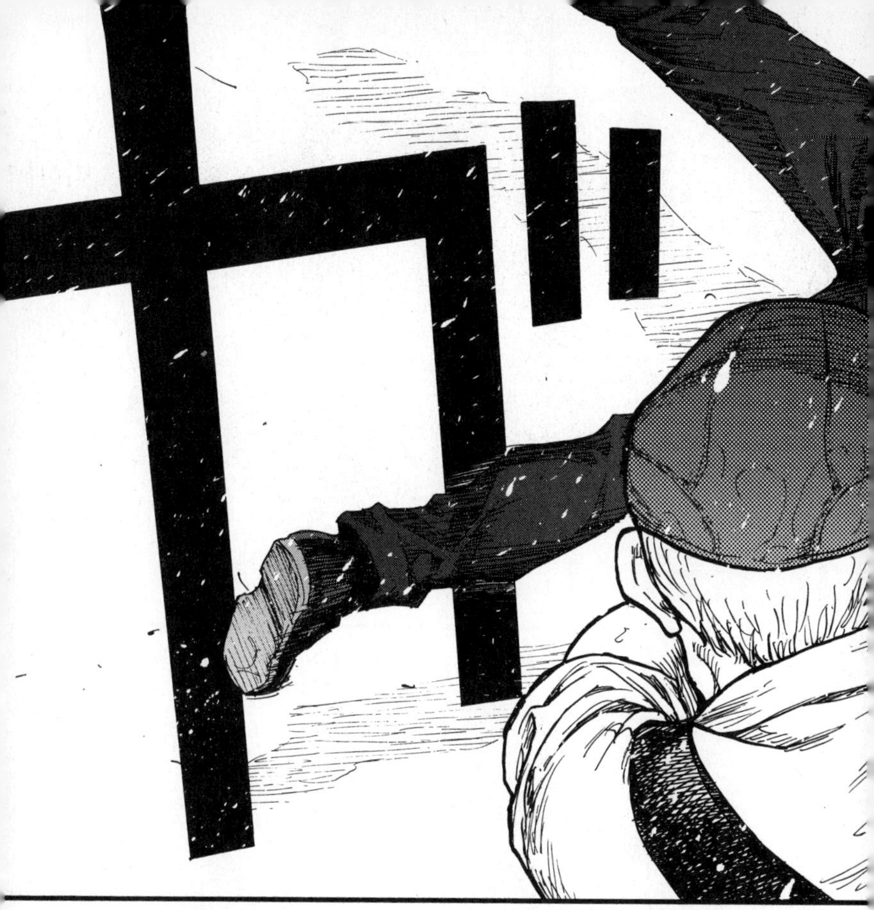

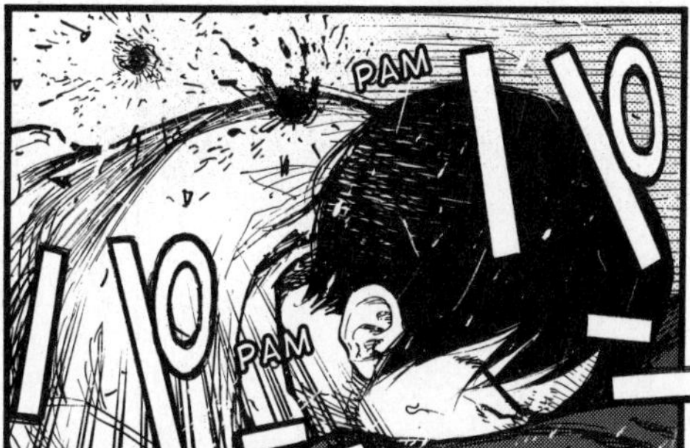
PAM
PAM

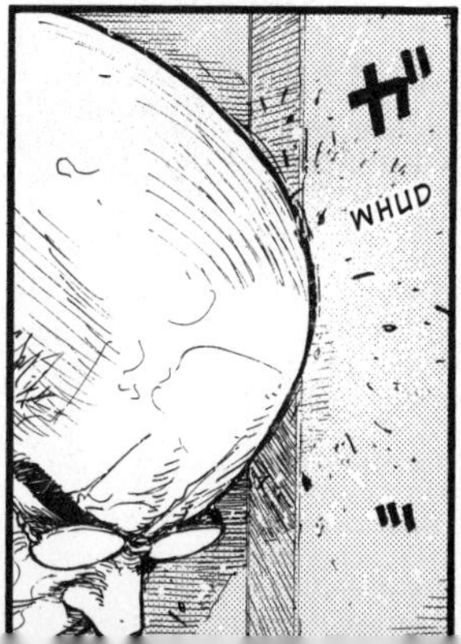
WHUD

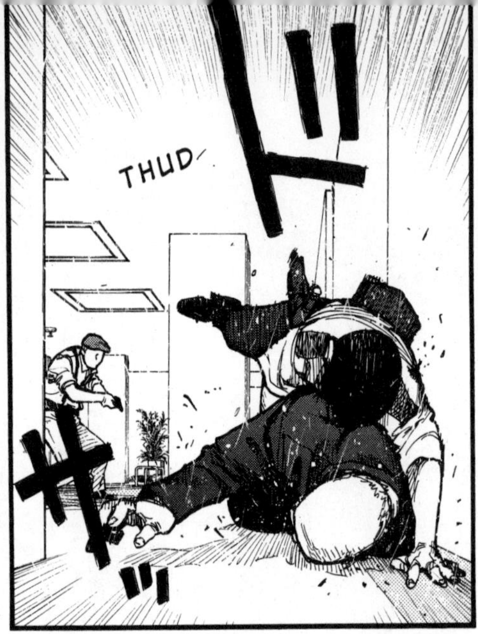
THUD
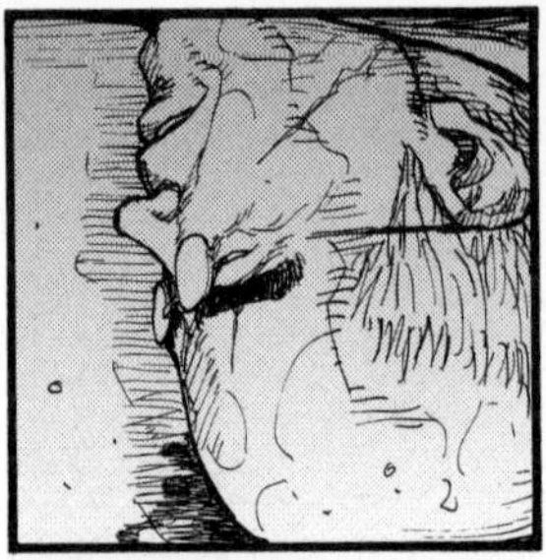
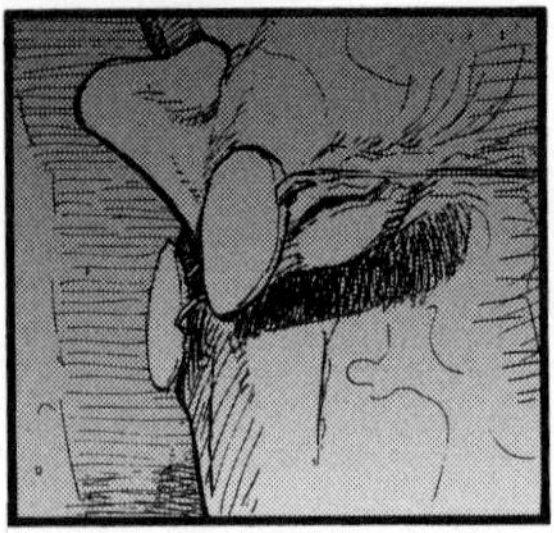
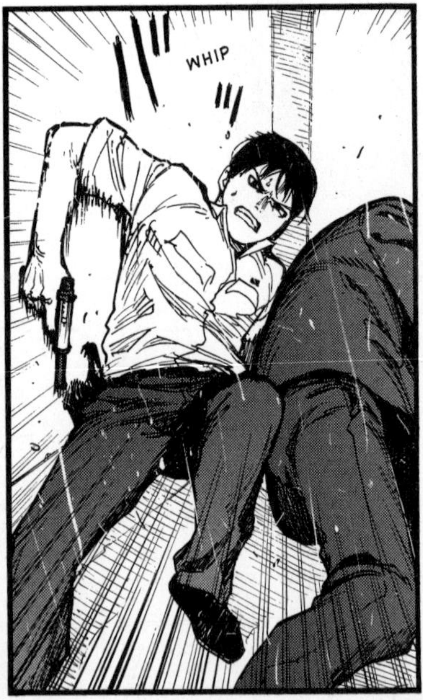
WHIP
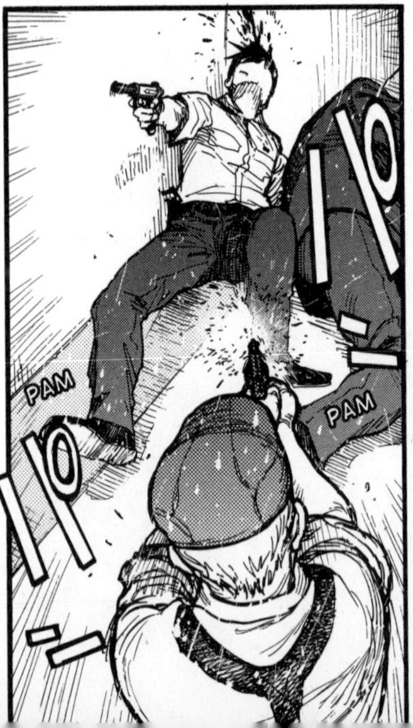
PAM
PAM

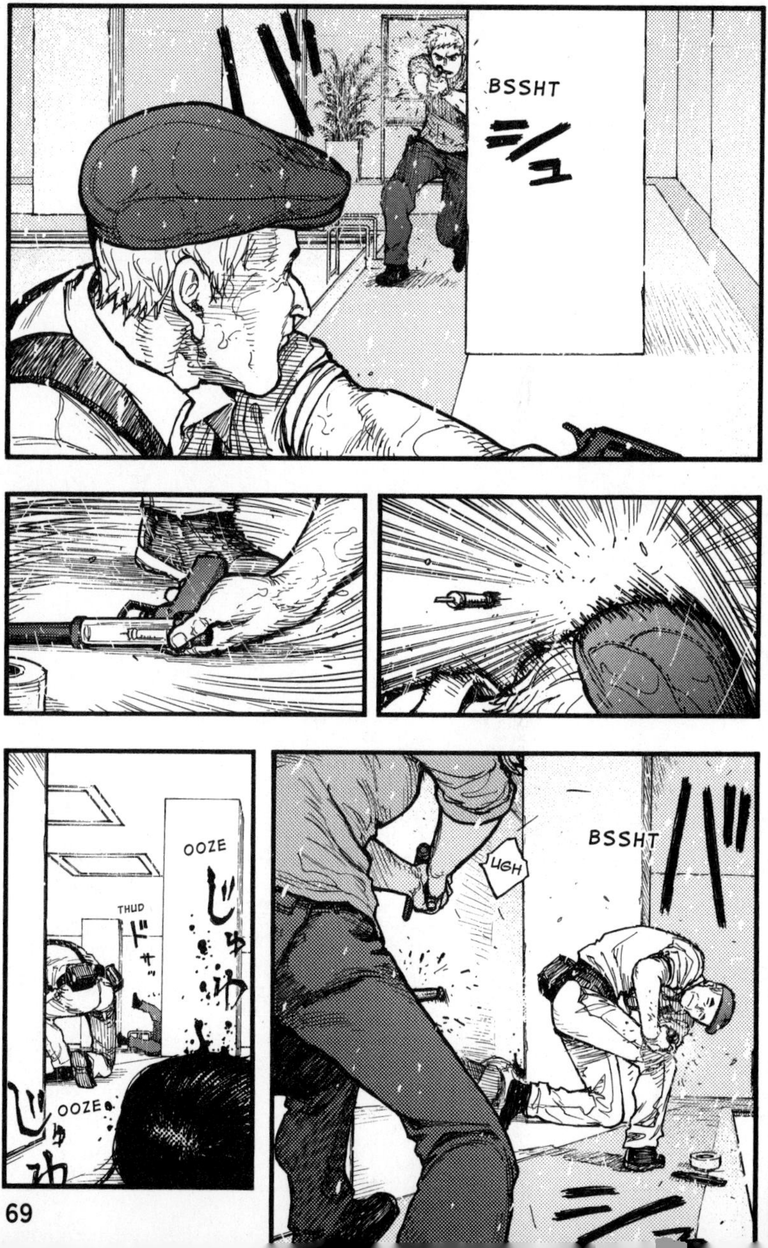
BSSHT
BSSHT
UGH
OOZE
じゅわ
THUD
ドサッ
OOZE
じゅわ

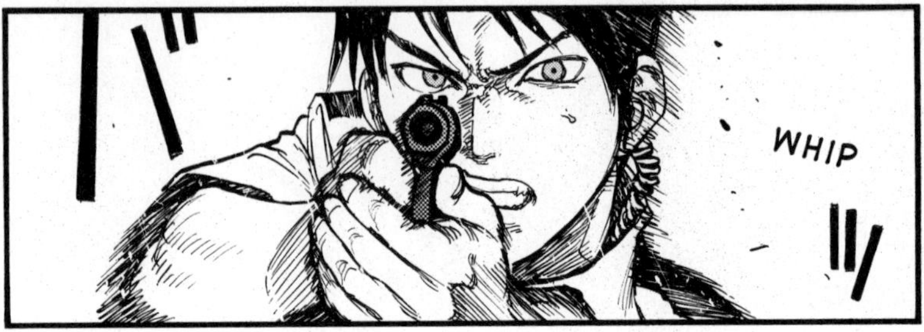
WHIP
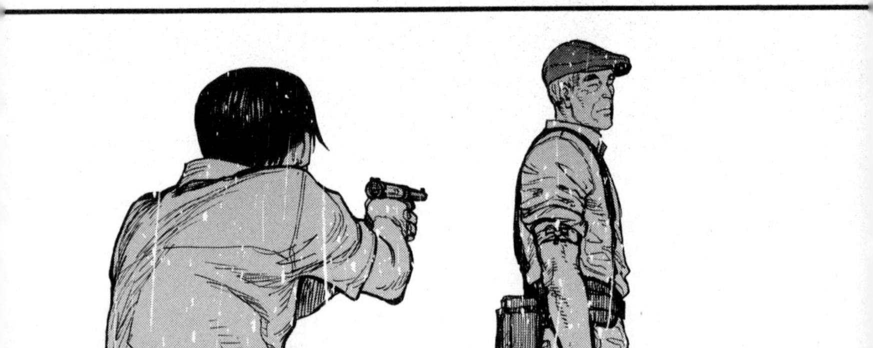
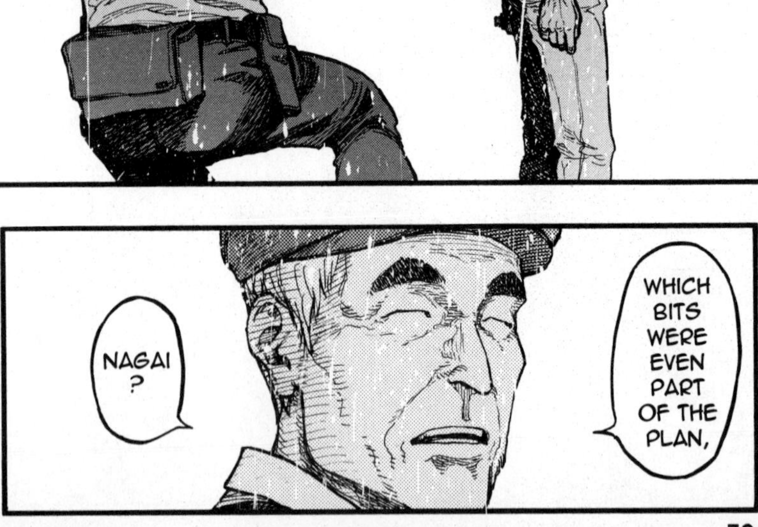
WHICH BITS WERE EVEN PART OF THE PLAN,
NAGAI?

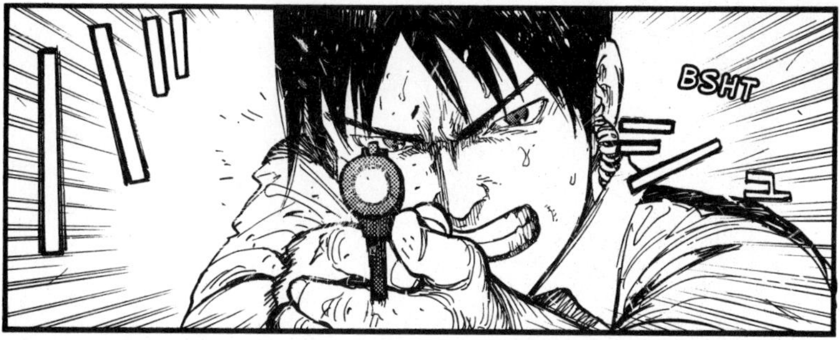
バジ
BSHT
ジュ
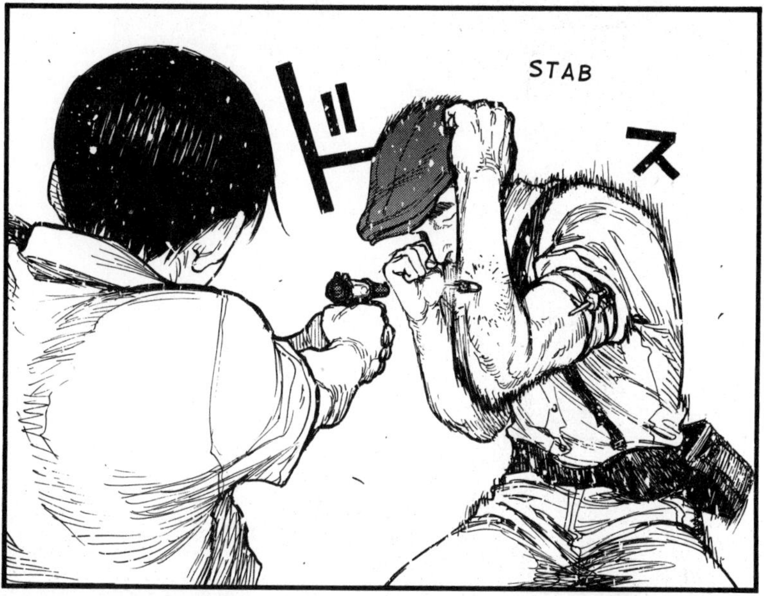
STAB
ドス
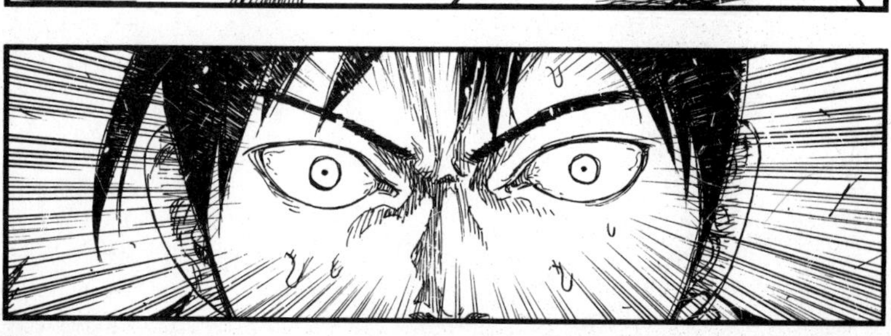

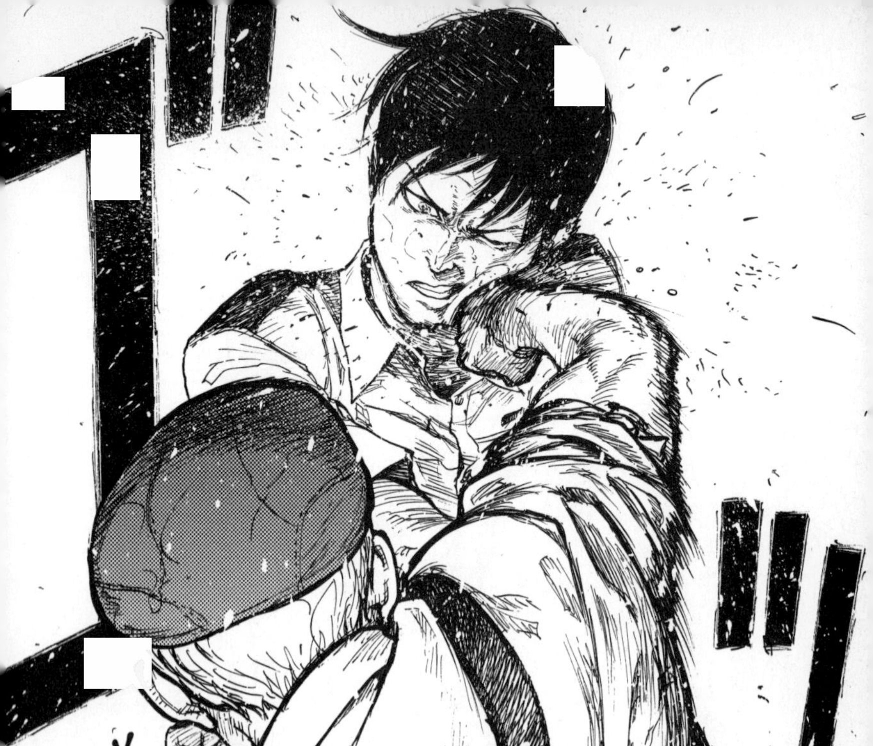
GWOK
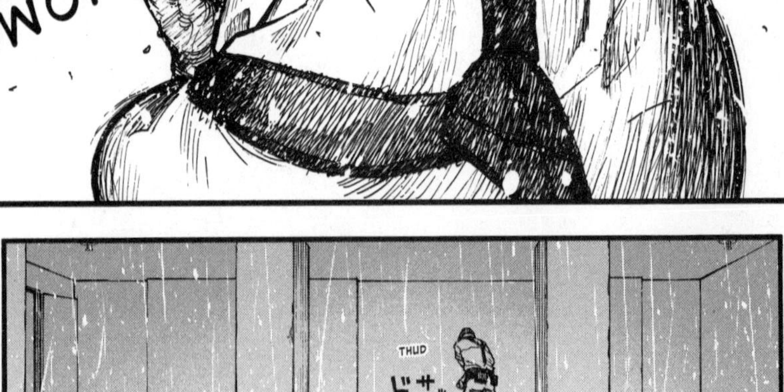
THUD
ドサッ
File:40 End

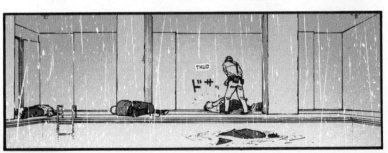

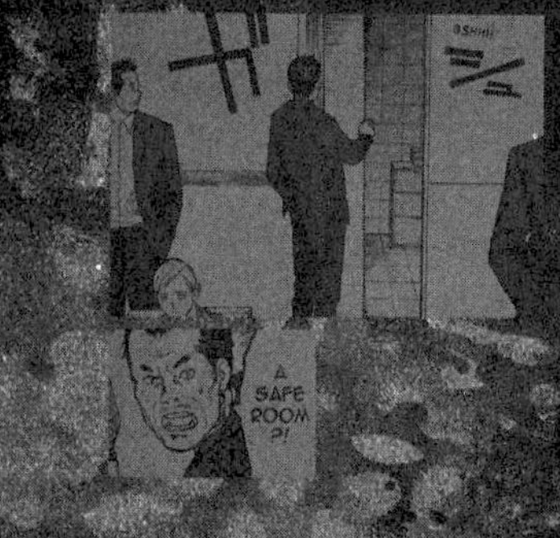
A SAFE ROOM ?!

File:41

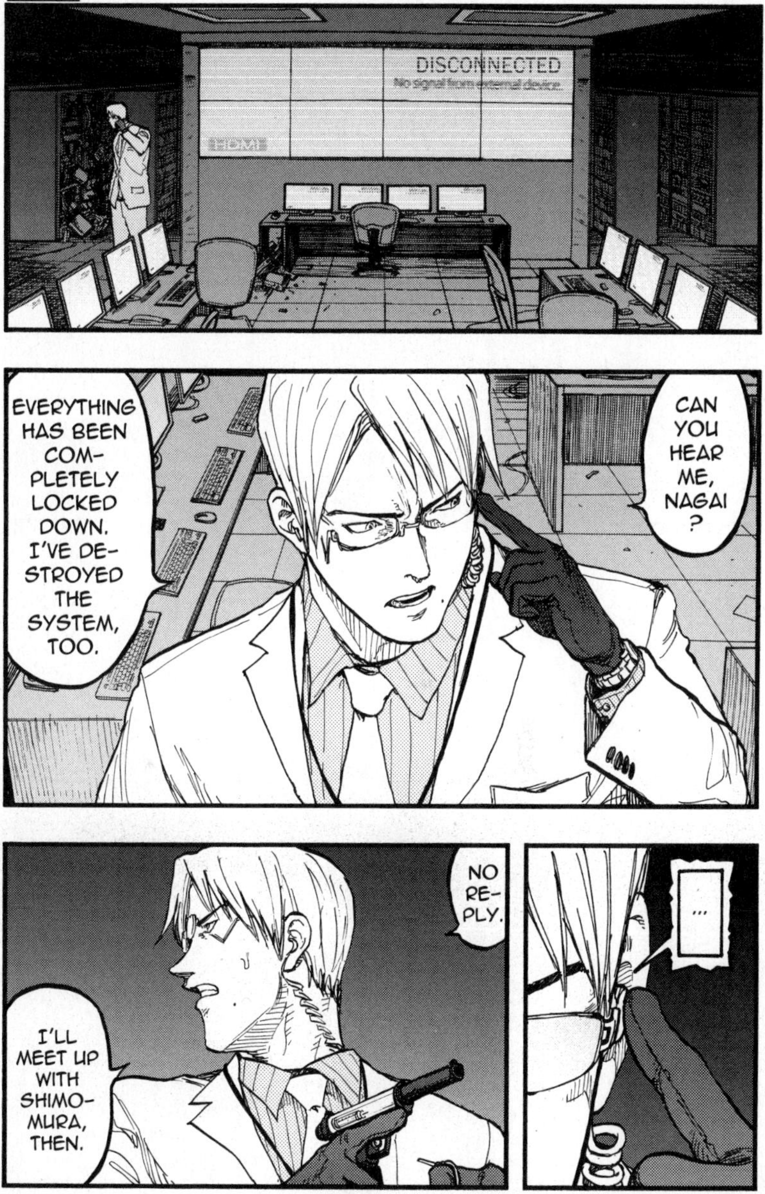
DISCONNECTED
No signal from external device...
HDMI
CAN YOU HEAR ME, NAGAI?
EVERYTHING HAS BEEN COM-PLETELY LOCKED DOWN. I'VE DE-STROYED THE SYSTEM, TOO.
...
NO RE-PLY.
I'LL MEET UP WITH SHIMO-MURA, THEN.

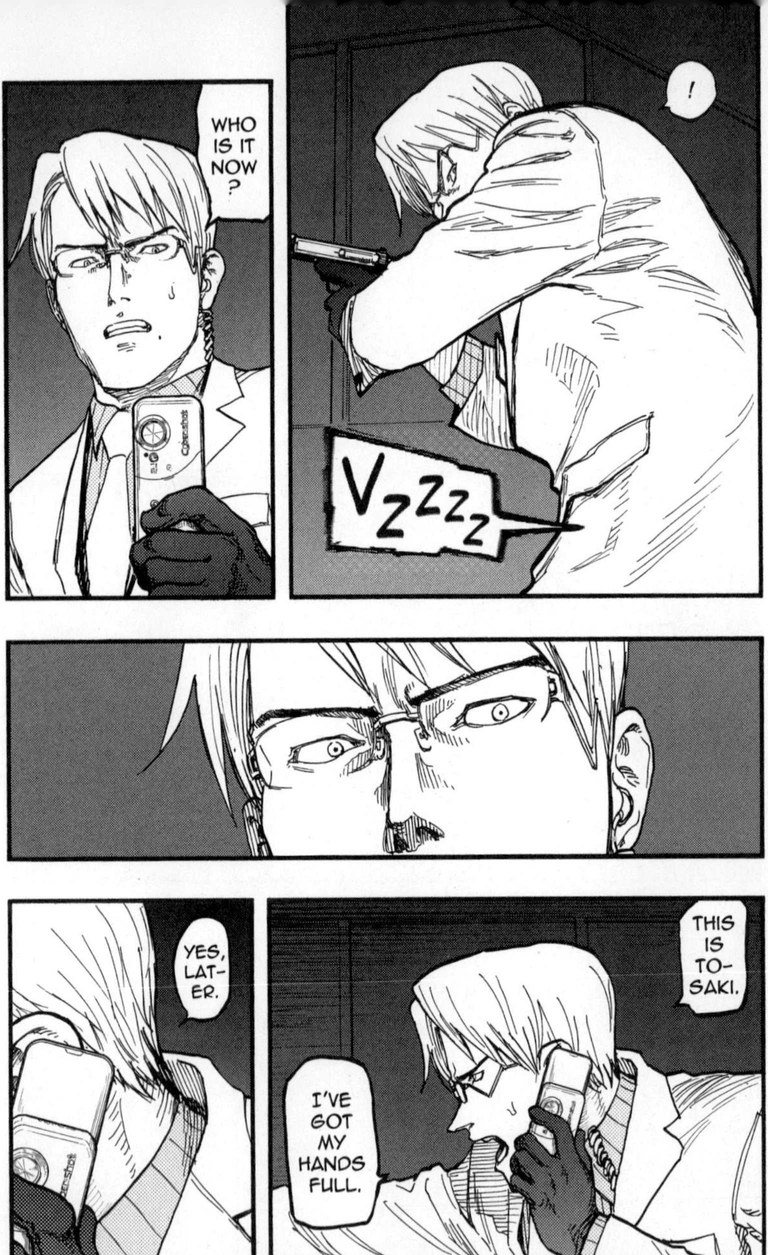
!
VZZZZ
WHO IS IT NOW?
THIS IS TO-SAKI.
I'VE GOT MY HANDS FULL.
YES, LATER.

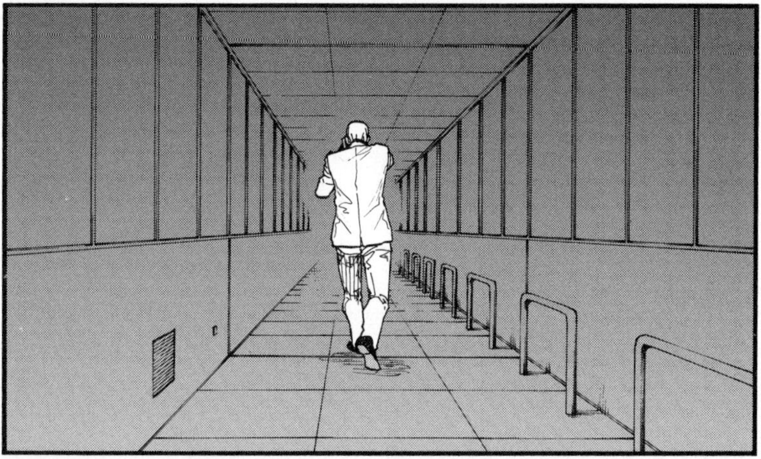

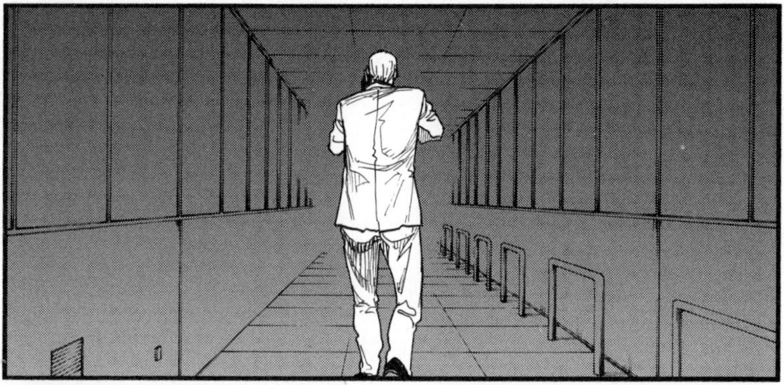

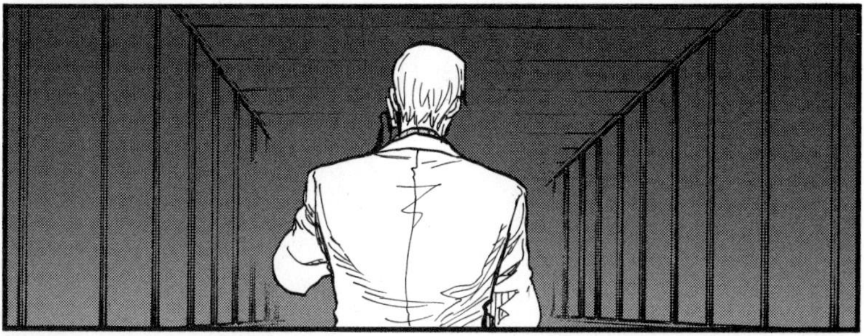

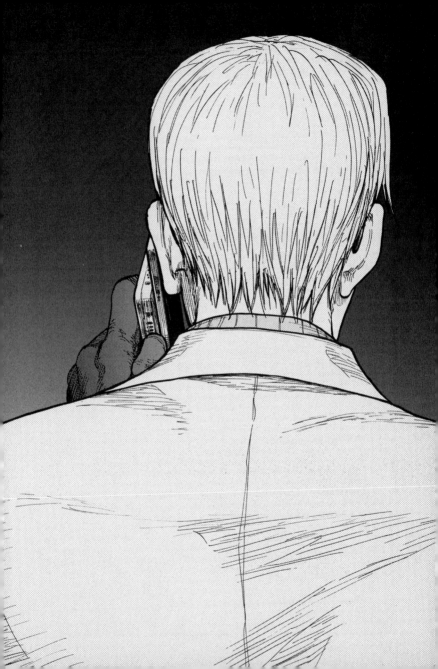

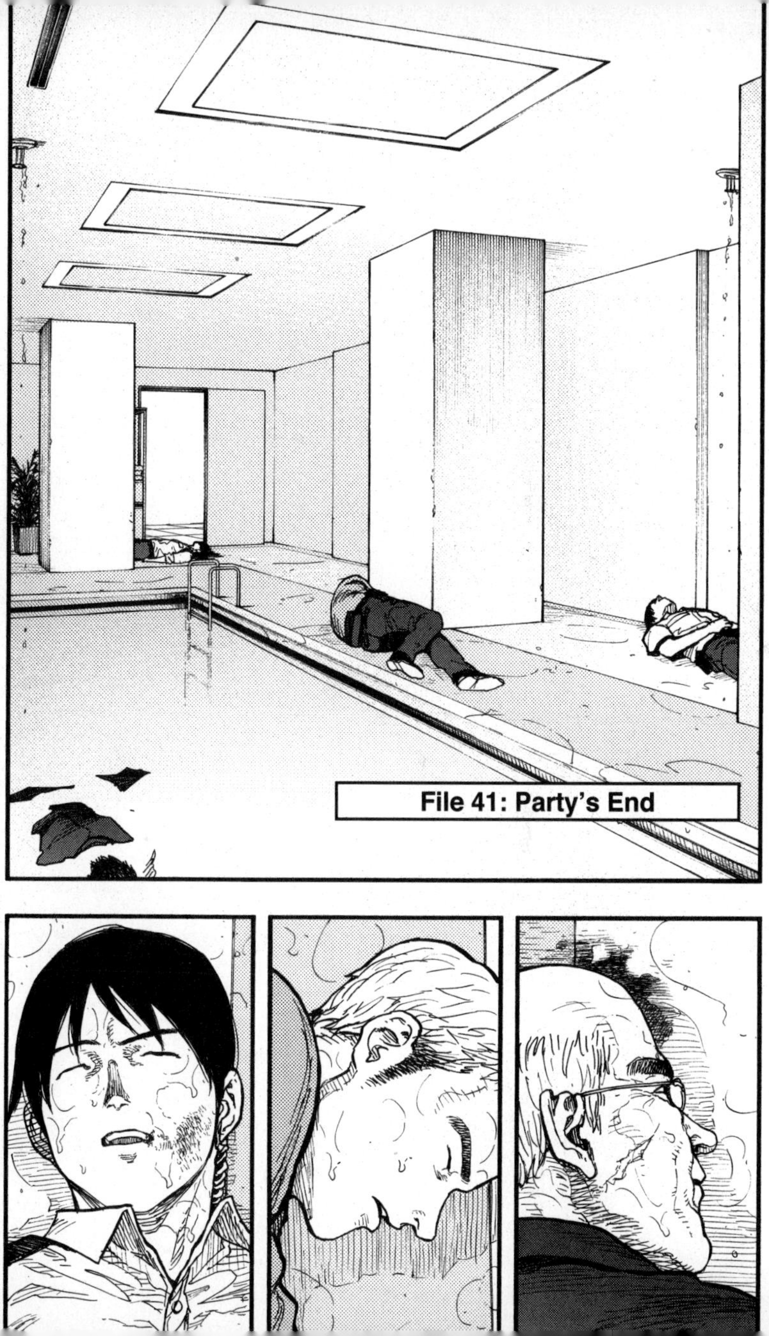
File 41: Party's End

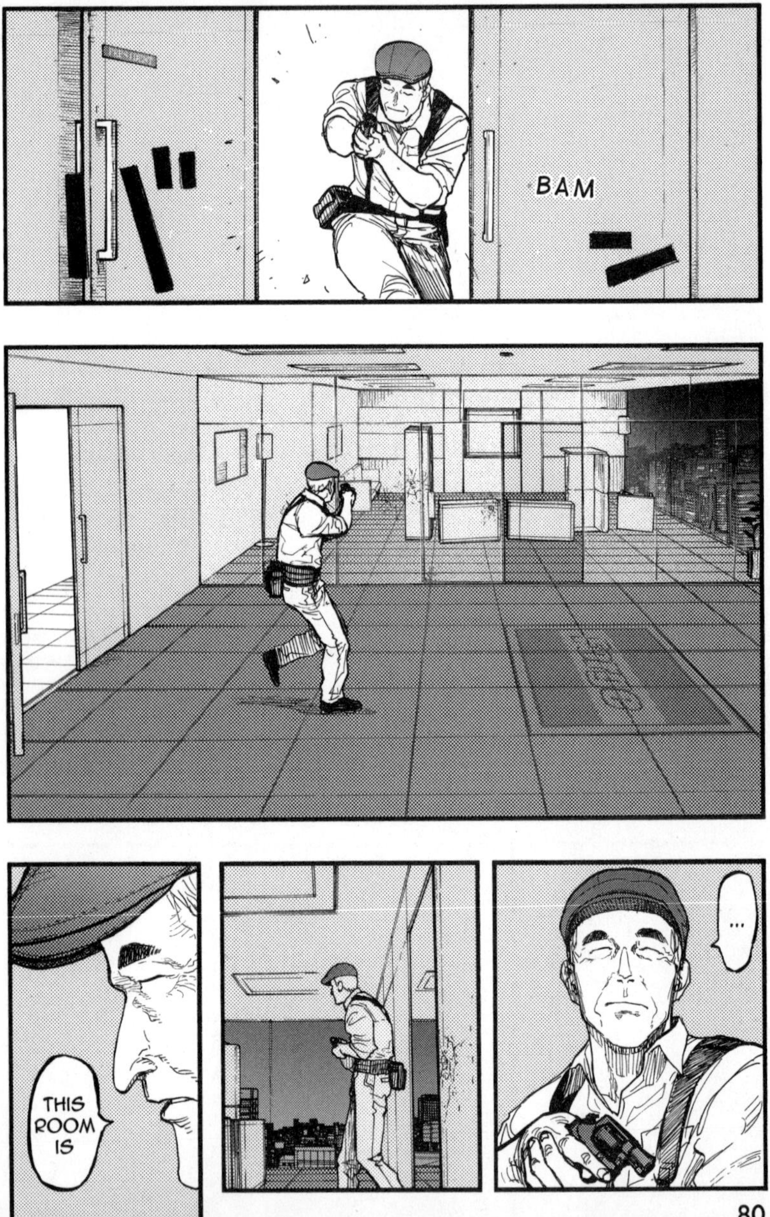
BAM
...
THIS ROOM IS

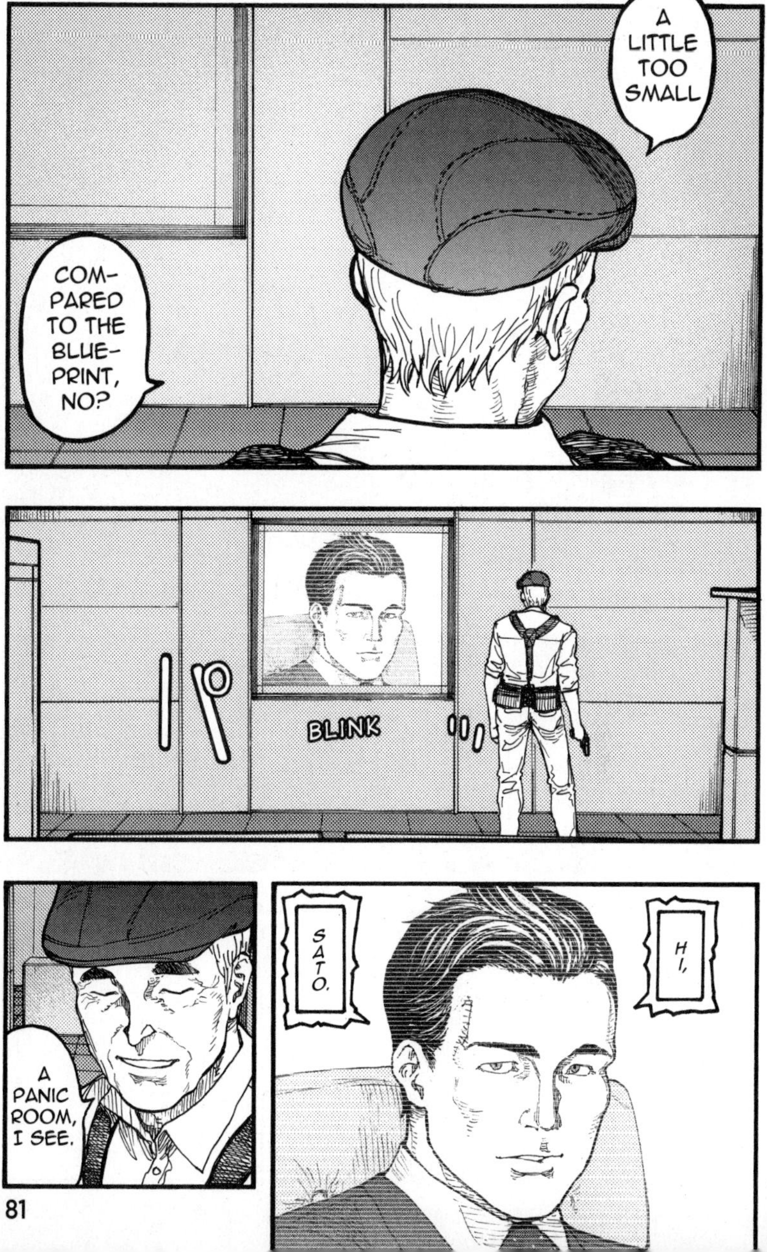
A LITTLE TOO SMALL
COMPARED TO THE BLUEPRINT, NO?
BLINK
HI,
SATO.
A PANIC ROOM, I SEE.

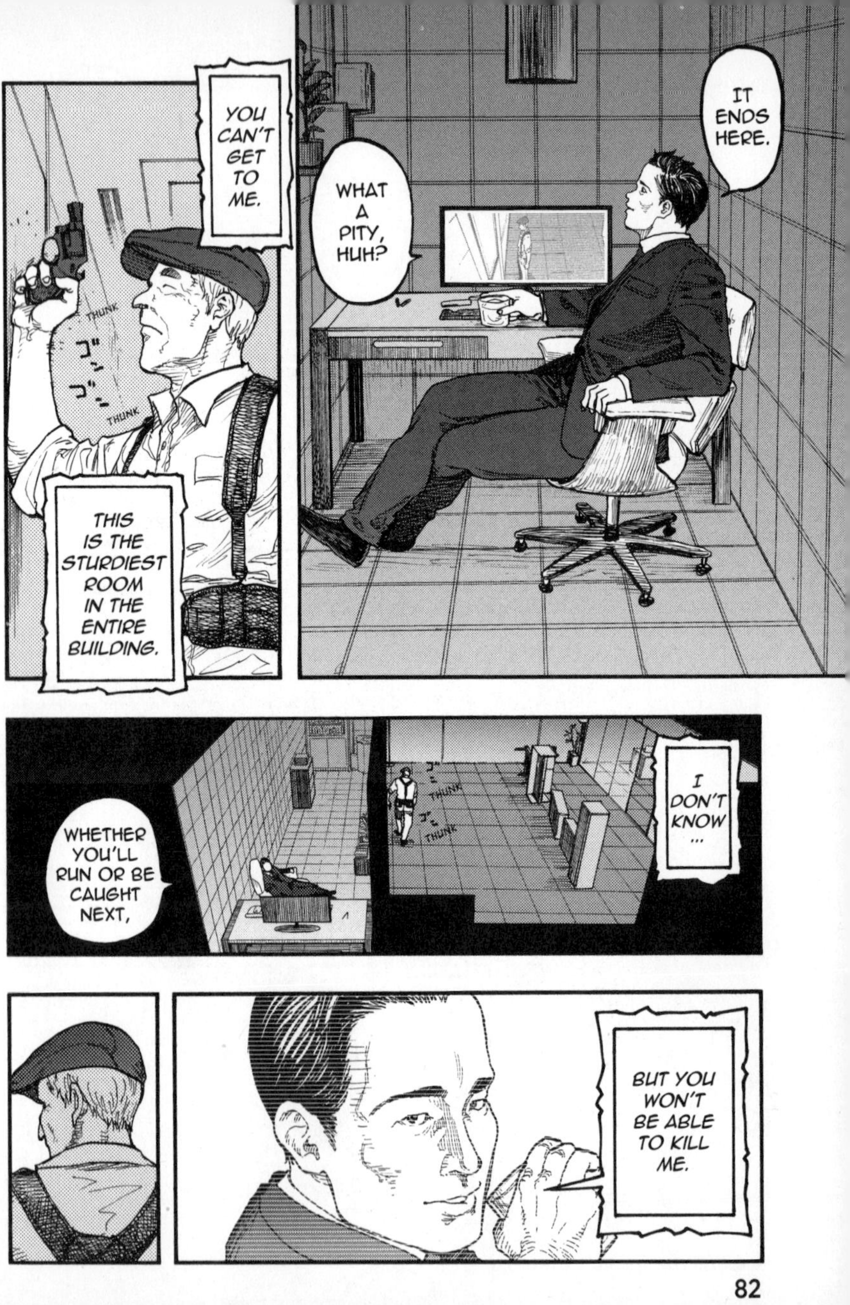
IT ENDS HERE.
WHAT A PITY, HUH?
YOU CAN'T GET TO ME.
THUNK
THUNK
THIS IS THE STURDIEST ROOM IN THE ENTIRE BUILDING.
I DON'T KNOW...
THUNK
THUNK
WHETHER YOU'LL RUN OR BE CAUGHT NEXT,
BUT YOU WON'T BE ABLE TO KILL ME.

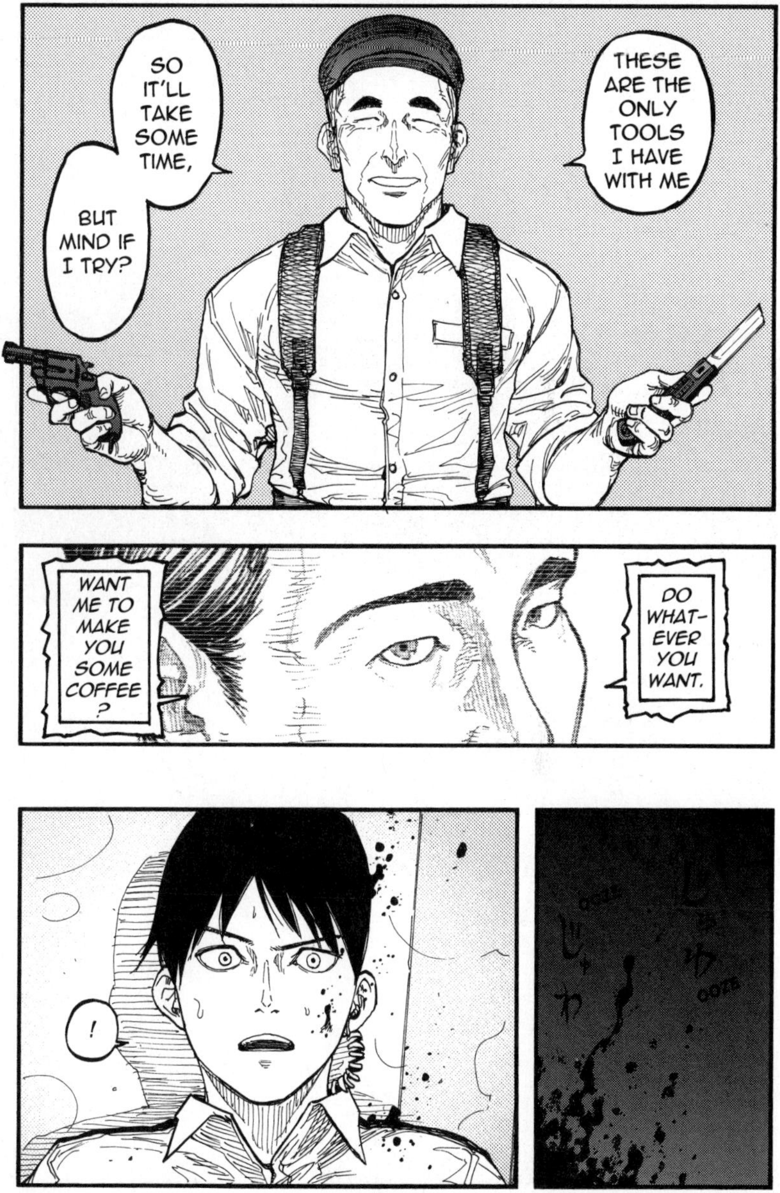
THESE ARE THE ONLY TOOLS I HAVE WITH ME
SO IT'LL TAKE SOME TIME,
BUT MIND IF I TRY?
DO WHATEVER YOU WANT.
WANT ME TO MAKE YOU SOME COFFEE?
OOZE
OOZE
!

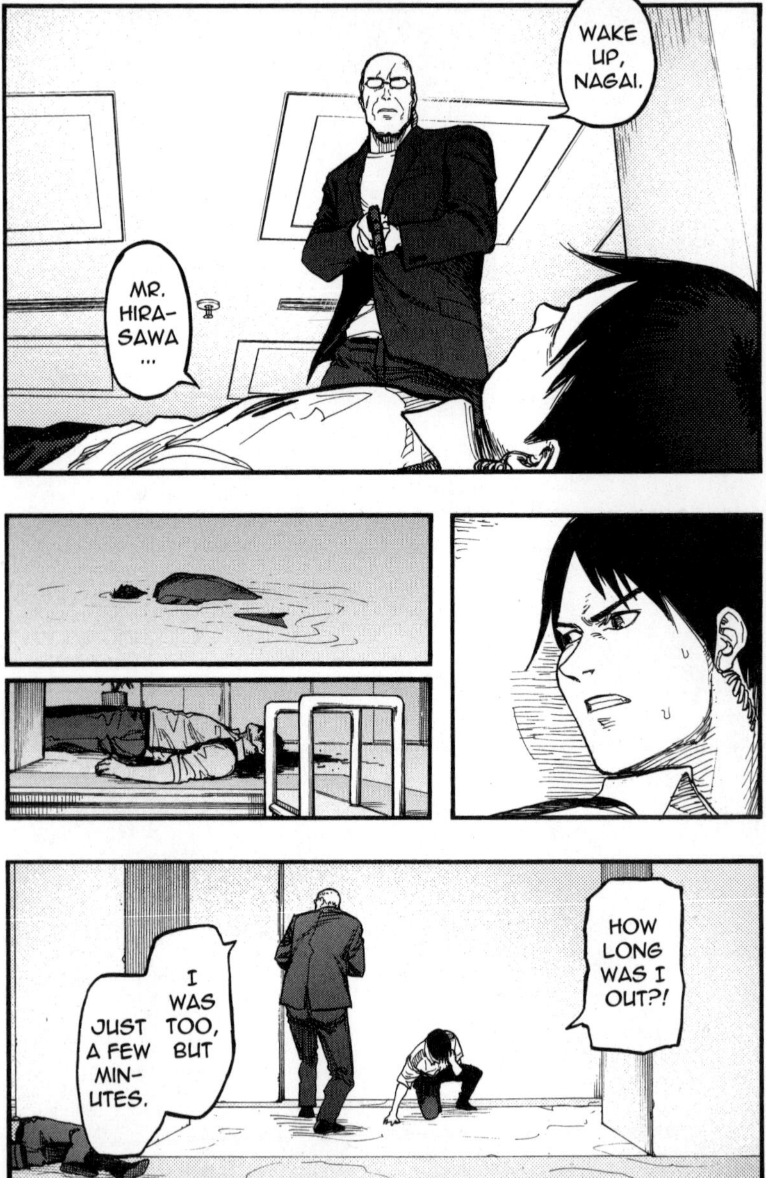
WAKE UP, NAGAI.
MR. HIRA-SAWA ...
HOW LONG WAS I OUT?!
I WAS TOO, BUT
JUST A FEW MIN-UTES.

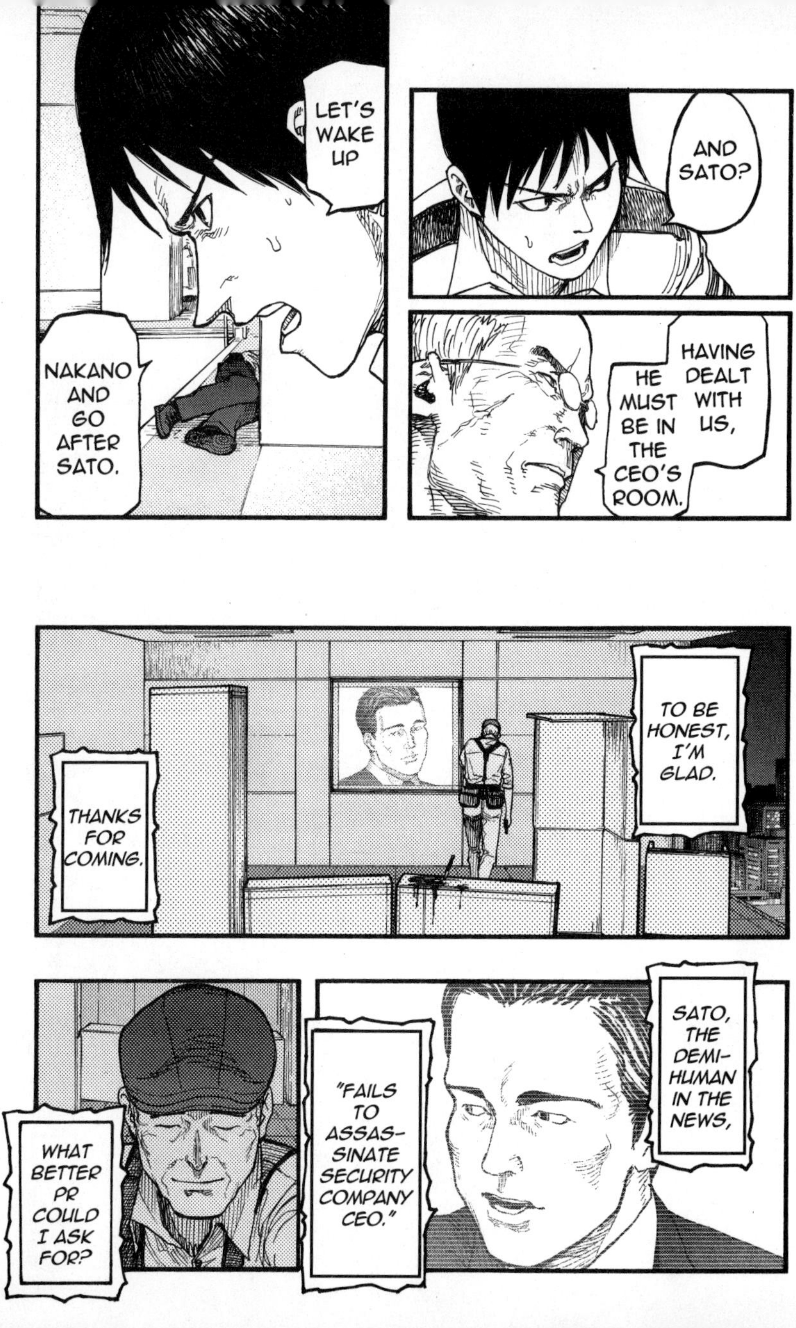
AND SATO?
HAVING DEALT WITH US, HE MUST BE IN THE CEO'S ROOM.
LET'S WAKE UP NAKANO AND GO AFTER SATO.
TO BE HONEST, I'M GLAD.
THANKS FOR COMING.
SATO, THE DEMI-HUMAN IN THE NEWS,
"FAILS TO ASSAS-SINATE SECURITY COMPANY CEO."
WHAT BETTER PR COULD I ASK FOR?

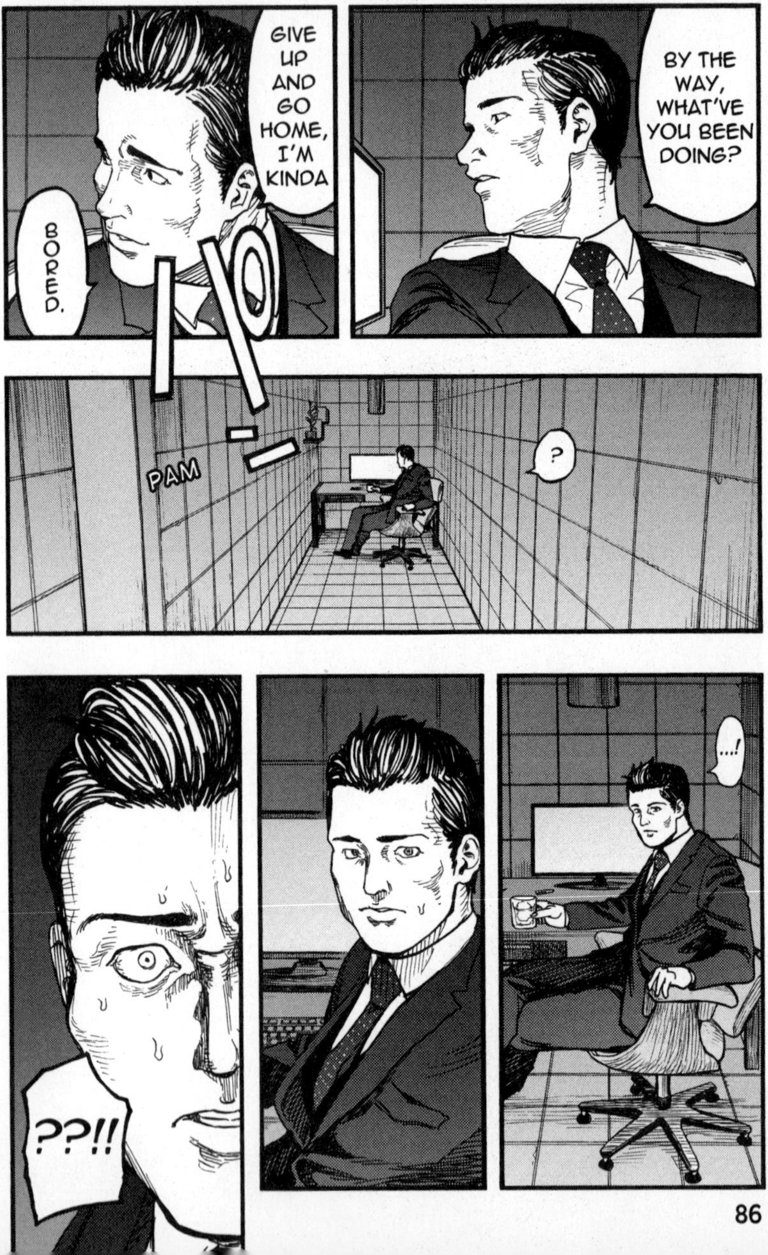
BY THE WAY, WHAT'VE YOU BEEN DOING?
GIVE UP AND GO HOME, I'M KINDA
BORED.
?
PAM
...!
??!!

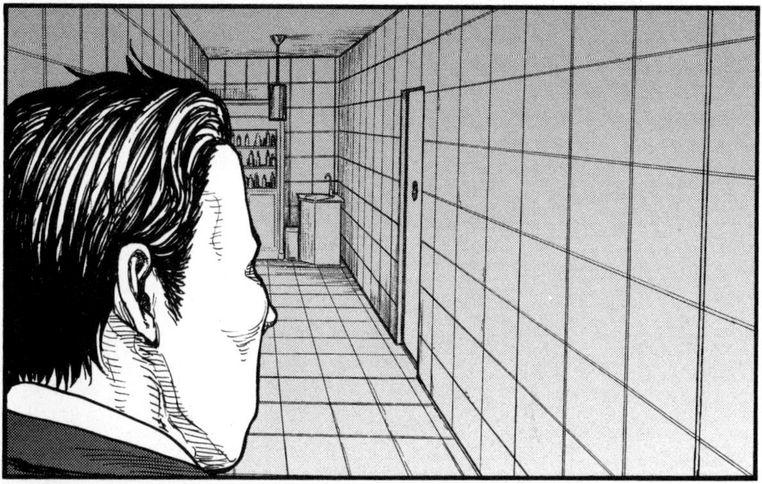
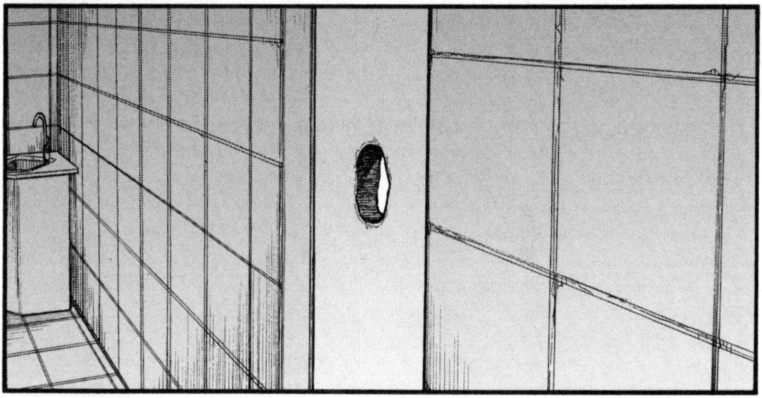
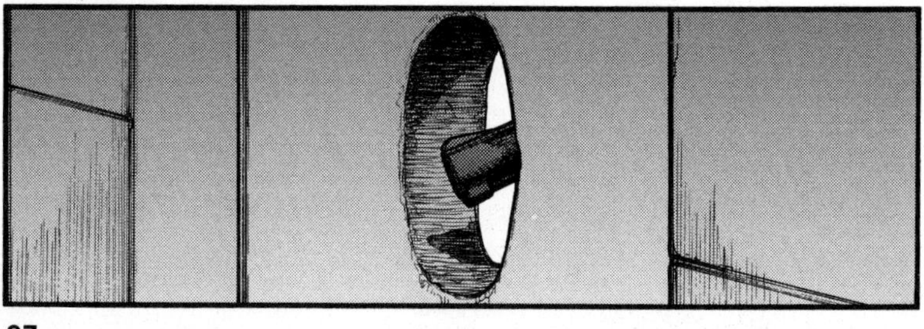

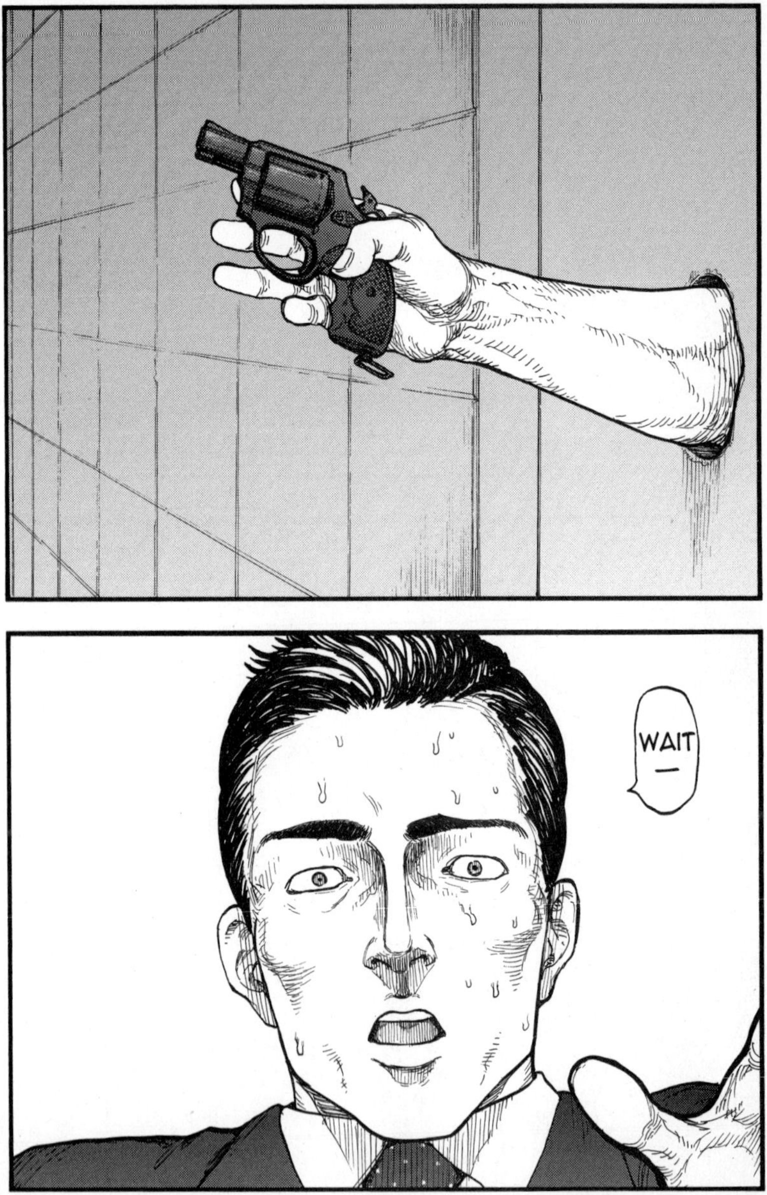
WAIT —

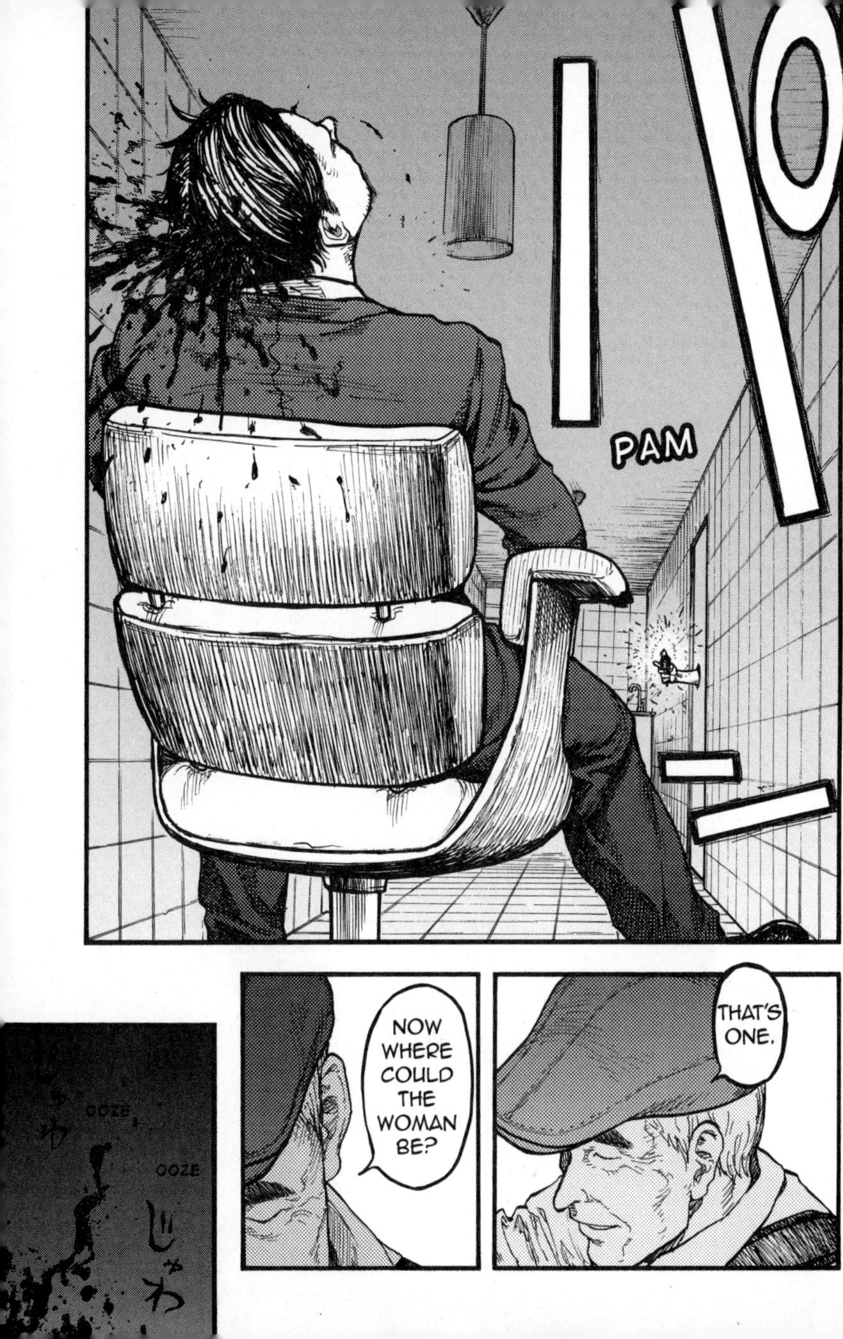
PAM
THAT'S ONE.
NOW WHERE COULD THE WOMAN BE?
OOZE
OOZE

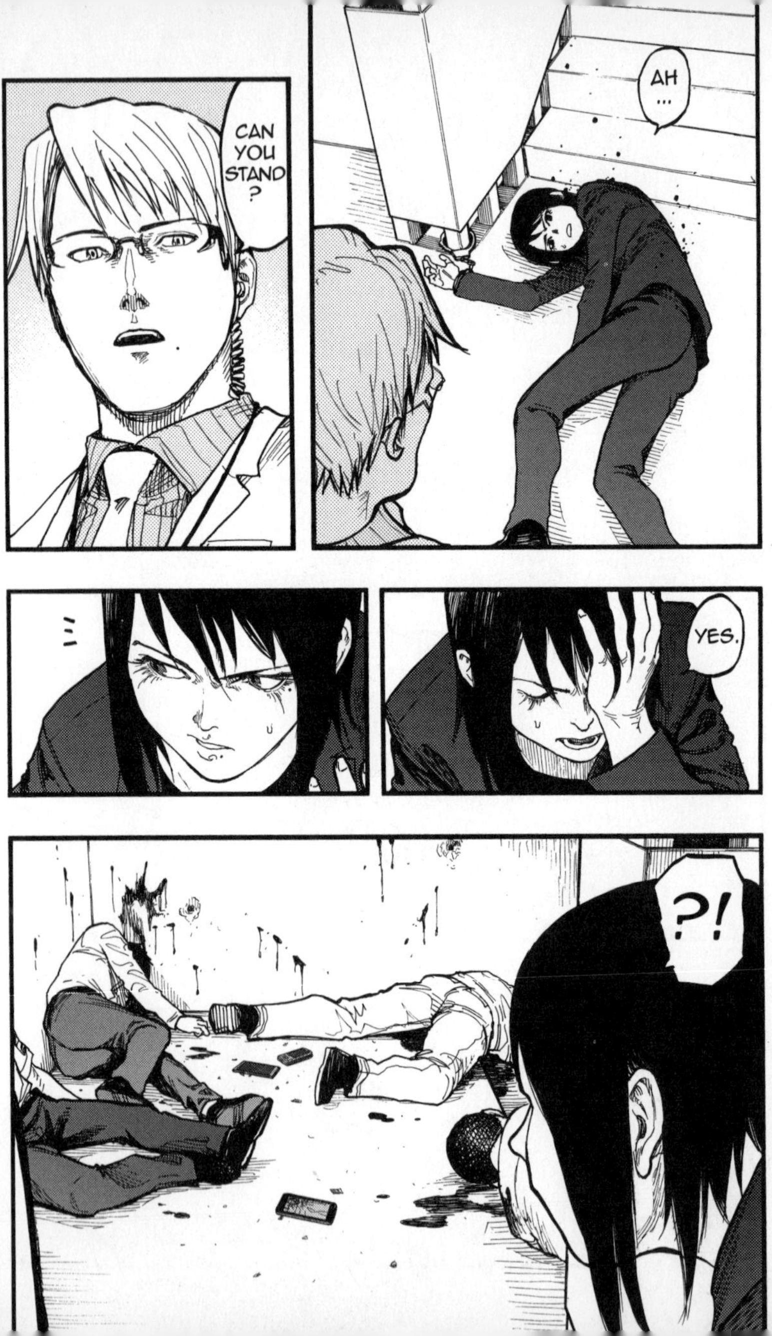
AH ...
CAN YOU STAND ?
YES.
?!

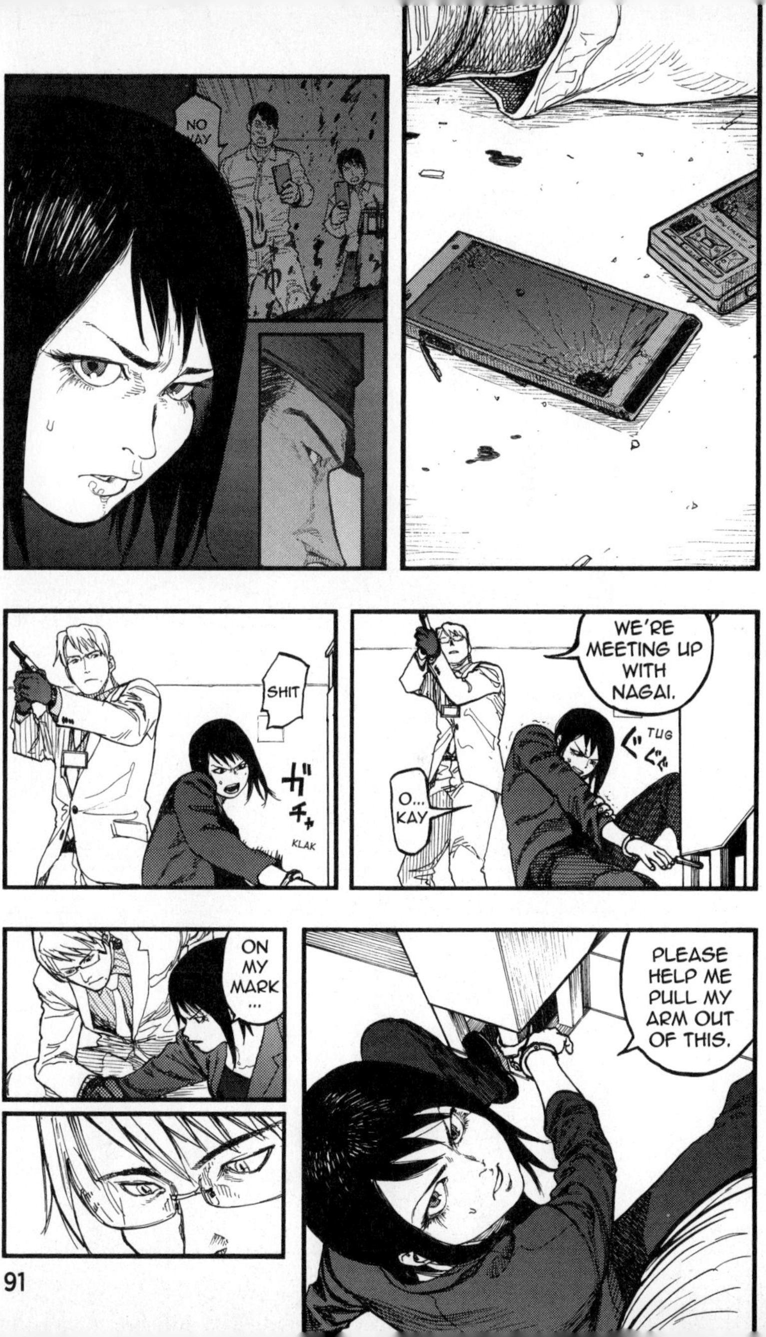
NO WAY
WE'RE MEETING UP WITH NAGAI.
TUG
O... KAY
SHIT
KLAK
PLEASE HELP ME PULL MY ARM OUT OF THIS.
ON MY MARK ...

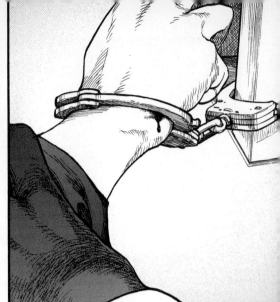

ス

SST

I'LL FIND THE KEY.

WHA ?!

MR. TOSAKI !

MR. TOSAKI ?!

HEY ...

92

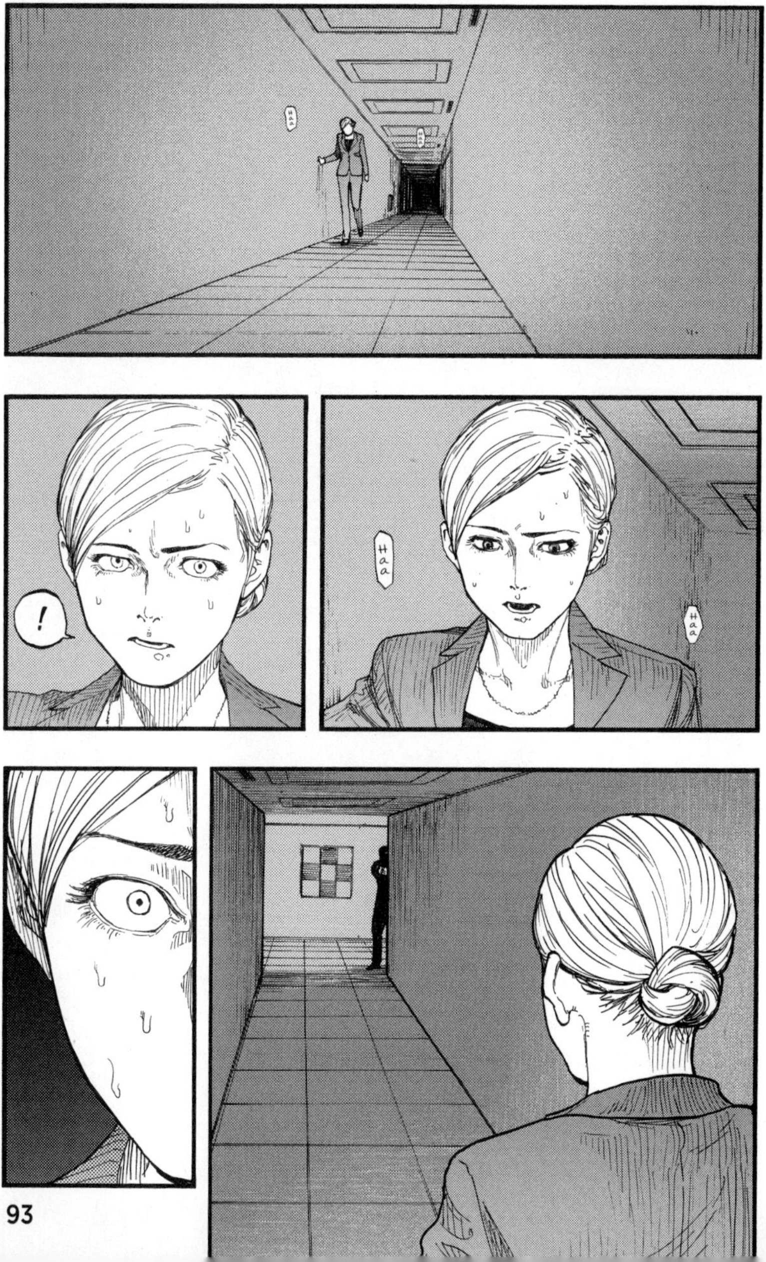
Haa
Haa
Haa
Haa
!

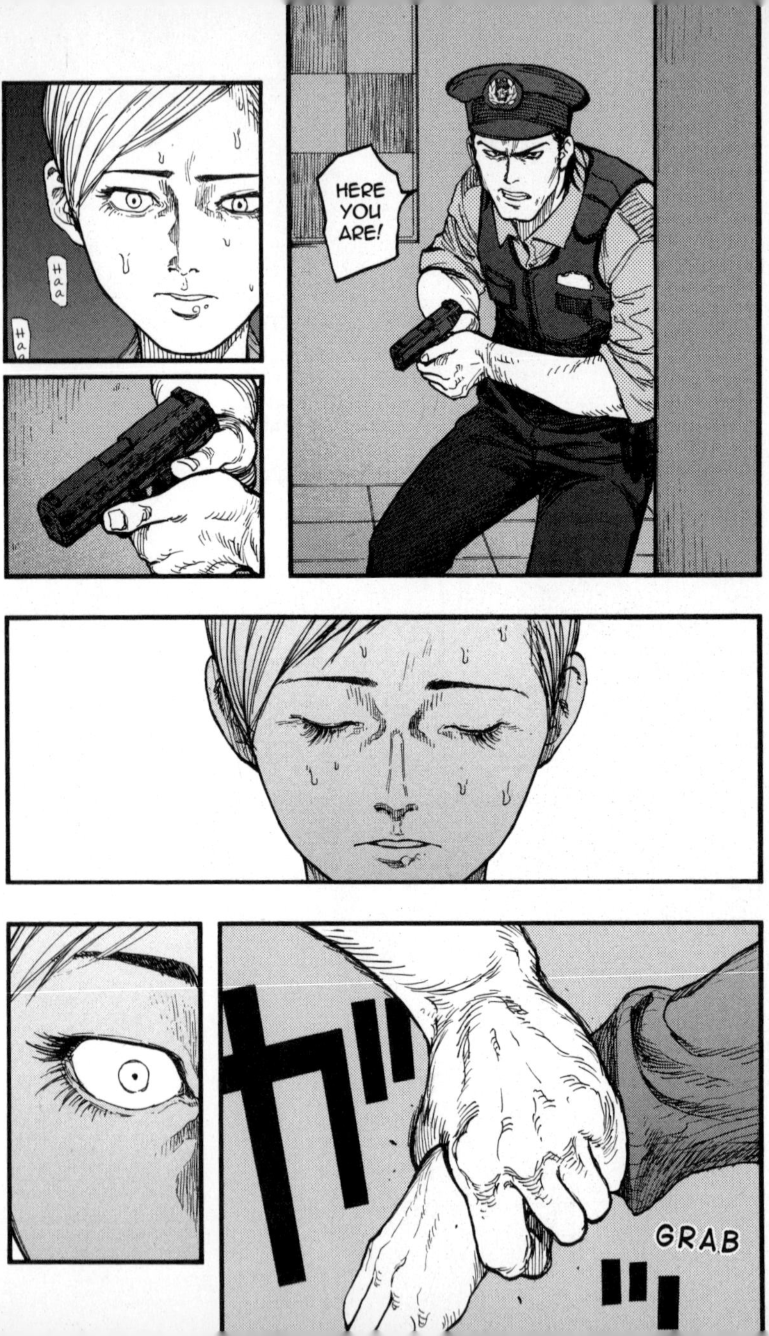
HERE YOU ARE!
Haa
Haa
GRAB

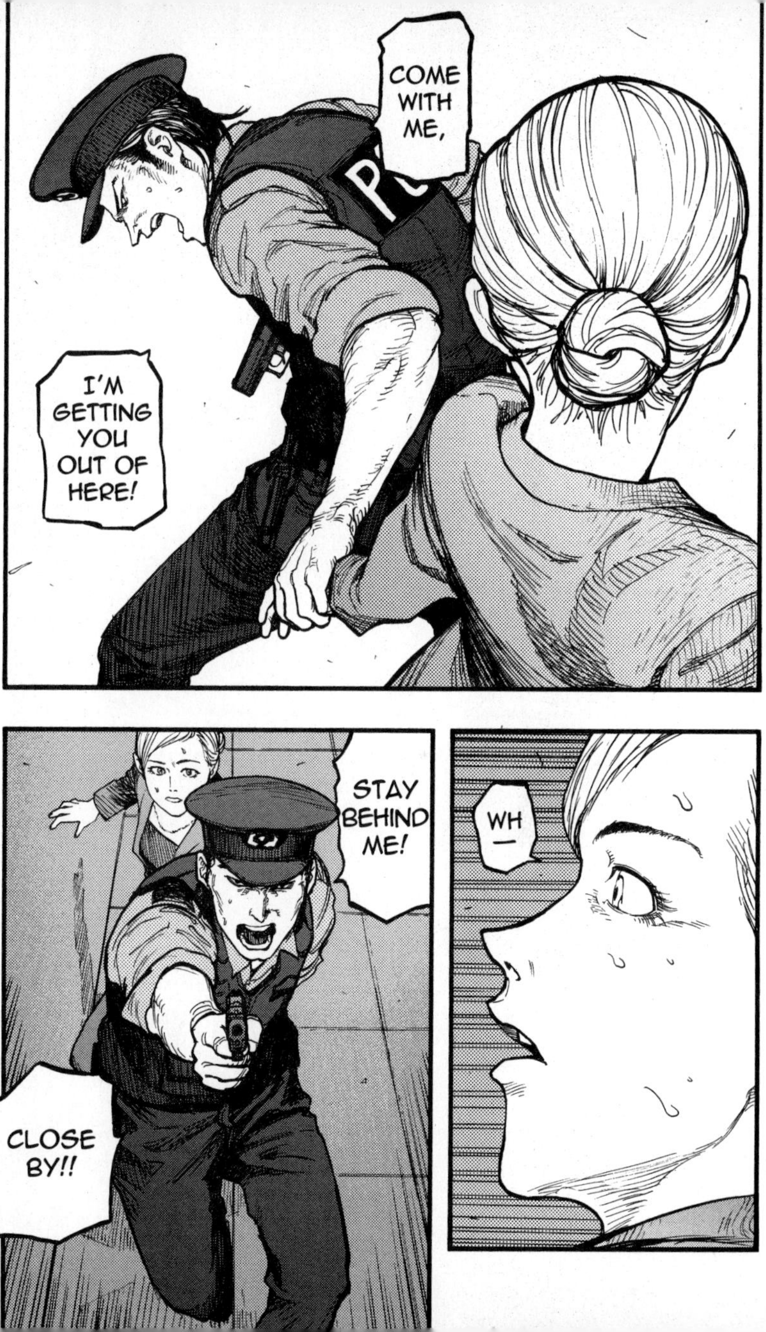
COME WITH ME,
I'M GETTING YOU OUT OF HERE!
WH—
STAY BEHIND ME!
CLOSE BY!!

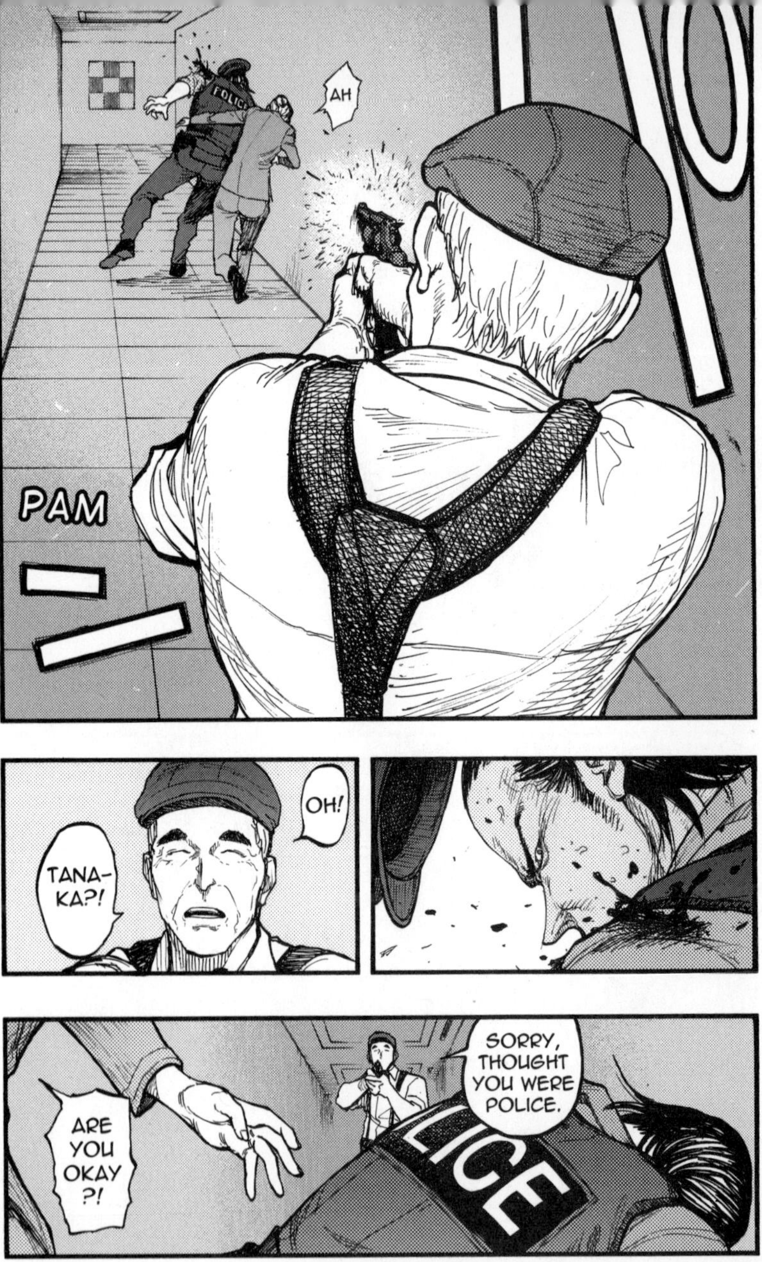
AH
PAM
OH!
TANA-KA?!
SORRY, THOUGHT YOU WERE POLICE.
ARE YOU OKAY ?!

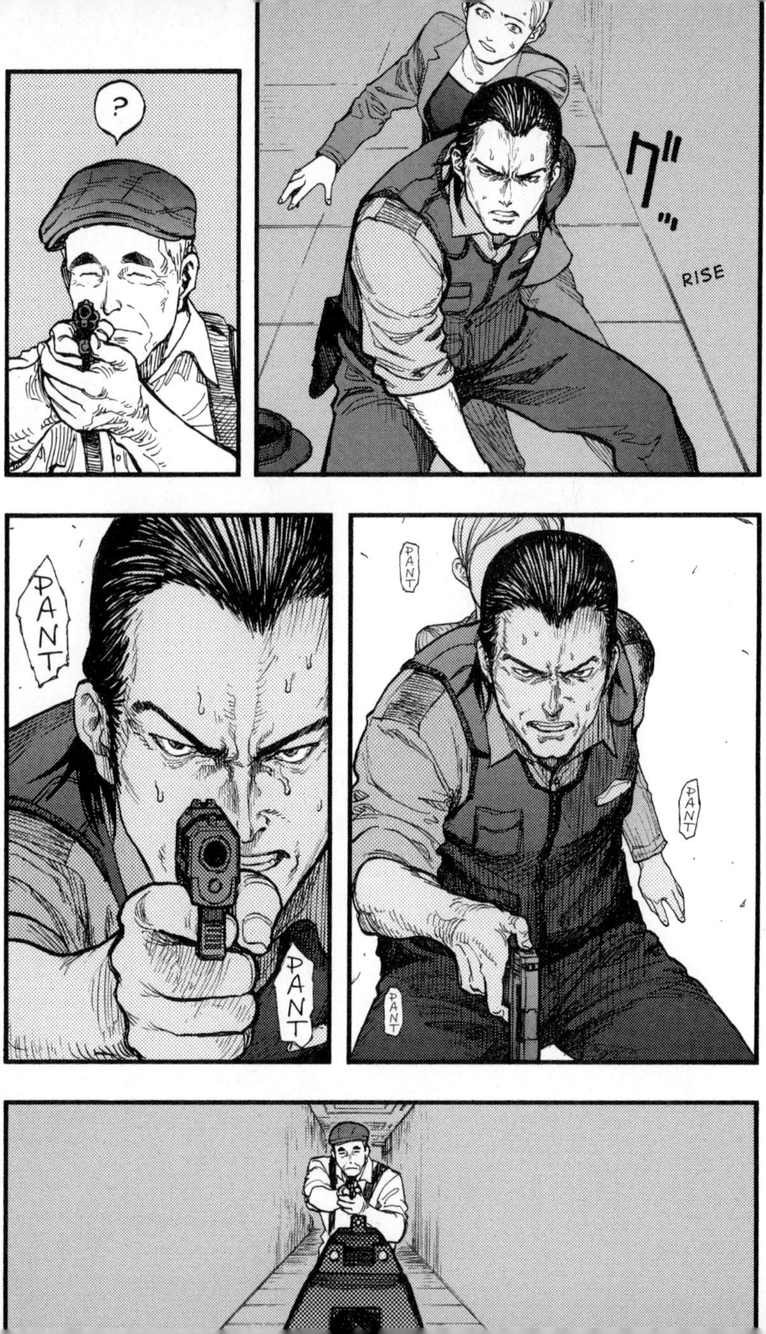
RISE
?
PANT
PANT
PANT
PANT
PANT

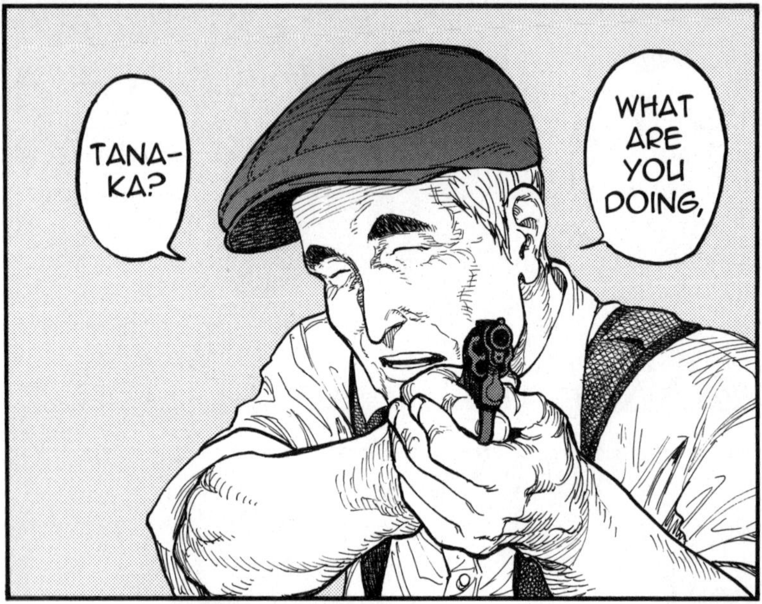
WHAT ARE YOU DOING,
TANA-KA?

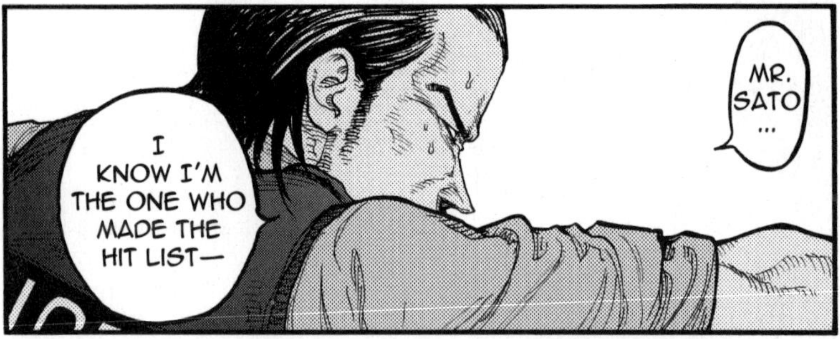
MR. SATO ...
I KNOW I'M THE ONE WHO MADE THE HIT LIST—

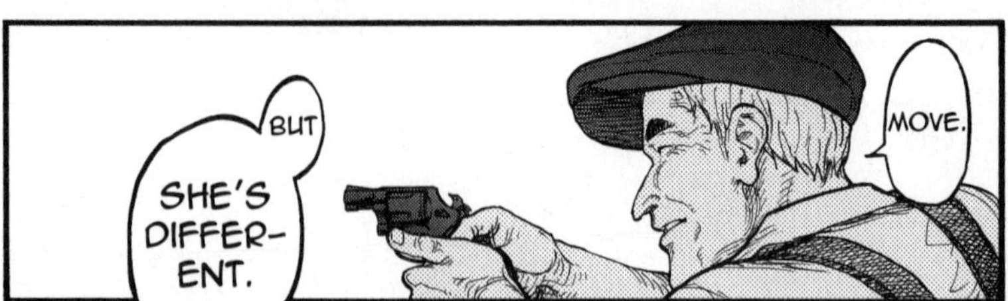
MOVE.
BUT
SHE'S DIFFER-ENT.

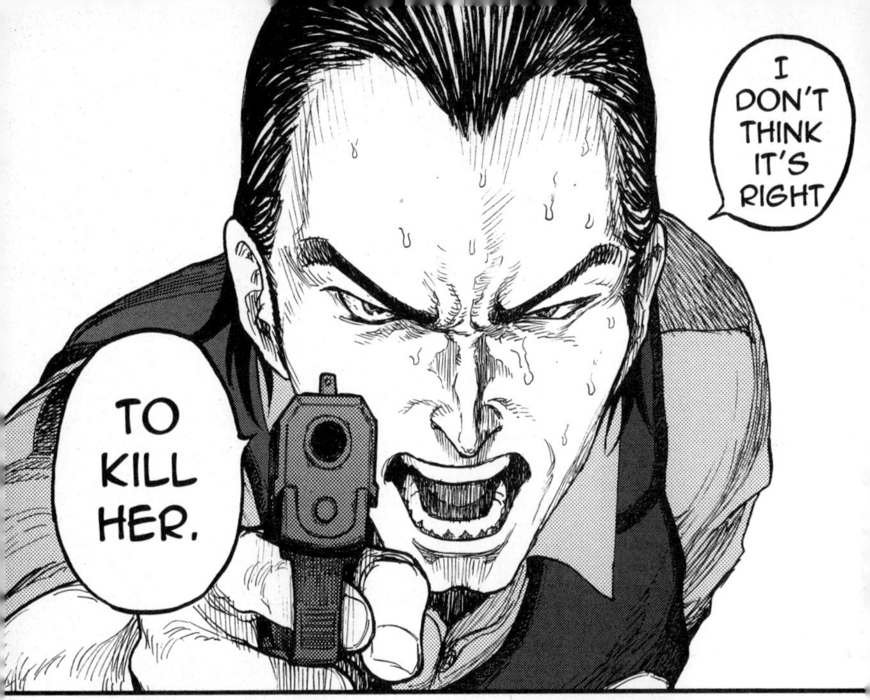
I DON'T THINK IT'S RIGHT
TO KILL HER.
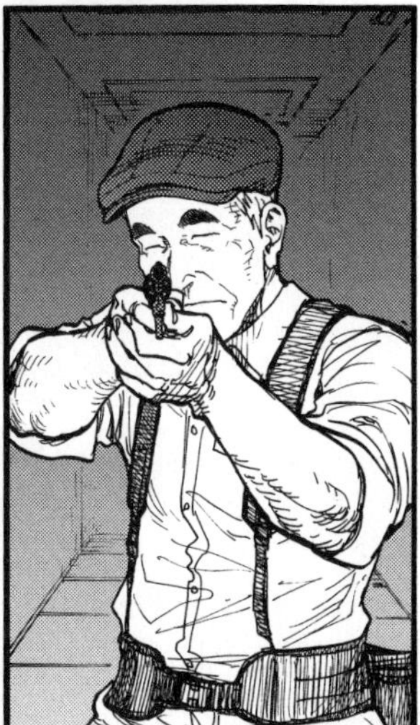
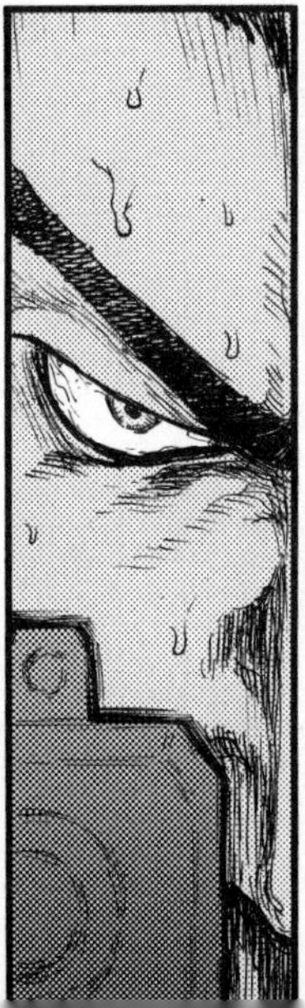
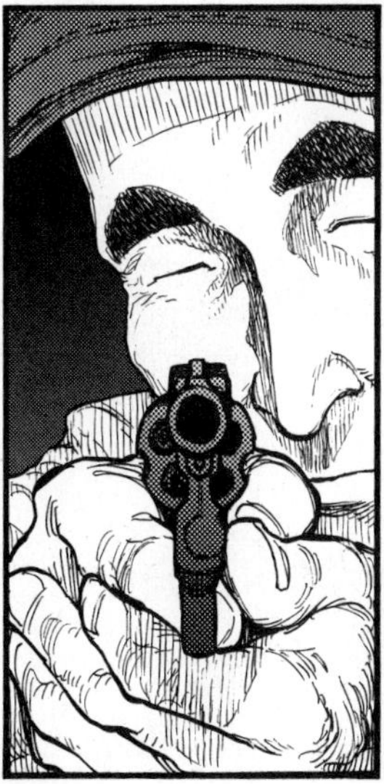

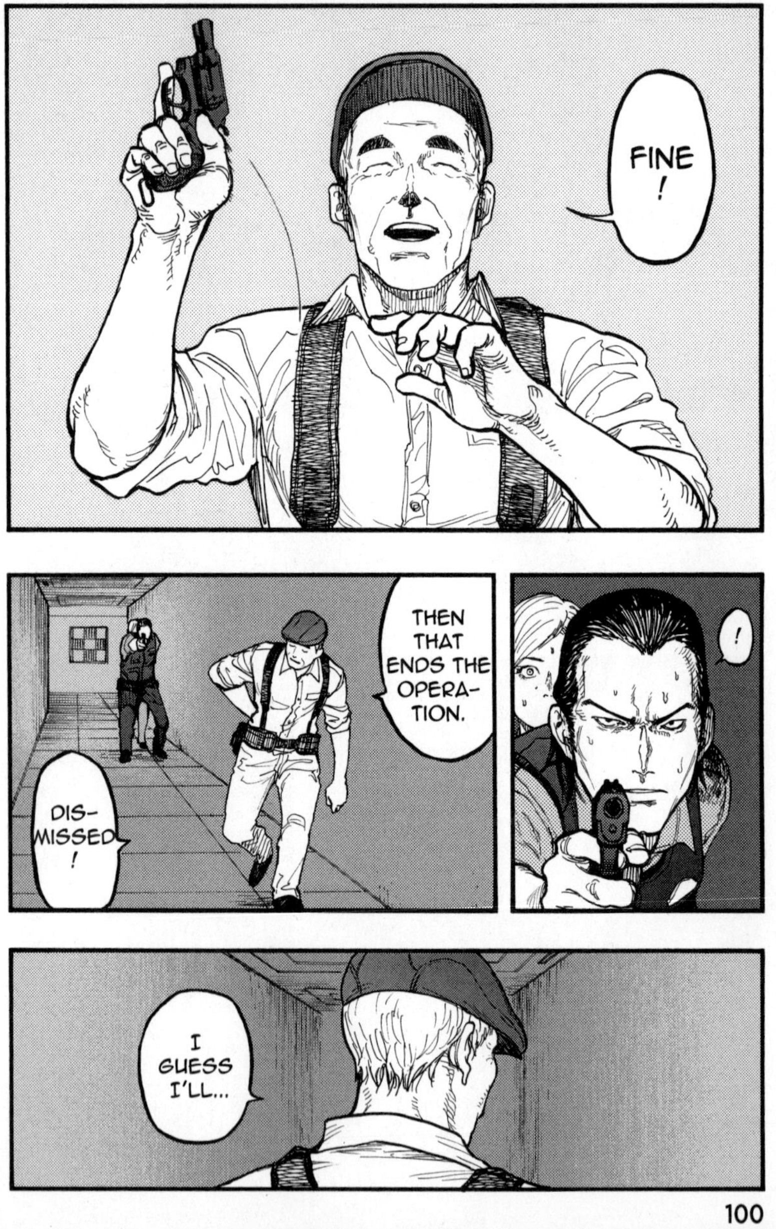
FINE!
!
THEN THAT ENDS THE OPERA-TION.
DIS-MISSED!
I GUESS I'LL...

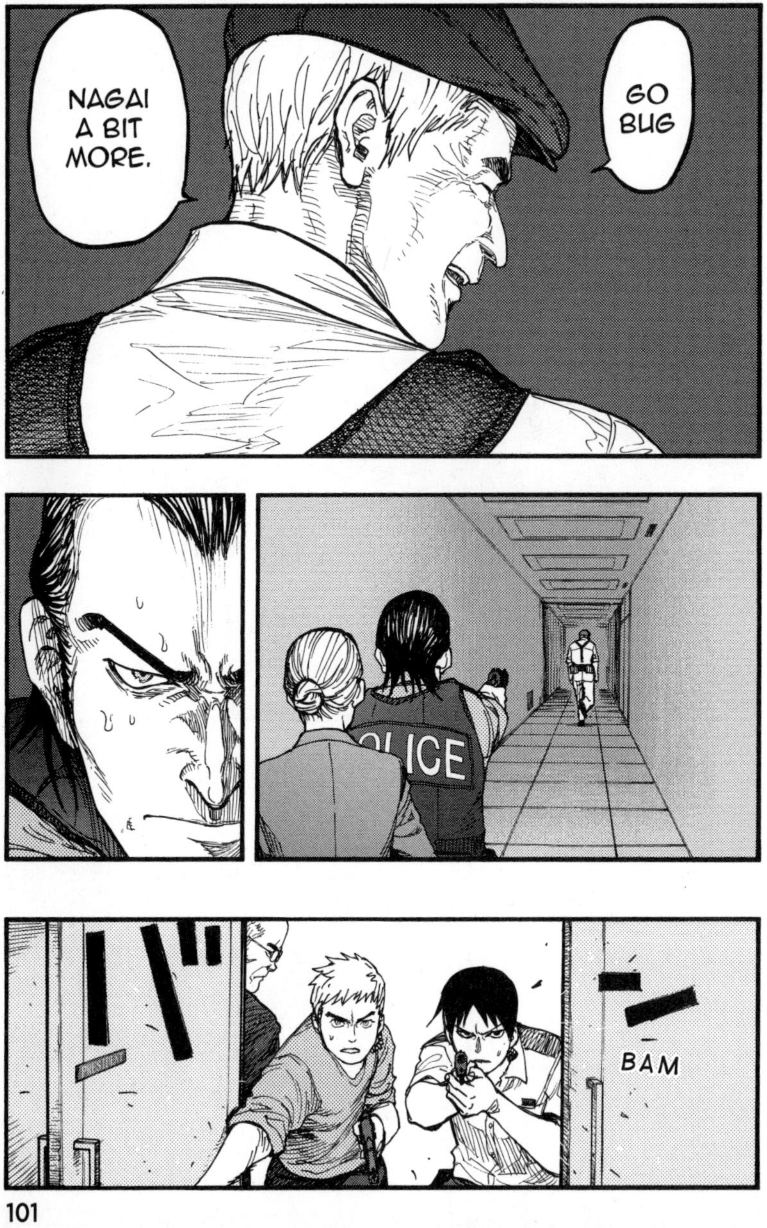
GO BUG
NAGAI A BIT MORE.
BAM

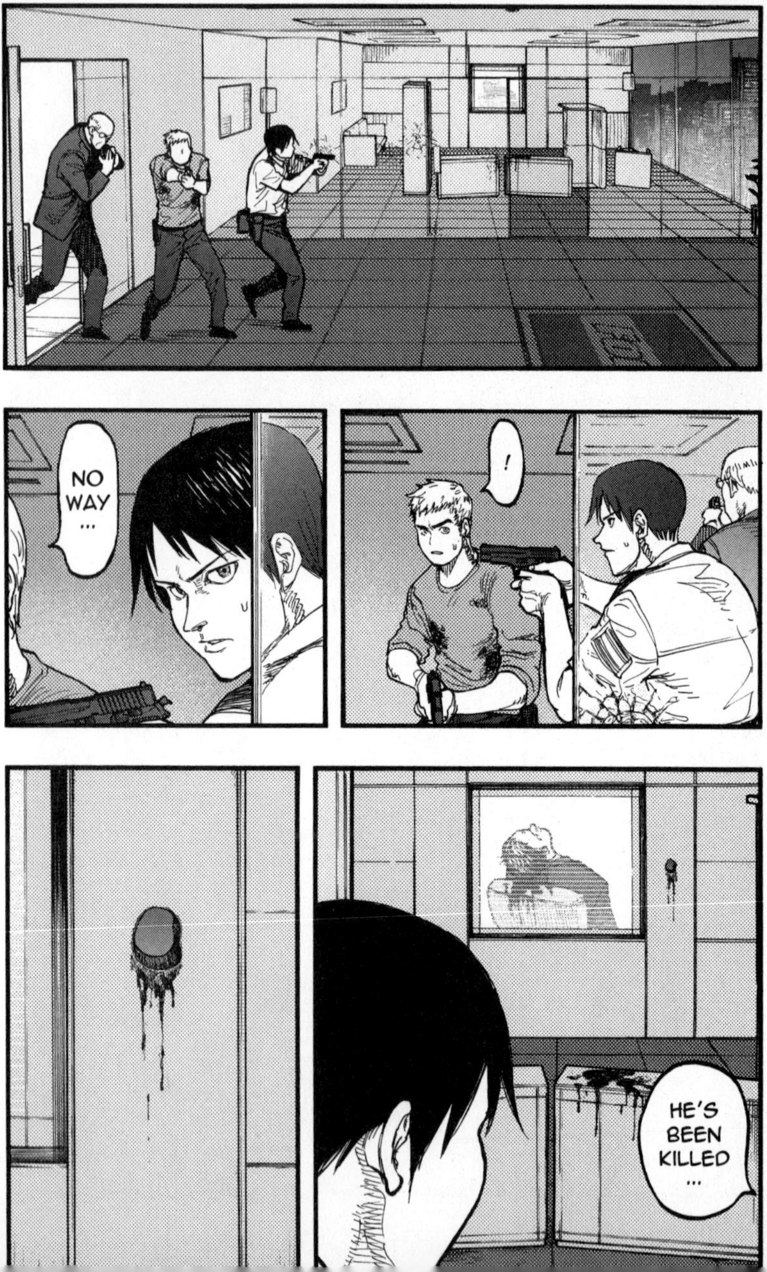
!
NO WAY ...
HE'S BEEN KILLED ...

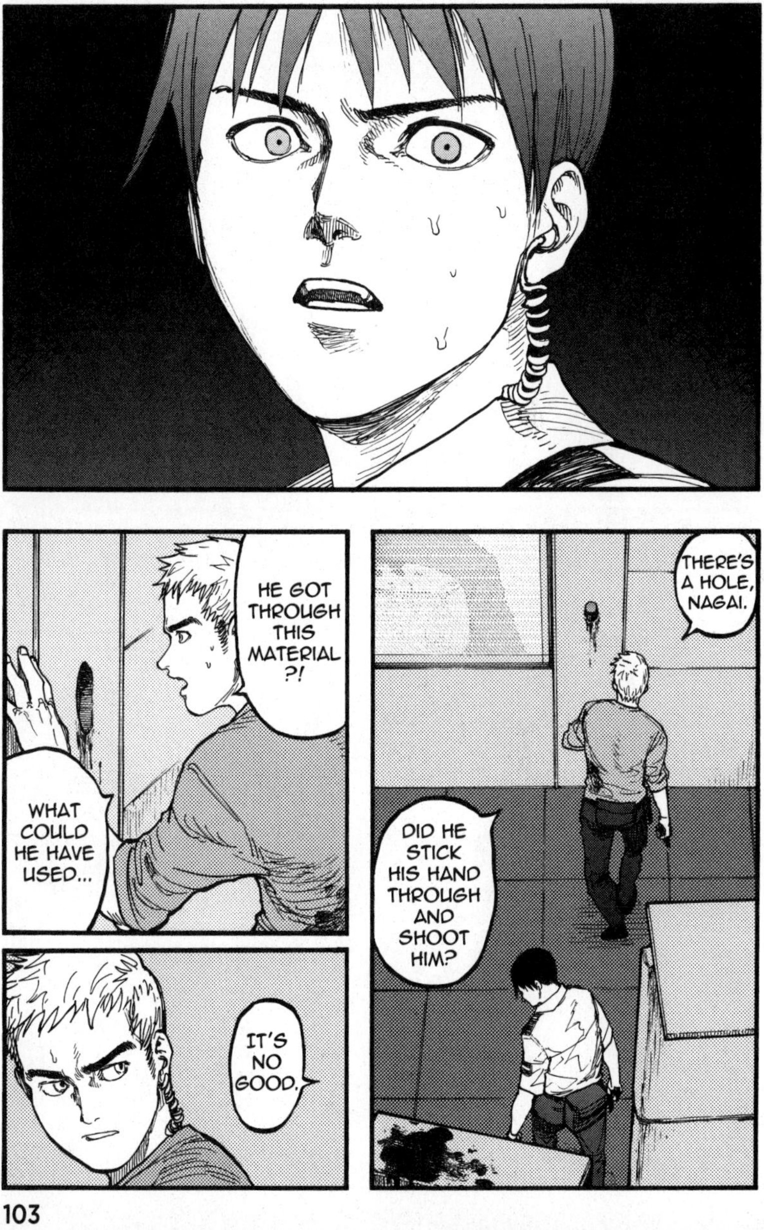
THERE'S A HOLE, NAGAI.
DID HE STICK HIS HAND THROUGH AND SHOOT HIM?
HE GOT THROUGH THIS MATERIAL ?!
WHAT COULD HE HAVE USED...
IT'S NO GOOD.

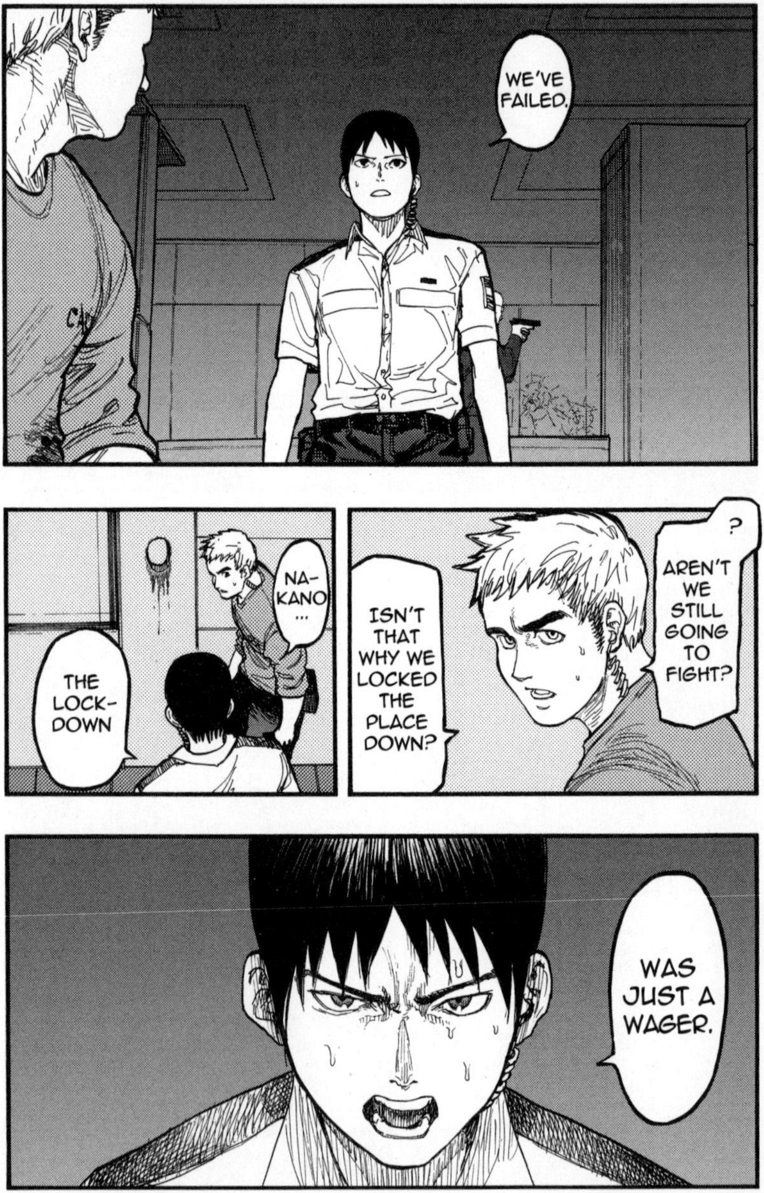
WE'VE FAILED.
?
AREN'T WE STILL GOING TO FIGHT?
ISN'T THAT WHY WE LOCKED THE PLACE DOWN?
NA-KANO ...
THE LOCK-DOWN
WAS JUST A WAGER.

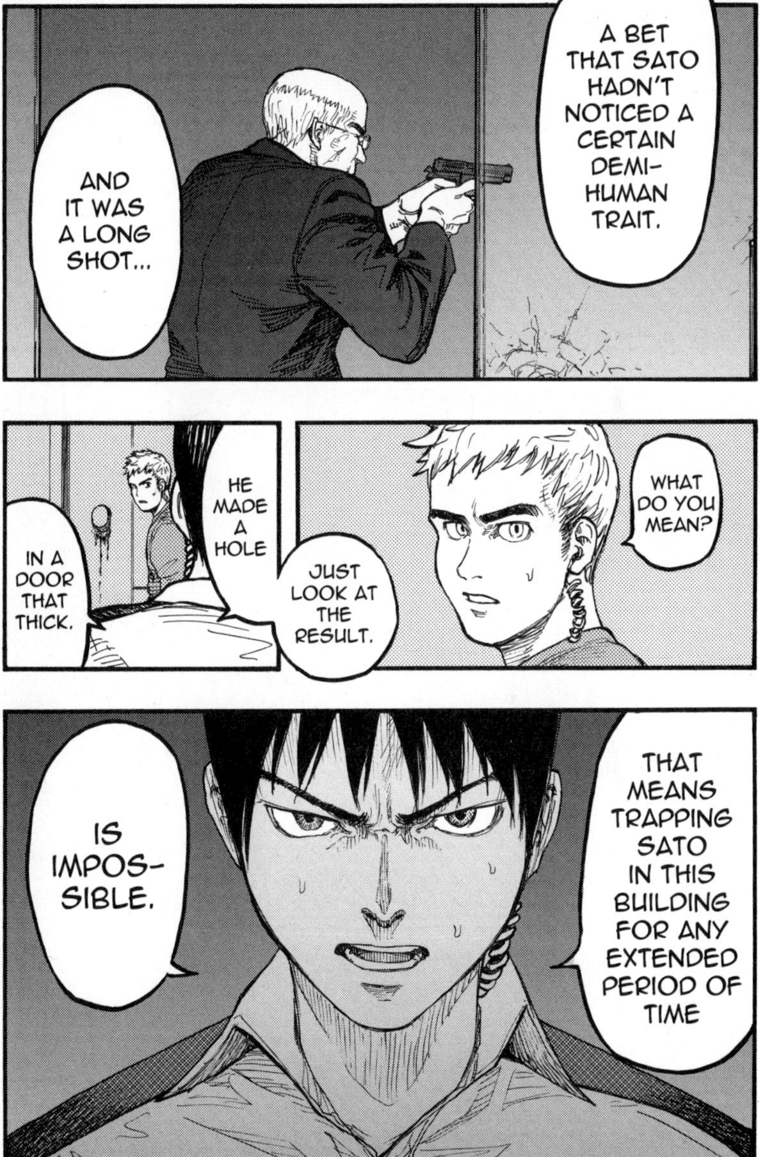
A BET THAT SATO HADN'T NOTICED A CERTAIN DEMI-HUMAN TRAIT.
AND IT WAS A LONG SHOT...
WHAT DO YOU MEAN?
JUST LOOK AT THE RESULT.
HE MADE A HOLE
IN A DOOR THAT THICK.
THAT MEANS TRAPPING SATO IN THIS BUILDING FOR ANY EXTENDED PERIOD OF TIME
IS IMPOSSIBLE.

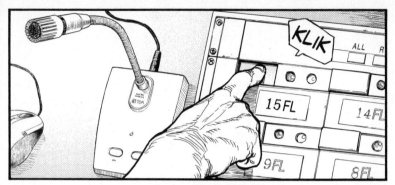

KLIK
ALL
15FL
14FL
9FL
8FL
NAGAI
IF YOU CAN HEAR THIS,
YOU MUST STILL BE ON THE FIFTEENTH FLOOR.

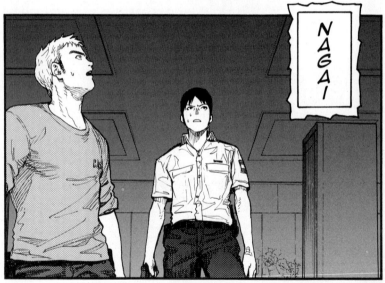

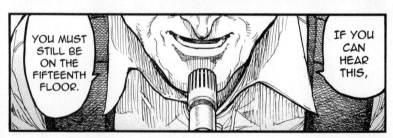

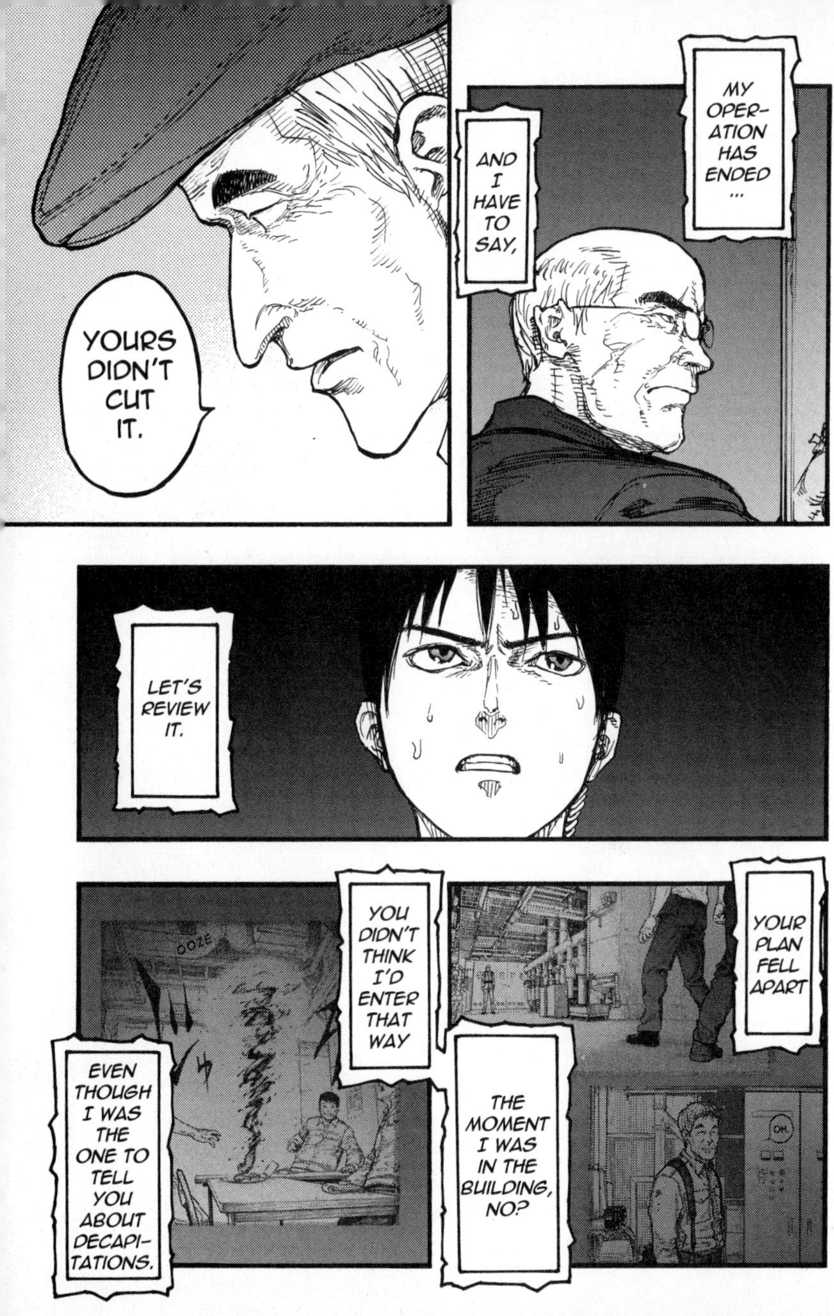
MY OPERATION HAS ENDED...
AND I HAVE TO SAY,
YOURS DIDN'T CUT IT.
LET'S REVIEW IT.
YOUR PLAN FELL APART
THE MOMENT I WAS IN THE BUILDING, NO?
OH.
YOU DIDN'T THINK I'D ENTER THAT WAY
EVEN THOUGH I WAS THE ONE TO TELL YOU ABOUT DECAPITATIONS.
OOZE

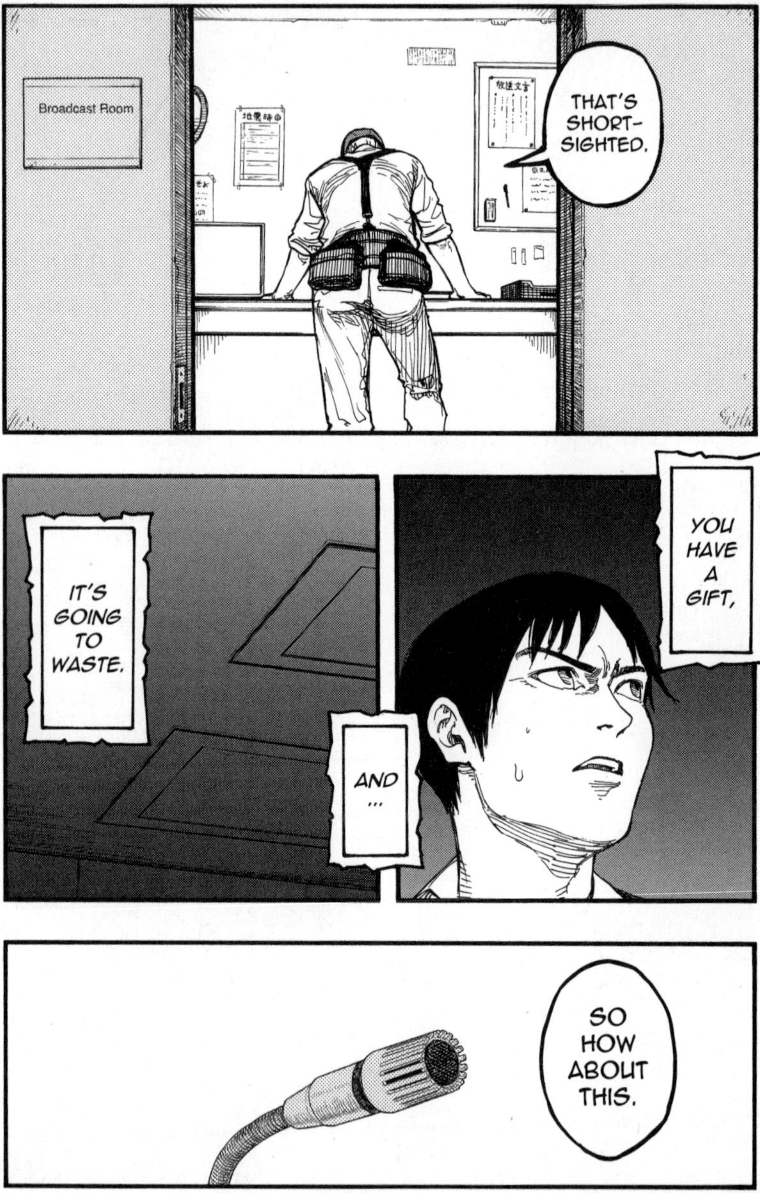
Broadcast Room
THAT'S SHORT-SIGHTED.
YOU HAVE A GIFT,
AND ...
IT'S GOING TO WASTE.
SO HOW ABOUT THIS.

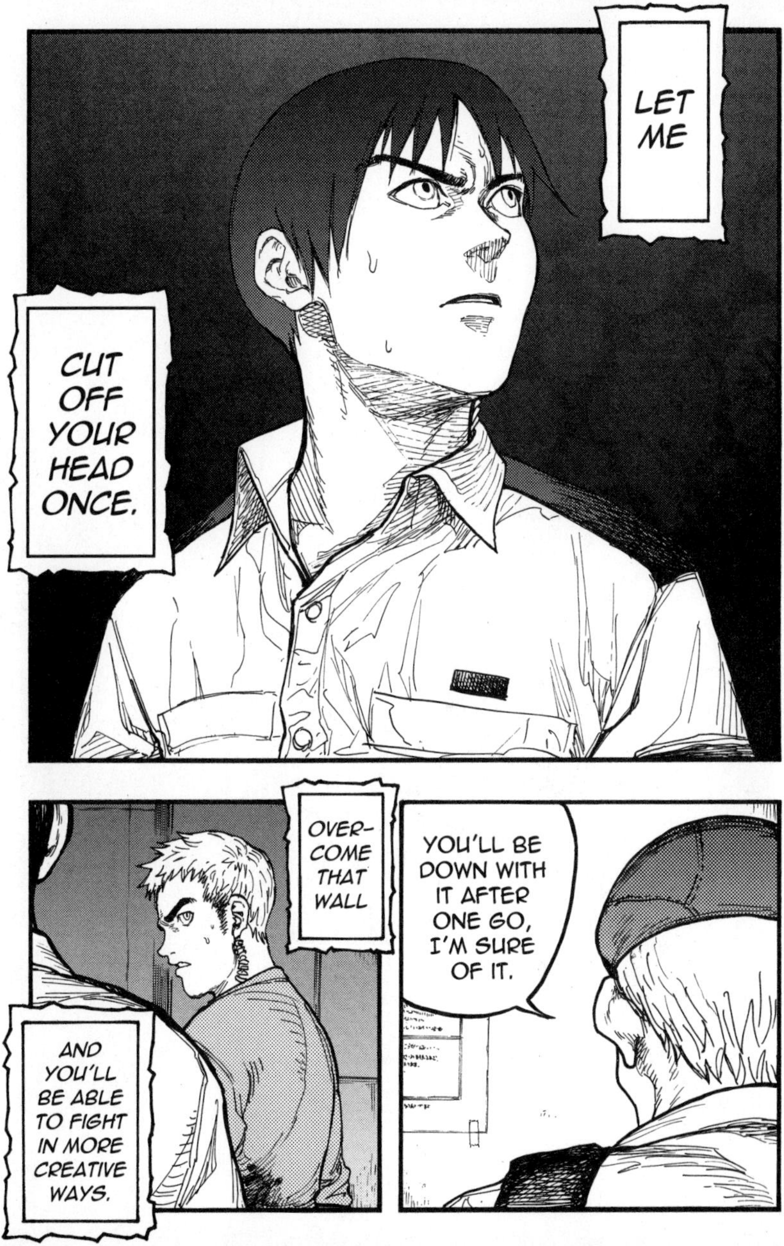
LET ME
CUT OFF YOUR HEAD ONCE.
YOU'LL BE DOWN WITH IT AFTER ONE GO, I'M SURE OF IT.
OVER-COME THAT WALL
AND YOU'LL BE ABLE TO FIGHT IN MORE CREATIVE WAYS.

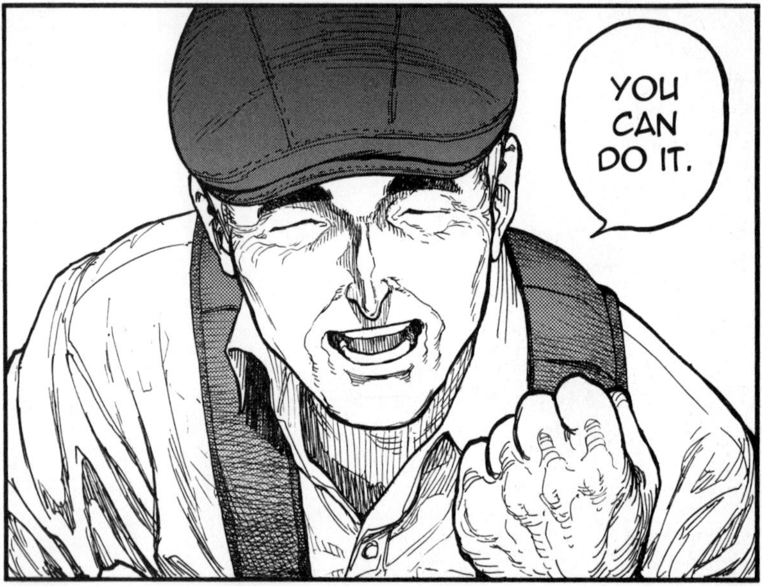
YOU CAN DO IT.

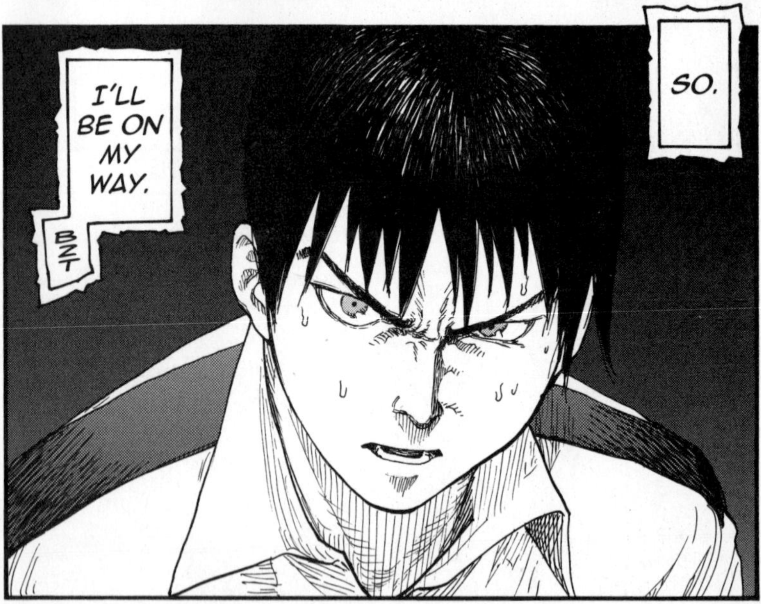
SO.
I'LL BE ON MY WAY.
BZT

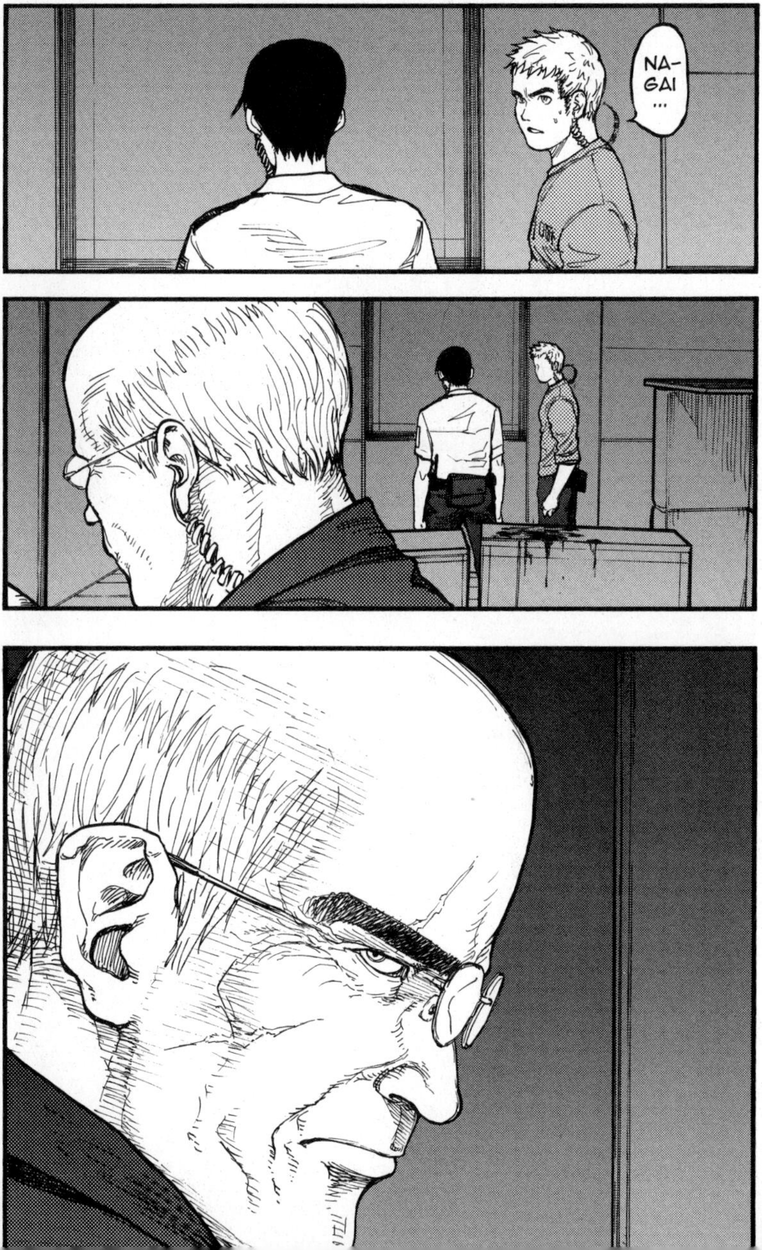
NA-
GAI
...

GA-CHIK

Landscaping Tools

CREAK

ギィイ

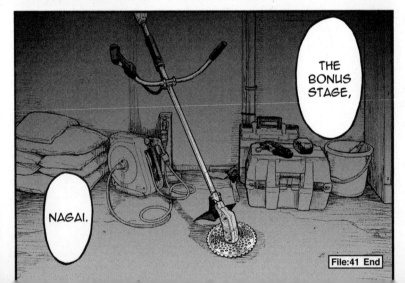

THE BONUS STAGE,

NAGAI.

File:41 End

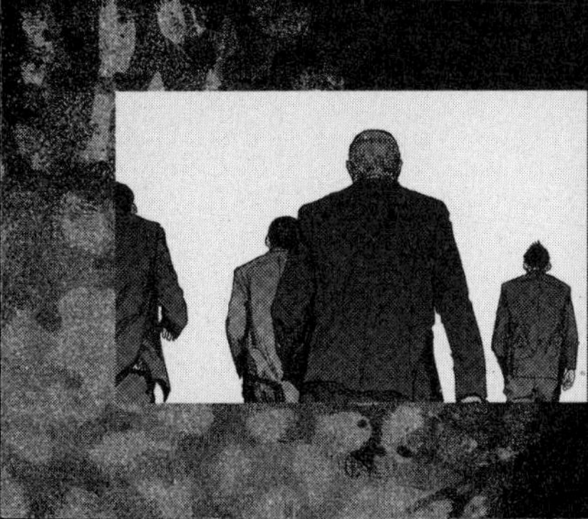

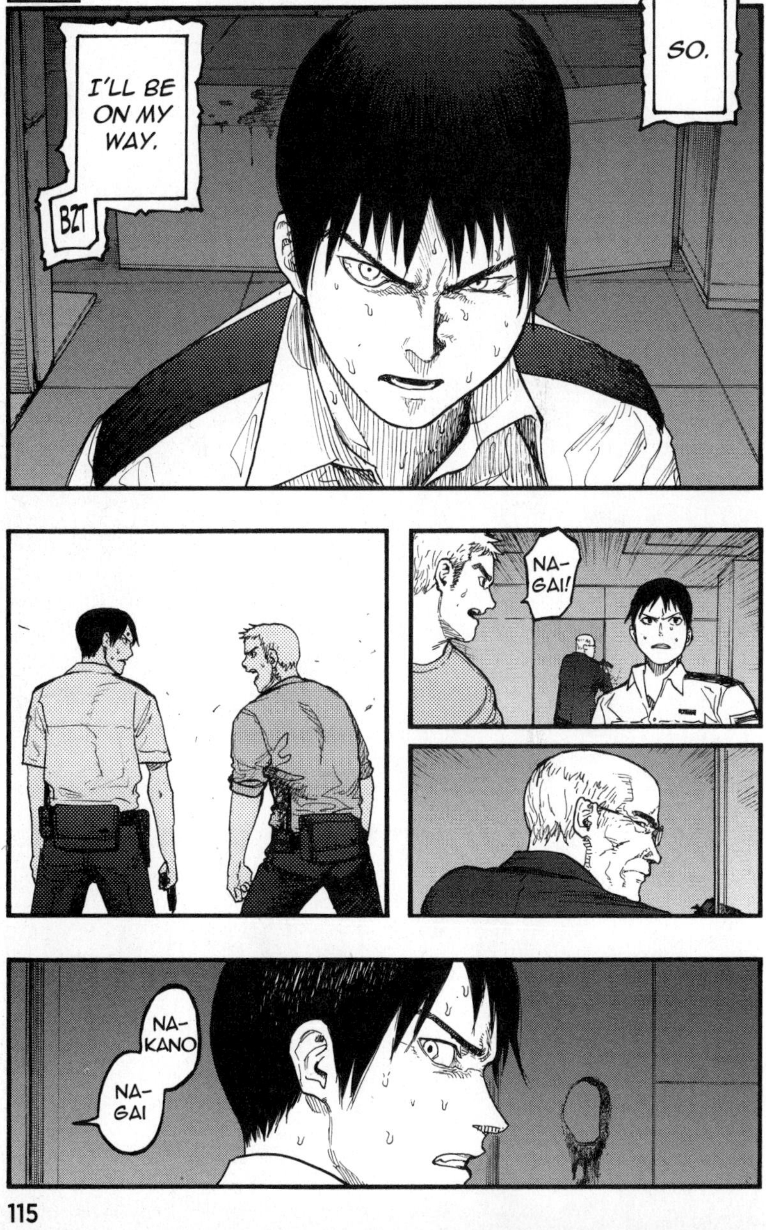
SO.
I'LL BE ON MY WAY.
BZT
NA-GAI!
NA-KANO
NA-GAI

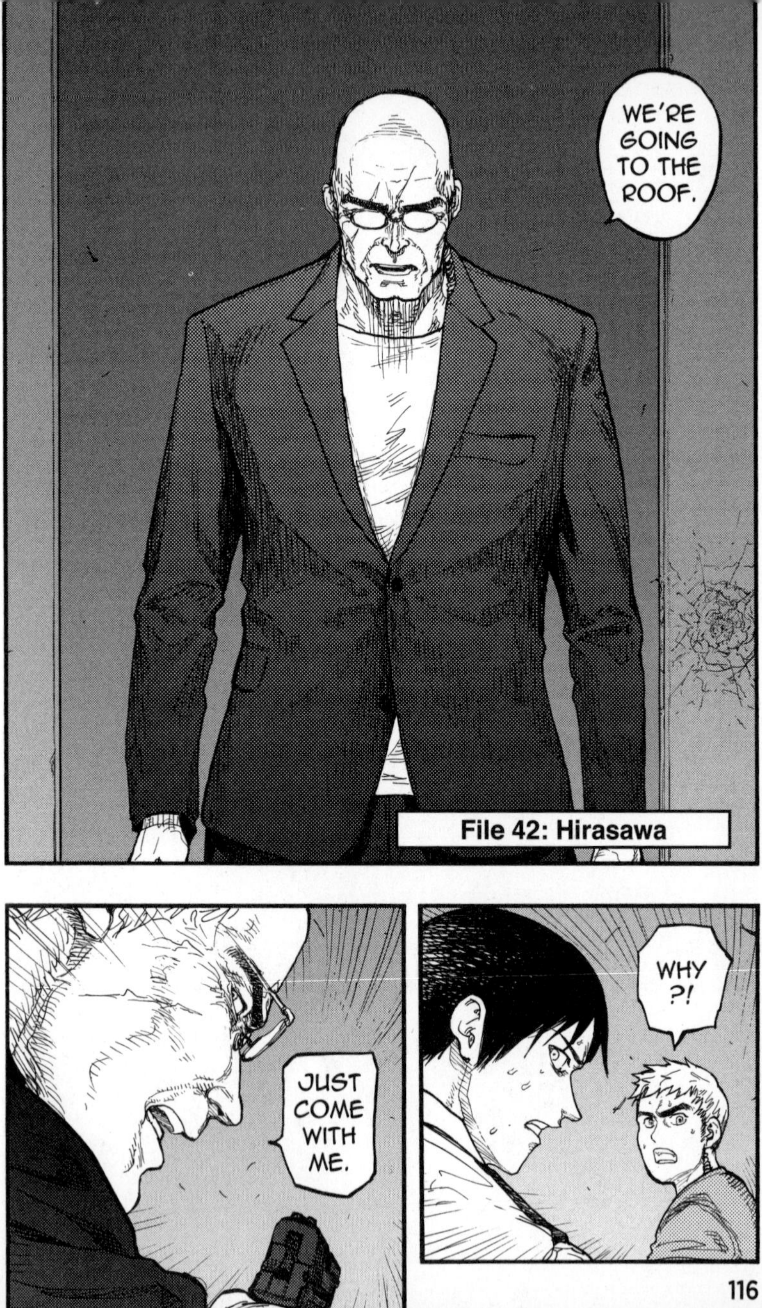
WE'RE GOING TO THE ROOF.
File 42: Hirasawa
WHY ?!
JUST COME WITH ME.

ガ
GCHAK
チャ
3.0Ah 18V
LOW SPEED
POWER
HIGH SPEED
6000 RPM
カチ
KLIK
カチ
カチ
カチ
KLIK
SGREEE

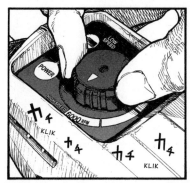

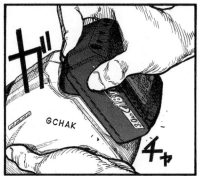

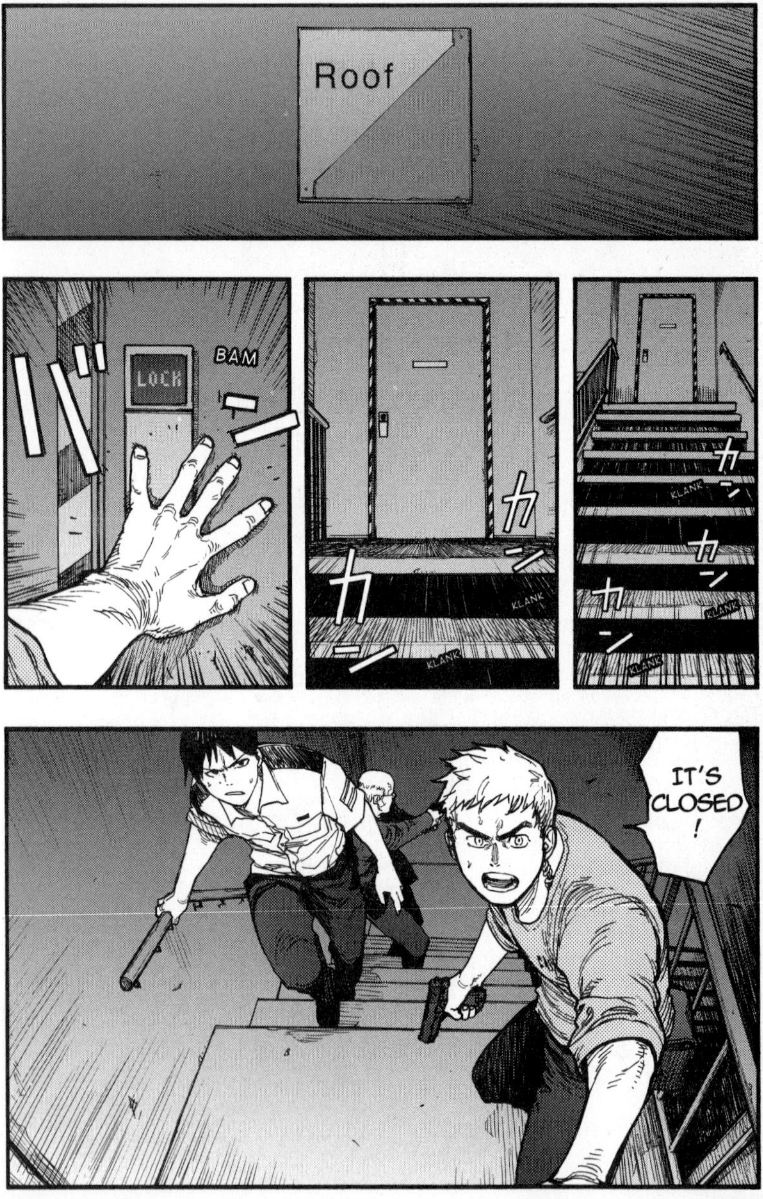
Roof
KLANK
KLANK
KLANK
KLANK
KLANK
LOCK
BAM
IT'S CLOSED!

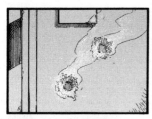

SHIT !!

PAM

PAM

THAT'S NOT GONNA WORK !

NOPE !

I'LL MAKE HOLES HERE AND HERE.

GOING BY THE BLUE-PRINT, THAT SHOULD OPEN IT.

BUT HOW ?

YEAH,

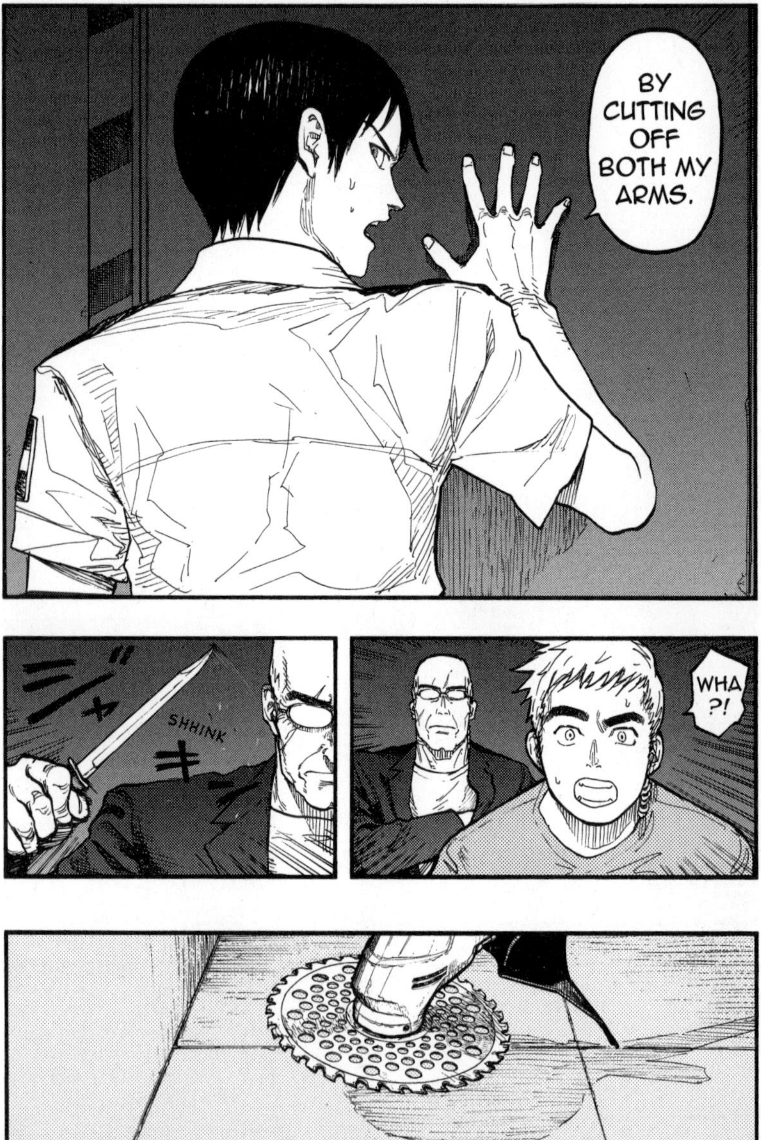
BY CUTTING OFF BOTH MY ARMS.
WHA ?!
SHHINK

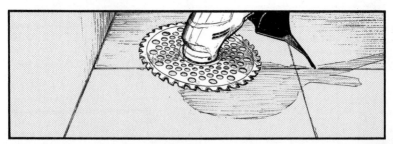

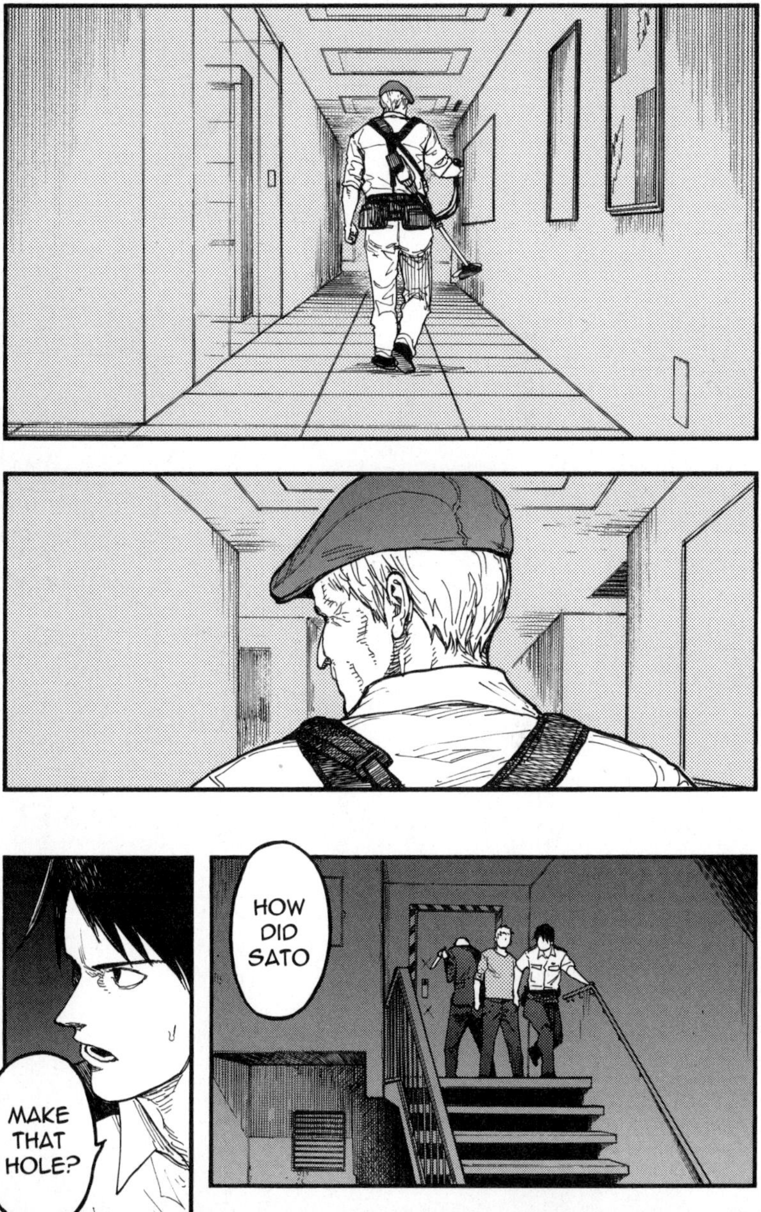
HOW DID SATO
MAKE THAT HOLE?

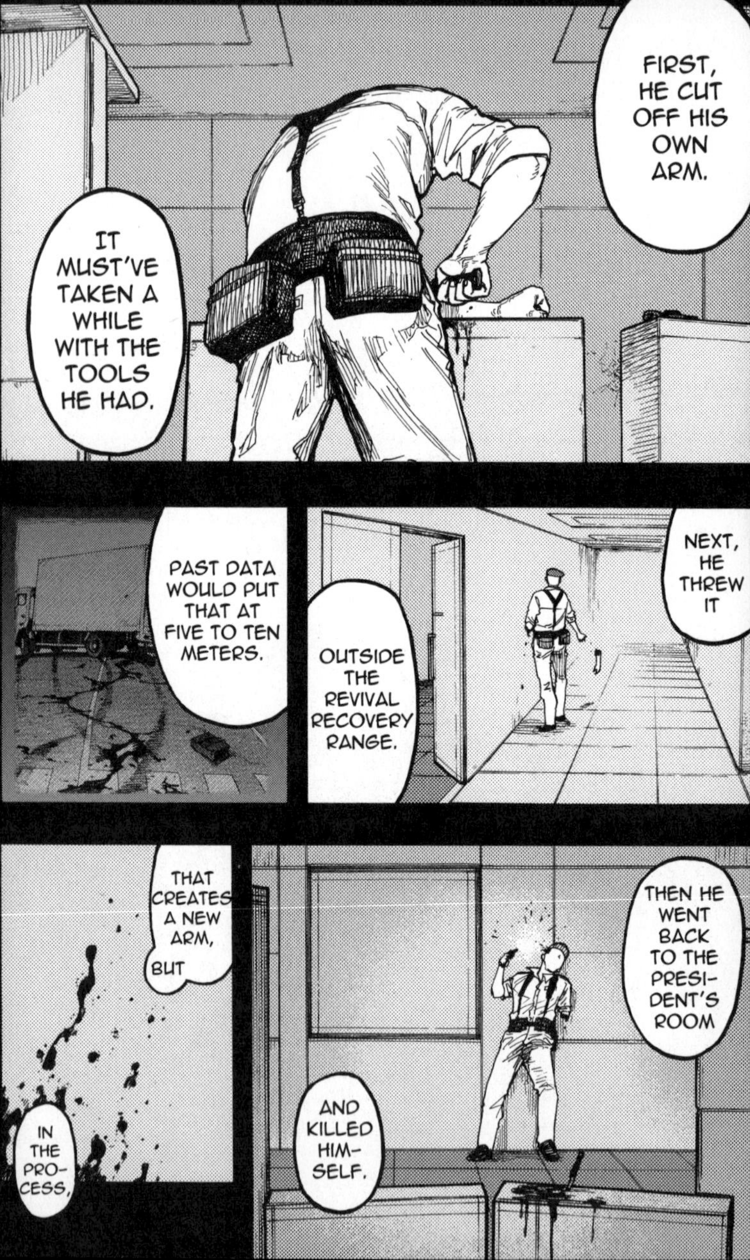
FIRST, HE CUT OFF HIS OWN ARM.
IT MUST'VE TAKEN A WHILE WITH THE TOOLS HE HAD.
NEXT, HE THREW IT
OUTSIDE THE REVIVAL RECOVERY RANGE.
PAST DATA WOULD PUT THAT AT FIVE TO TEN METERS.
THEN HE WENT BACK TO THE PRESIDENT'S ROOM
AND KILLED HIMSELF.
THAT CREATES A NEW ARM,
BUT
IN THE PROCESS,

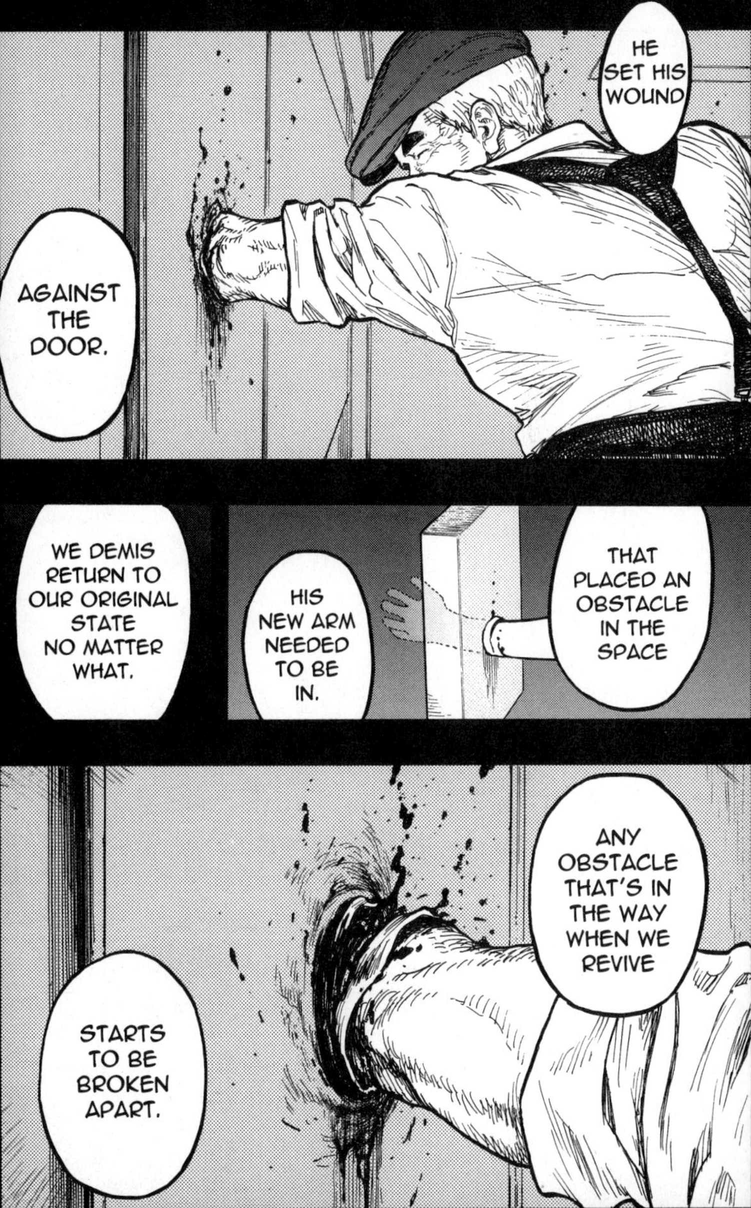
HE SET HIS WOUND
AGAINST THE DOOR.
THAT PLACED AN OBSTACLE IN THE SPACE
HIS NEW ARM NEEDED TO BE IN.
WE DEMIS RETURN TO OUR ORIGINAL STATE NO MATTER WHAT.
ANY OBSTACLE THAT'S IN THE WAY WHEN WE REVIVE
STARTS TO BE BROKEN APART.

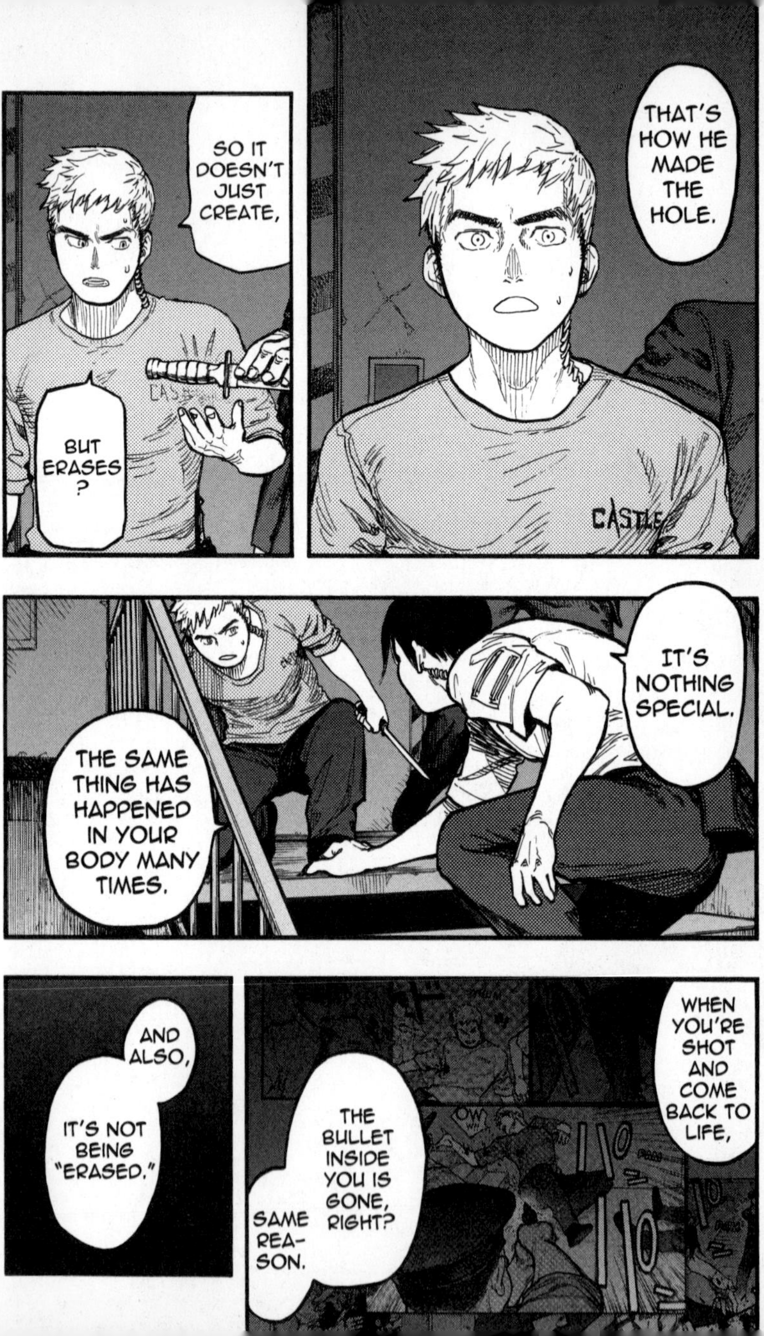
THAT'S HOW HE MADE THE HOLE.
SO IT DOESN'T JUST CREATE,
BUT ERASES?
CASTLE
IT'S NOTHING SPECIAL.
THE SAME THING HAS HAPPENED IN YOUR BODY MANY TIMES.
WHEN YOU'RE SHOT AND COME BACK TO LIFE,
THE BULLET INSIDE YOU IS GONE, RIGHT?
SAME REA-SON.
AND ALSO,
IT'S NOT BEING "ERASED."

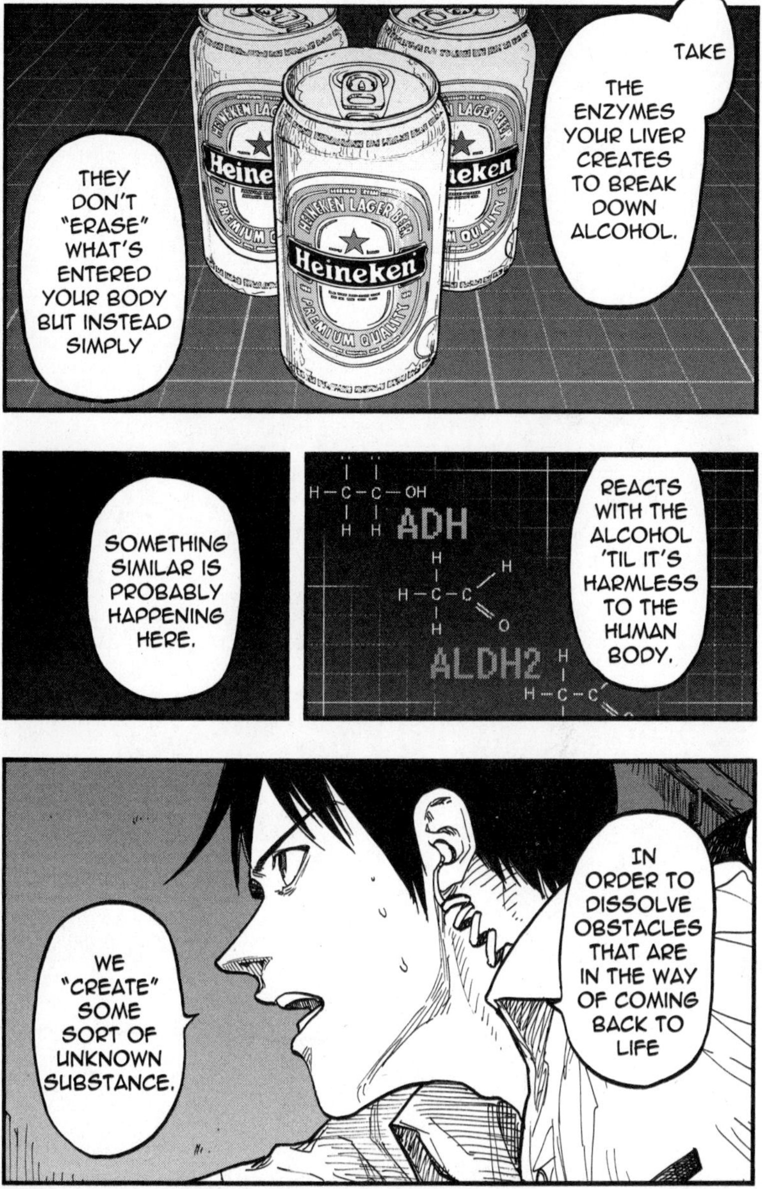
TAKE THE ENZYMES YOUR LIVER CREATES TO BREAK DOWN ALCOHOL.
THEY DON'T "ERASE" WHAT'S ENTERED YOUR BODY BUT INSTEAD SIMPLY
HEINEKEN LAGER BEER
Heineken
PREMIUM QUALITY
ADH
ALDH2
REACTS WITH THE ALCOHOL 'TIL IT'S HARMLESS TO THE HUMAN BODY.
SOMETHING SIMILAR IS PROBABLY HAPPENING HERE.
IN ORDER TO DISSOLVE OBSTACLES THAT ARE IN THE WAY OF COMING BACK TO LIFE
WE "CREATE" SOME SORT OF UNKNOWN SUBSTANCE.

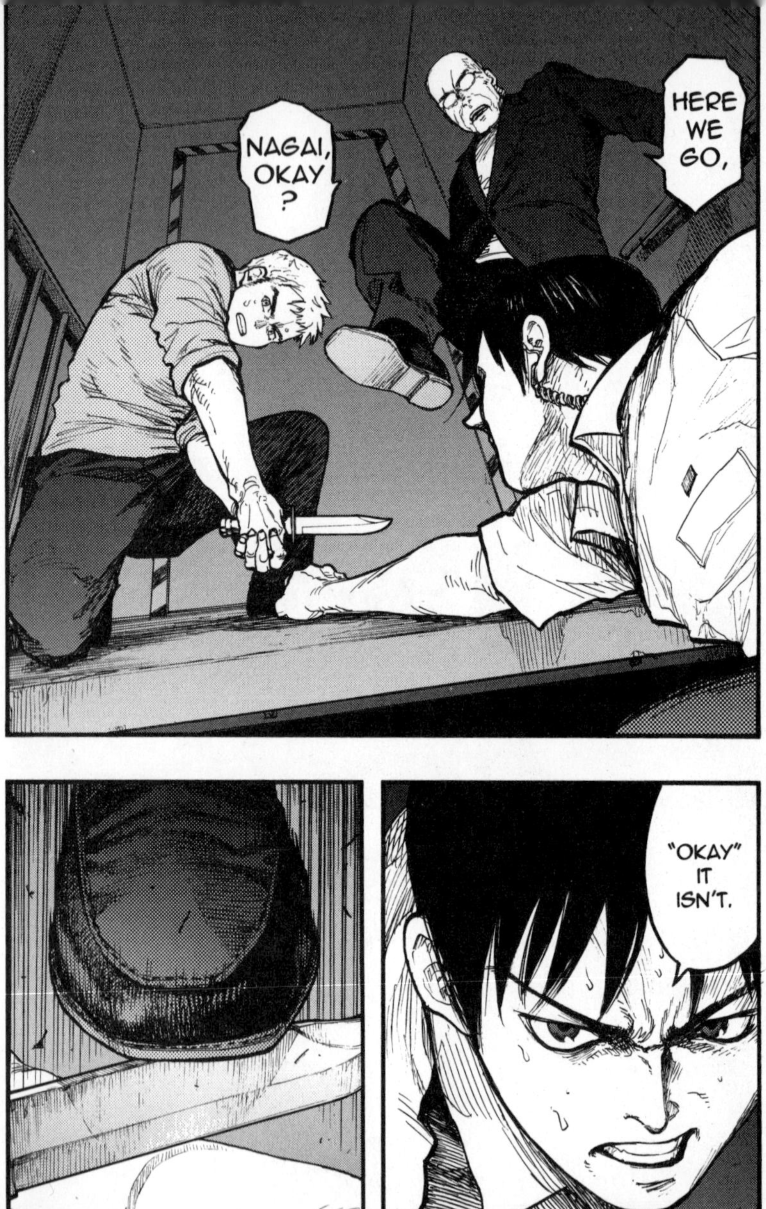
HERE WE GO,
NAGAI, OKAY ?
"OKAY" IT ISN'T.

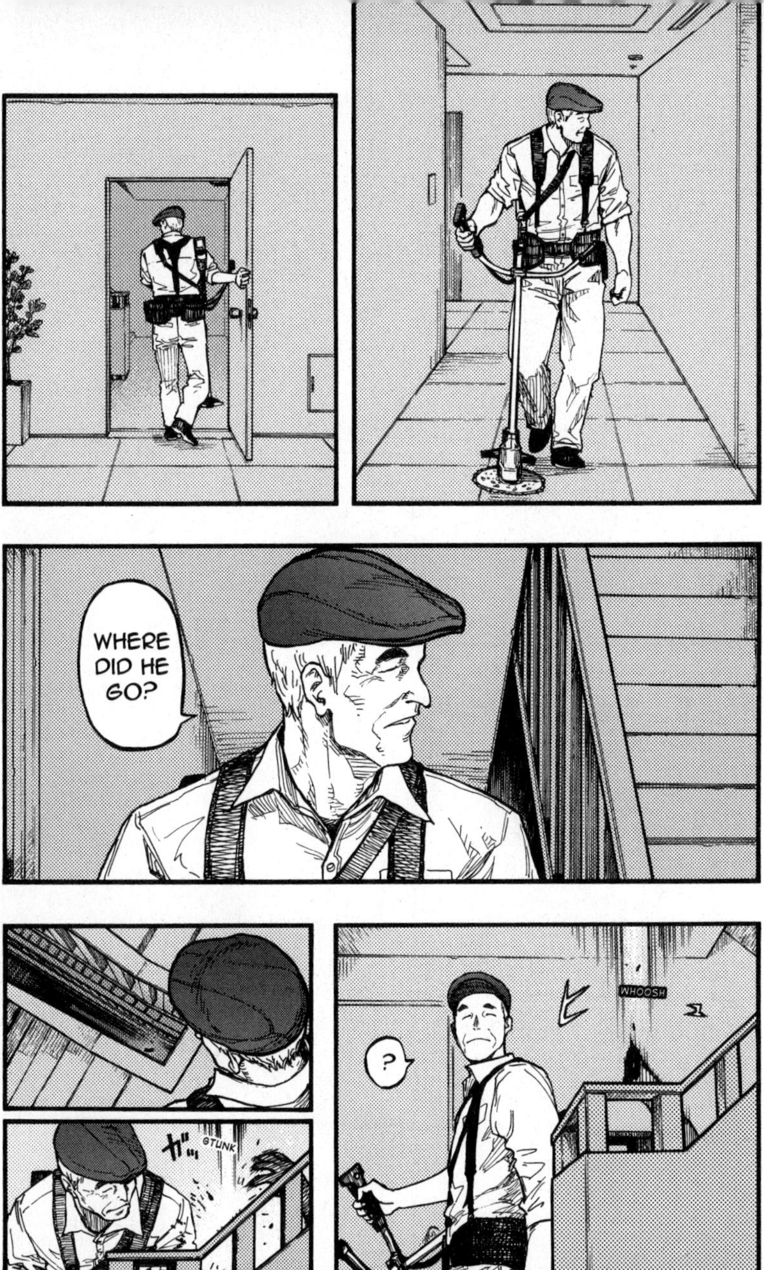
WHERE DID HE GO?
?
WHOOSH
GTUNK

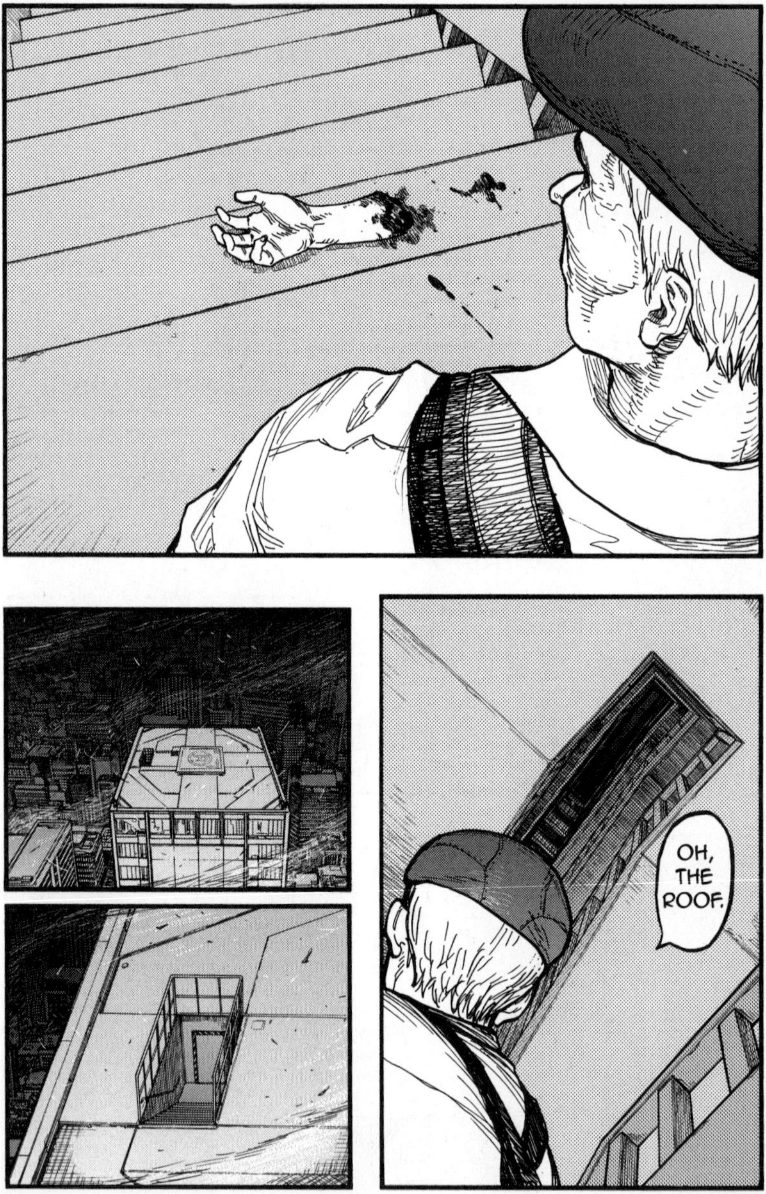
OH, THE ROOF.

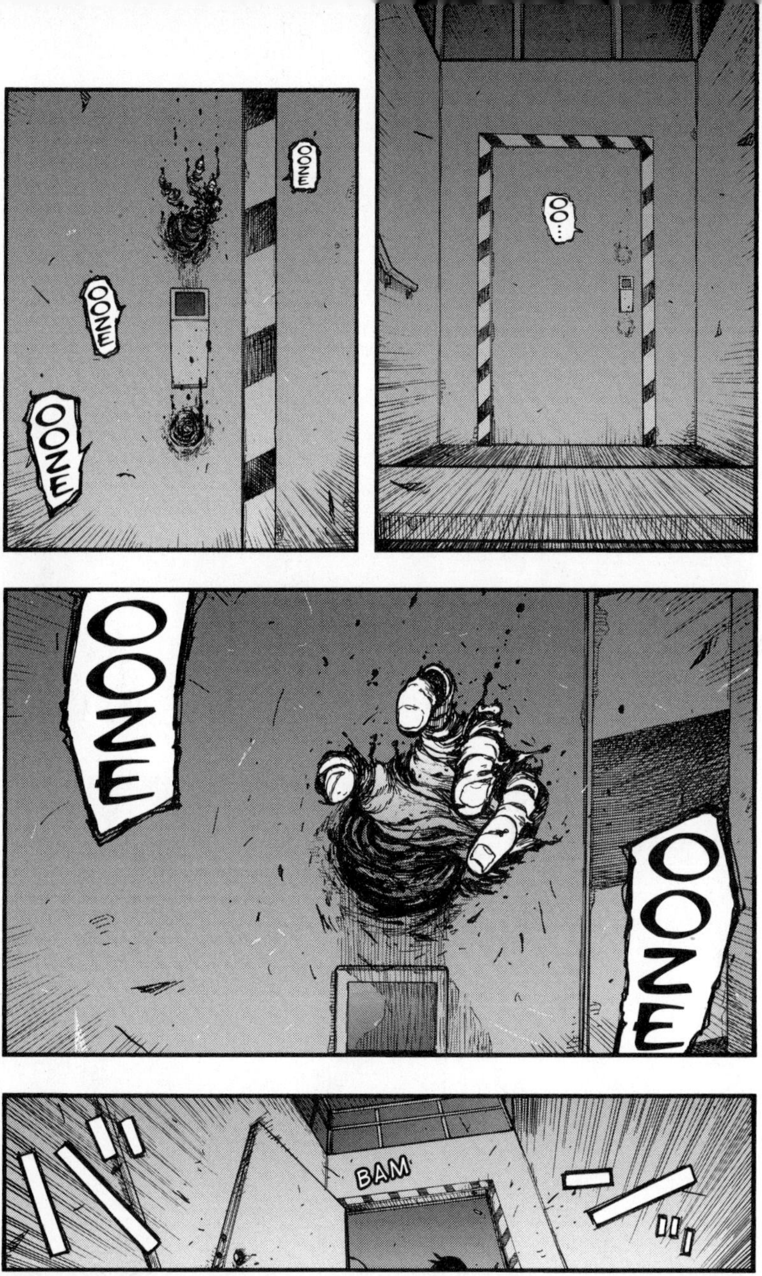
OO...
OOZE
OOZE
OOZE
OOZE
OOZE
BAM

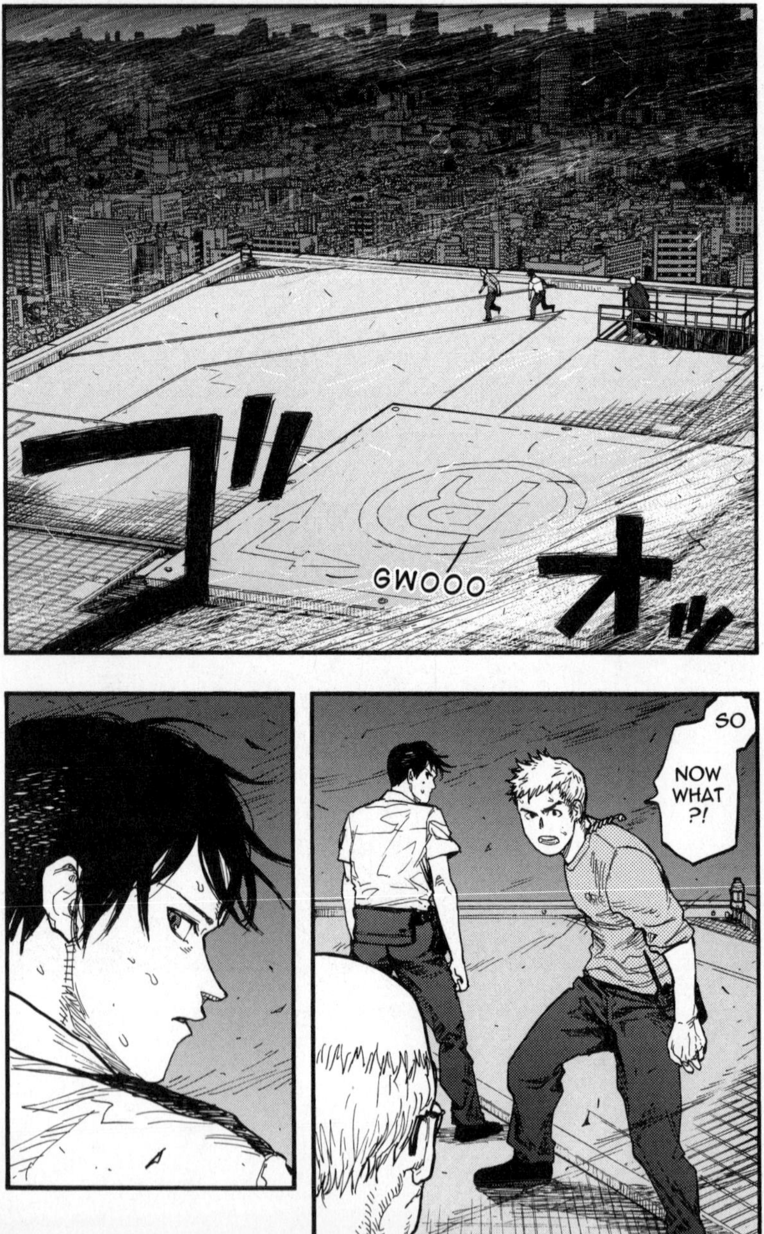
ゴオッ
GWOOO
SO
NOW WHAT ?!

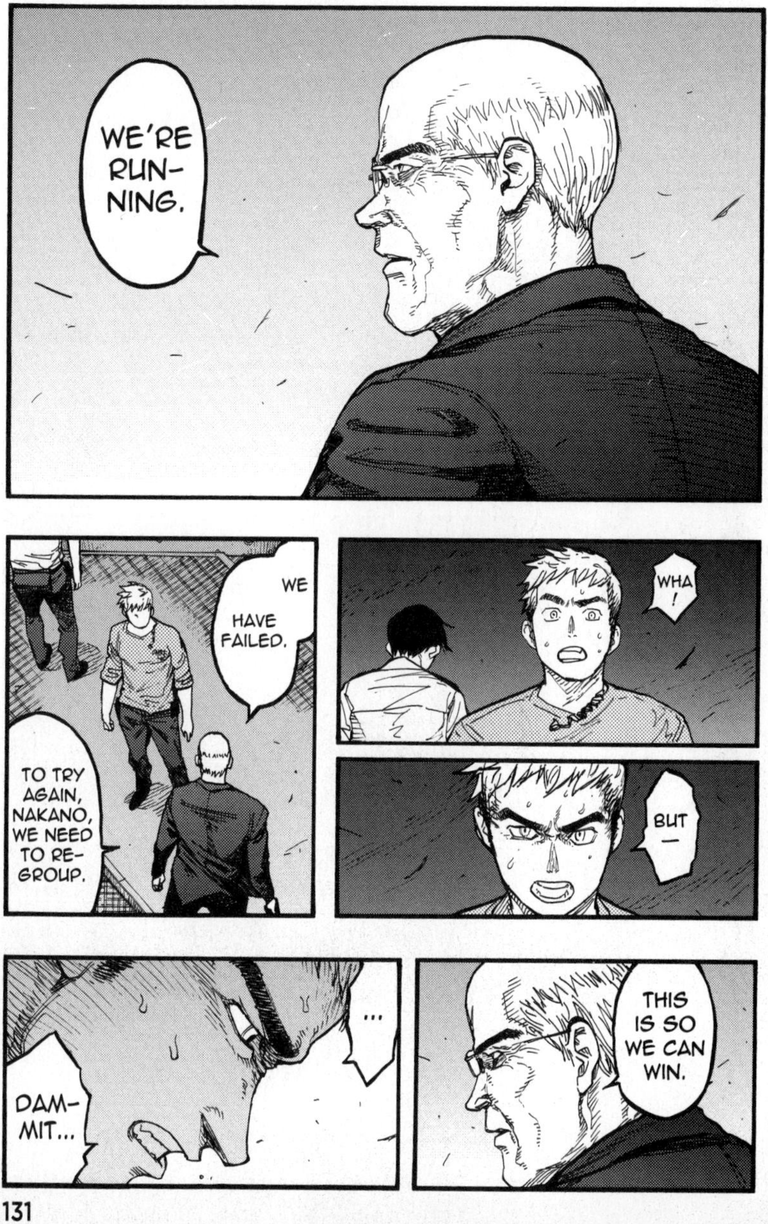
WE'RE RUN-NING.
WHA!
BUT—
WE HAVE FAILED.
TO TRY AGAIN, NAKANO, WE NEED TO RE-GROUP.
THIS IS SO WE CAN WIN.
...
DAM-MIT...

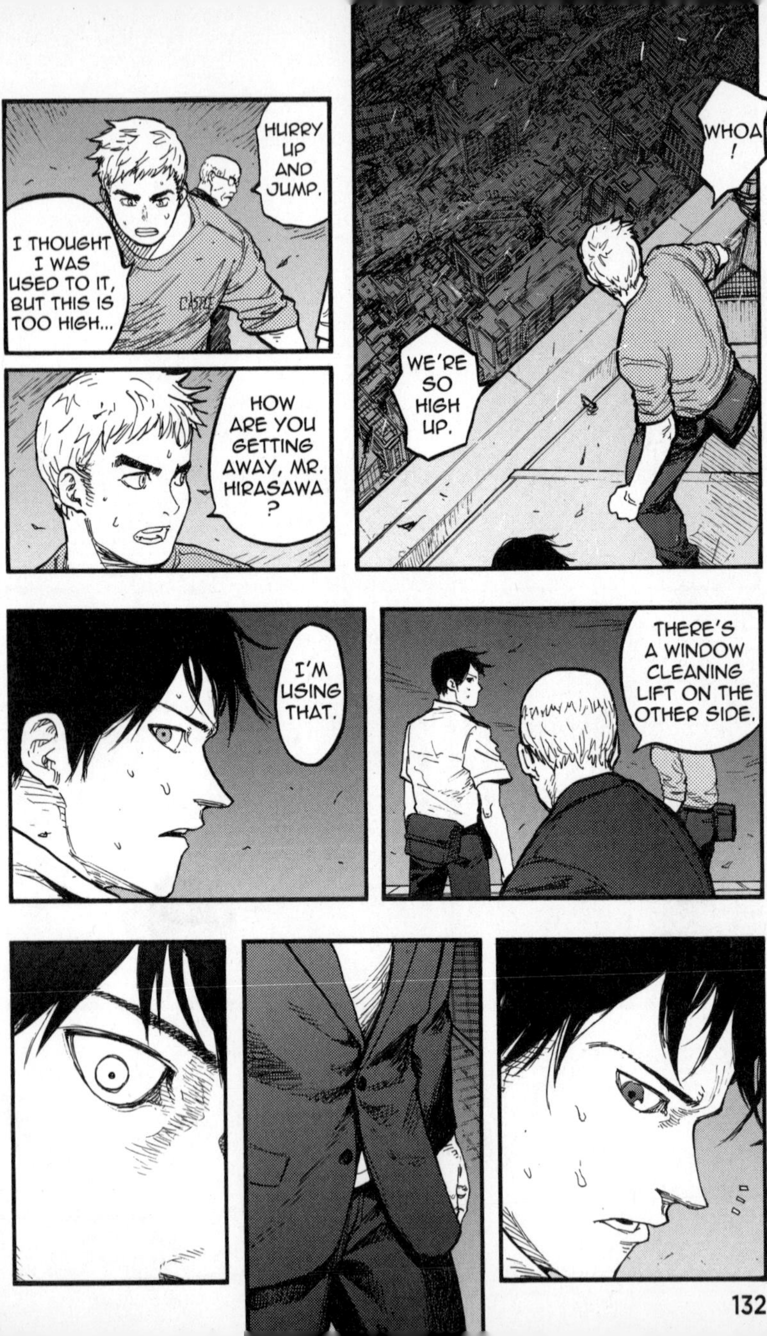
WHOA!
WE'RE SO HIGH UP.
HURRY UP AND JUMP.
I THOUGHT I WAS USED TO IT, BUT THIS IS TOO HIGH...
HOW ARE YOU GETTING AWAY, MR. HIRASAWA?
THERE'S A WINDOW CLEANING LIFT ON THE OTHER SIDE.
I'M USING THAT.

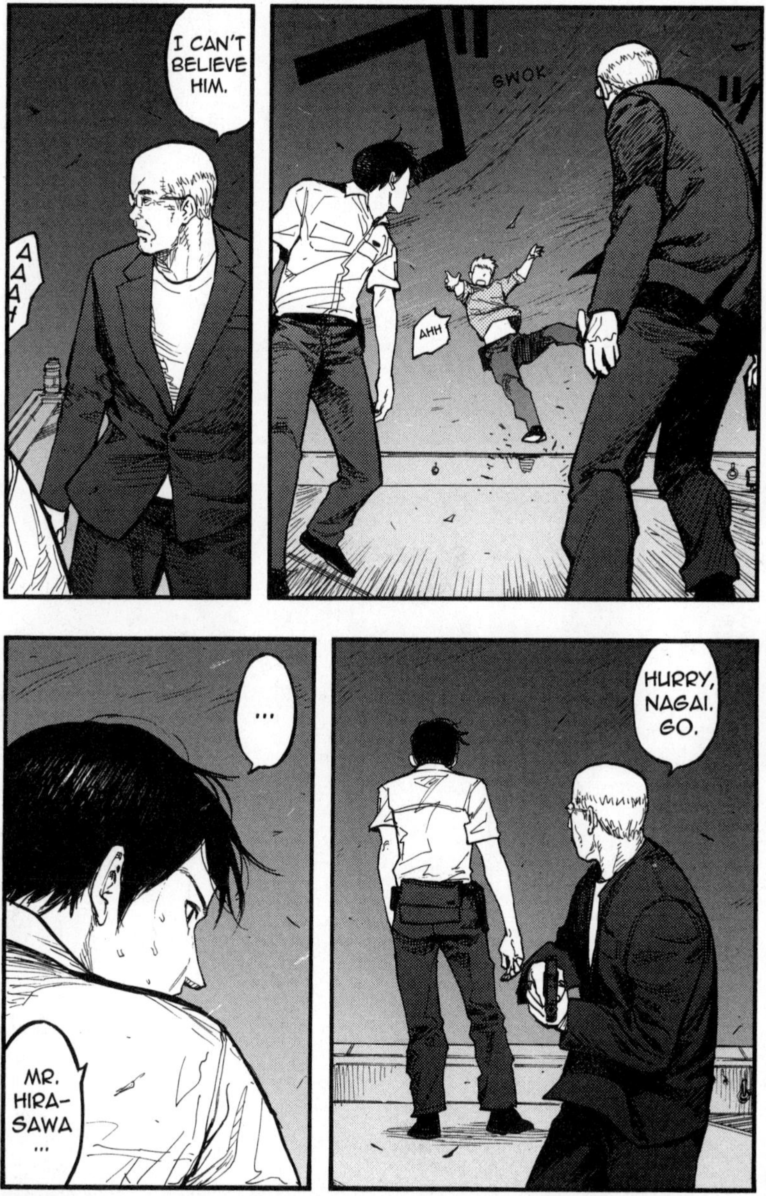
SWOK
AHH
I CAN'T BELIEVE HIM.
AAAH
HURRY, NAGAI. GO.
...
MR. HIRA-SAWA ...

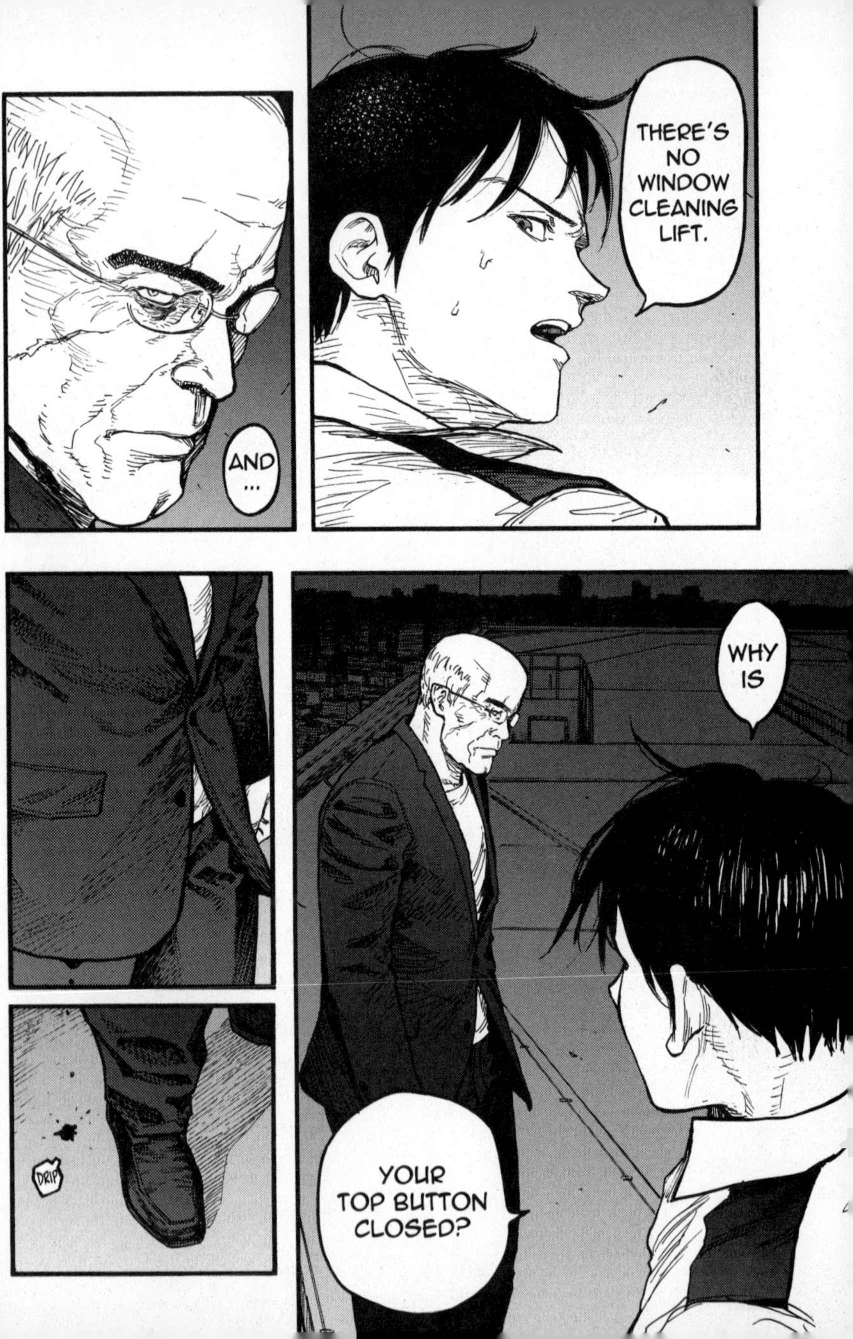
THERE'S NO WINDOW CLEANING LIFT.
AND ...
WHY IS
YOUR TOP BUTTON CLOSED?
DRIP

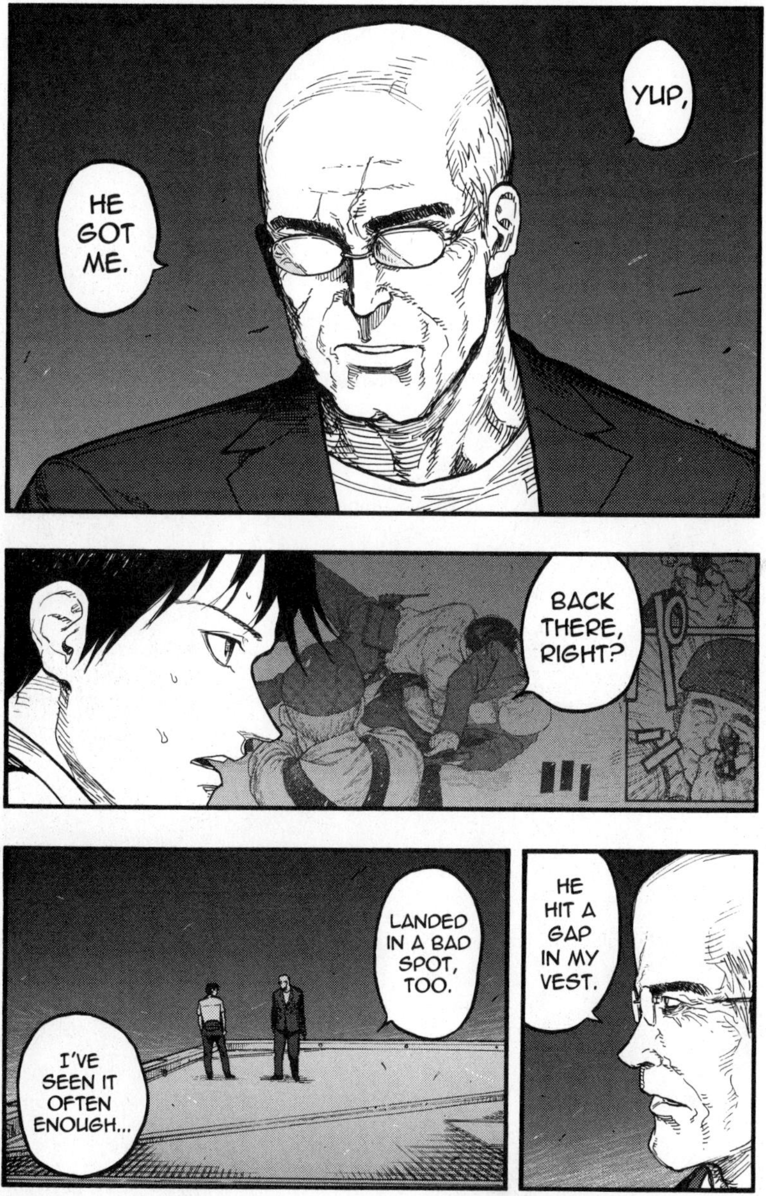
YUP,
HE GOT ME.
BACK THERE, RIGHT?
HE HIT A GAP IN MY VEST.
LANDED IN A BAD SPOT, TOO.
I'VE SEEN IT OFTEN ENOUGH...

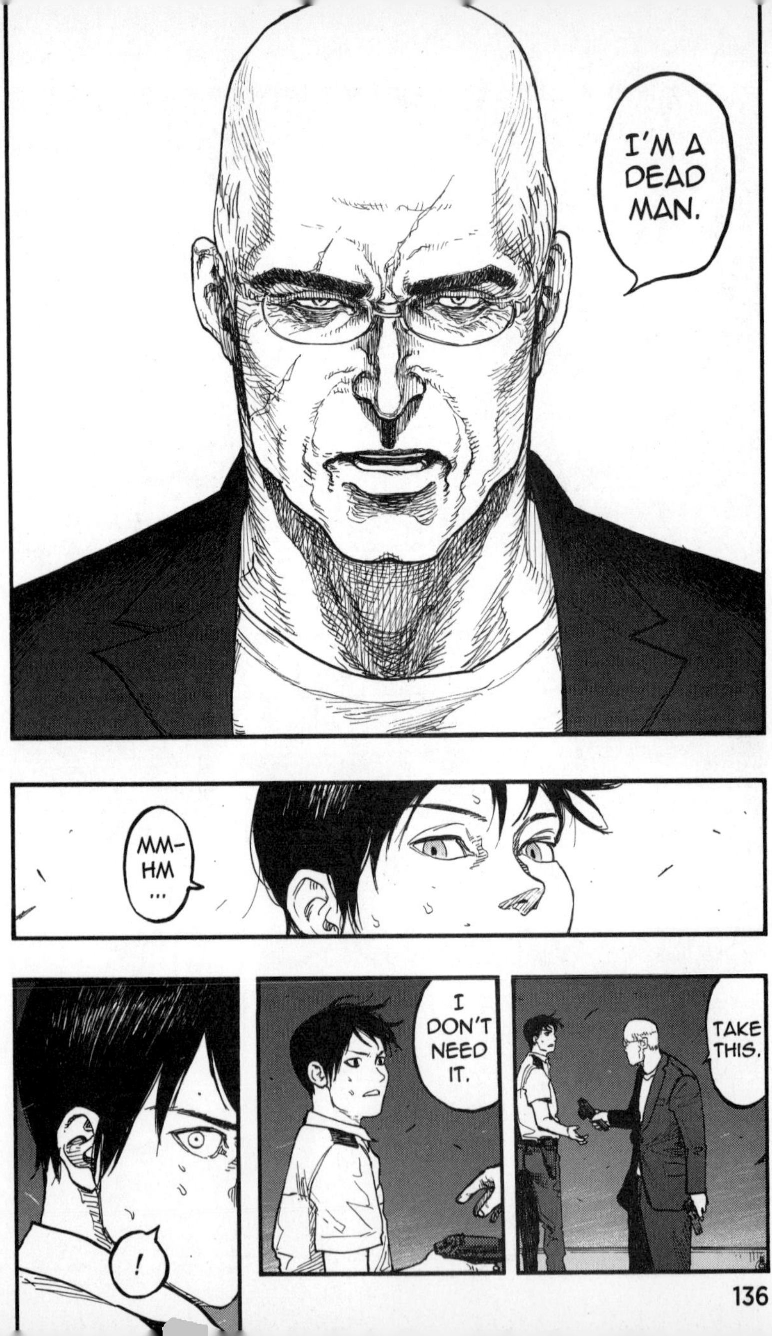
I'M A DEAD MAN.
MM-HM ...
TAKE THIS.
I DON'T NEED IT.
!

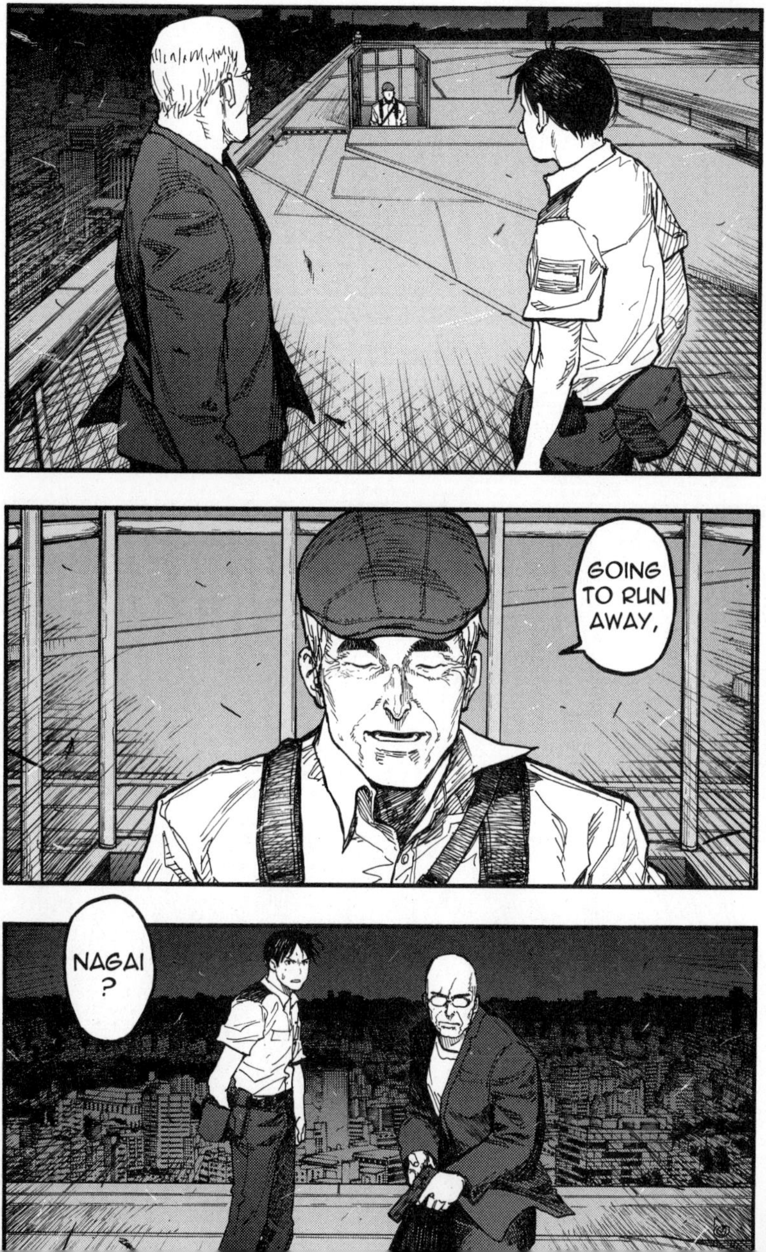
GOING TO RUN AWAY,
NAGAI ?

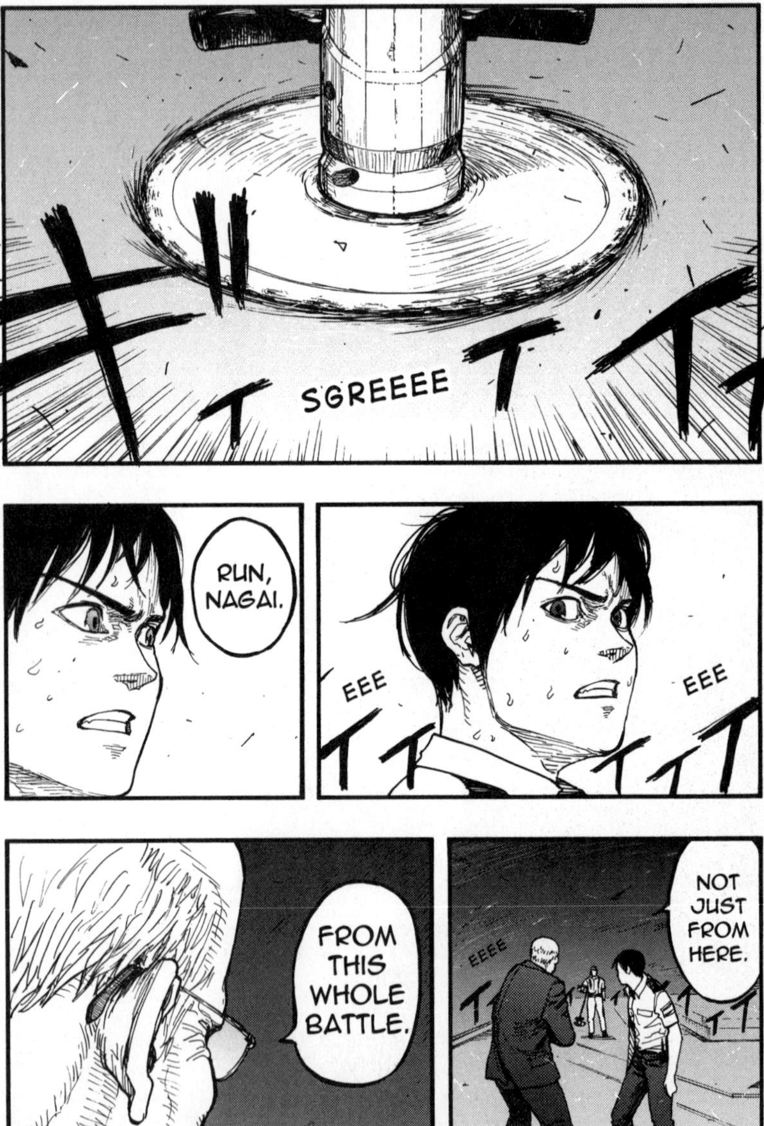
SGREEEE
EEE
EEE
RUN, NAGAI.
EEEE
NOT JUST FROM HERE.
FROM THIS WHOLE BATTLE.

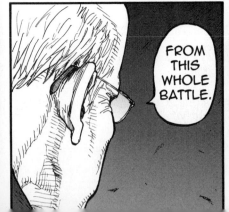

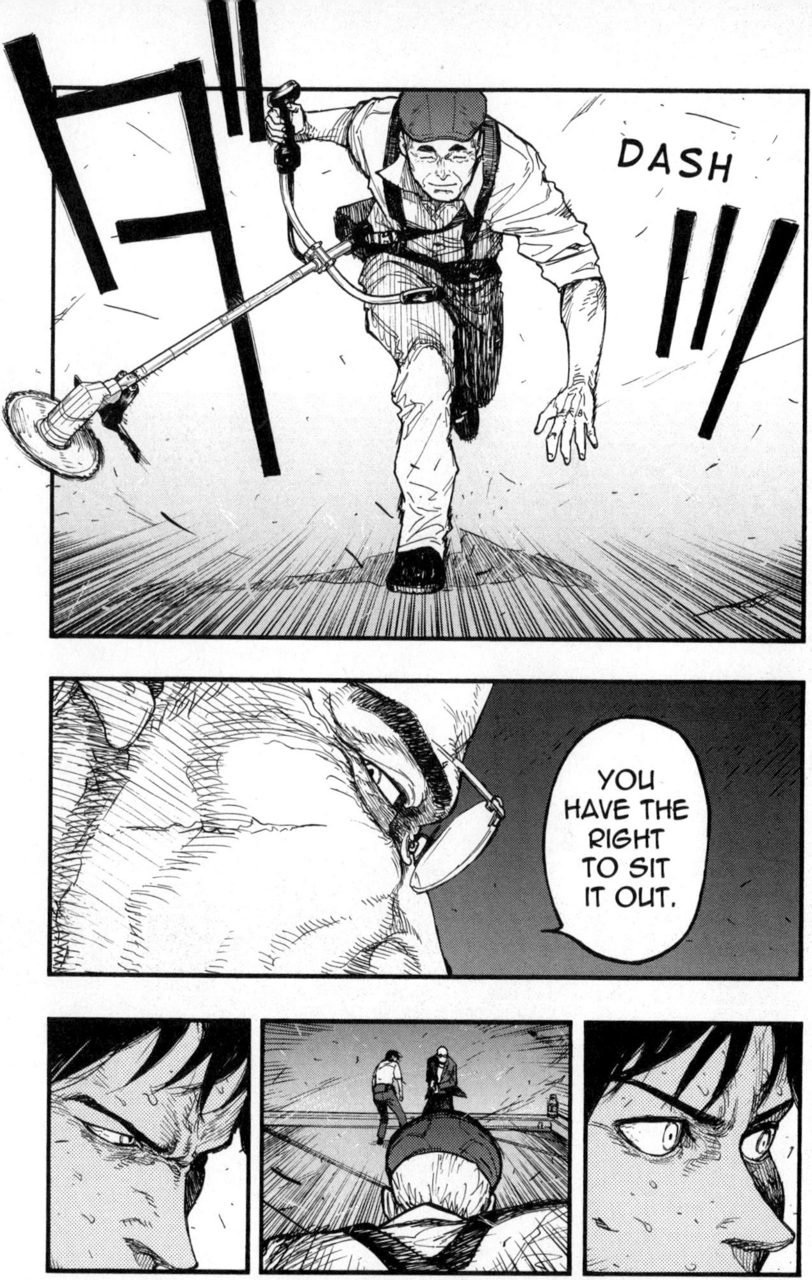
DASH
YOU HAVE THE RIGHT TO SIT IT OUT.

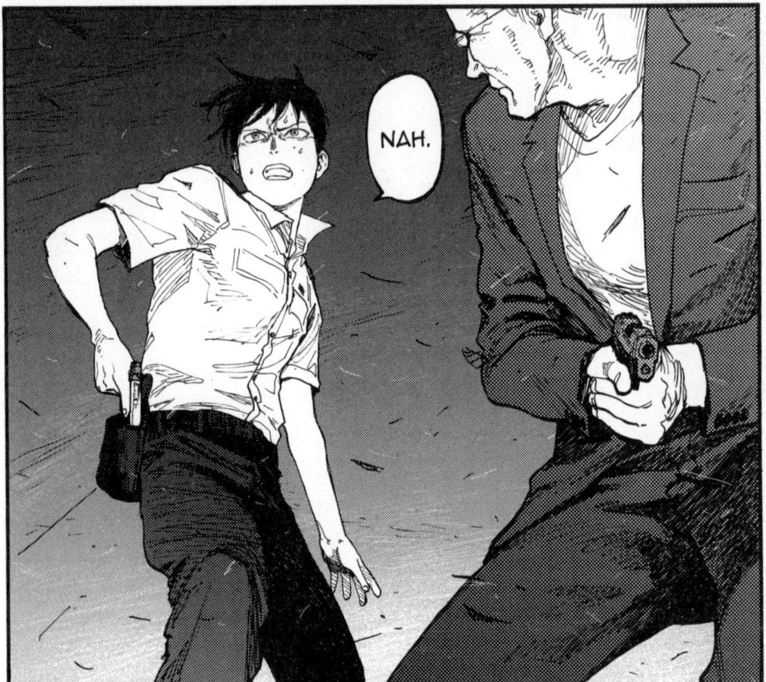
NAH.

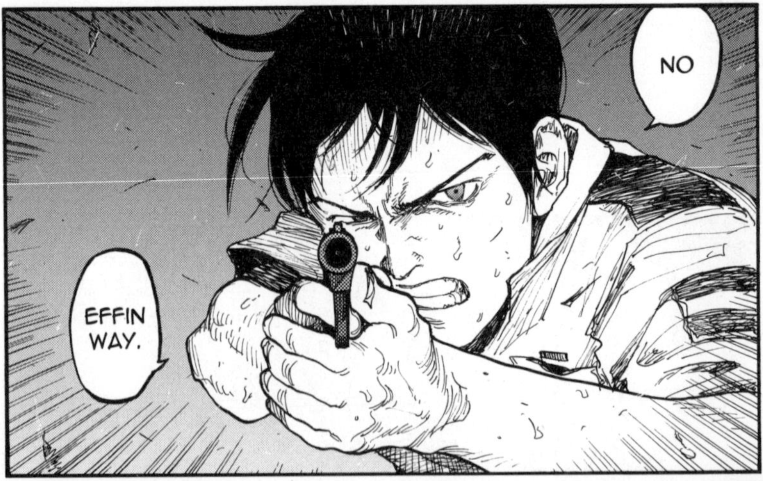
NO
EFFIN WAY.

IT WAS FUN.

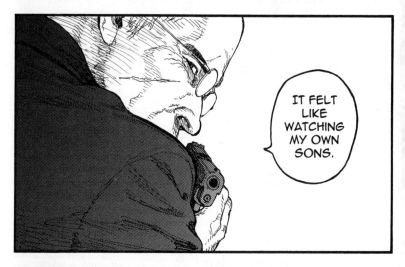

IT FELT LIKE WATCHING MY OWN SONS.

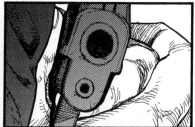

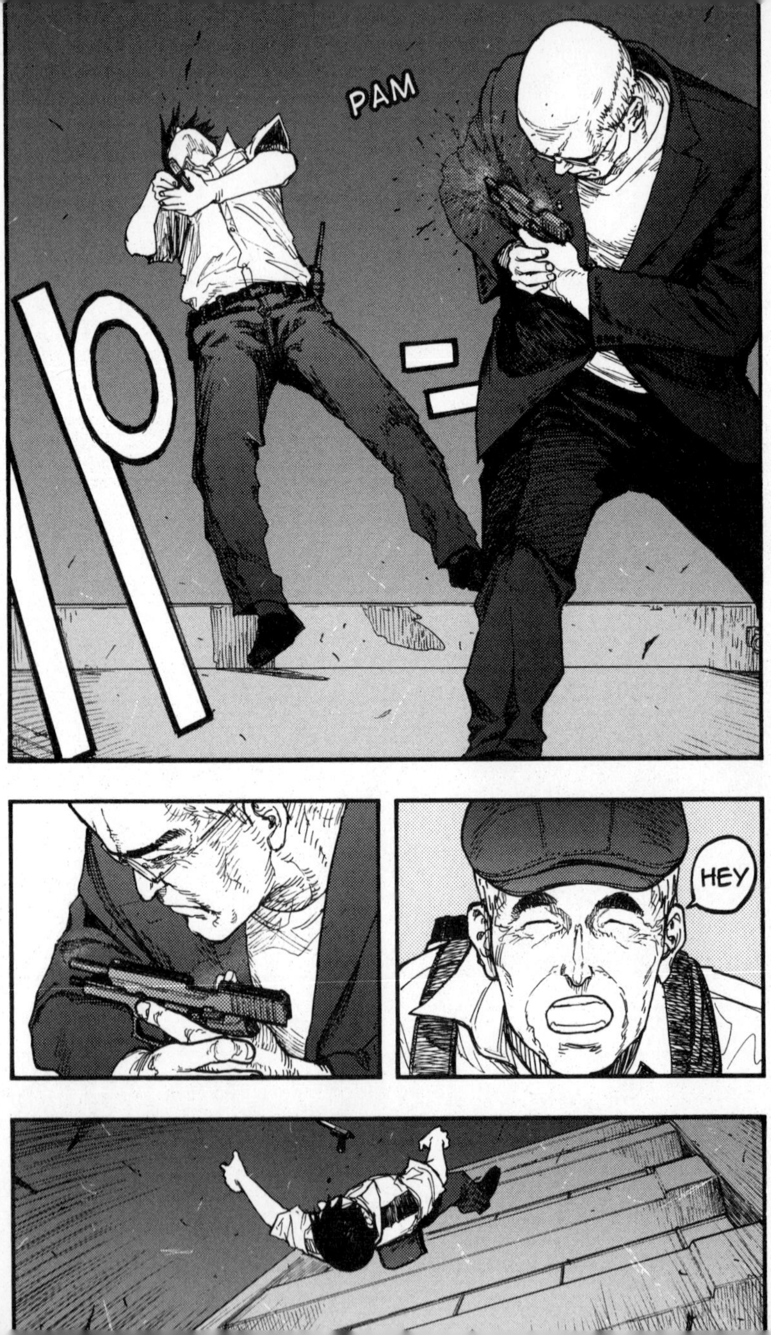
PAM
HEY

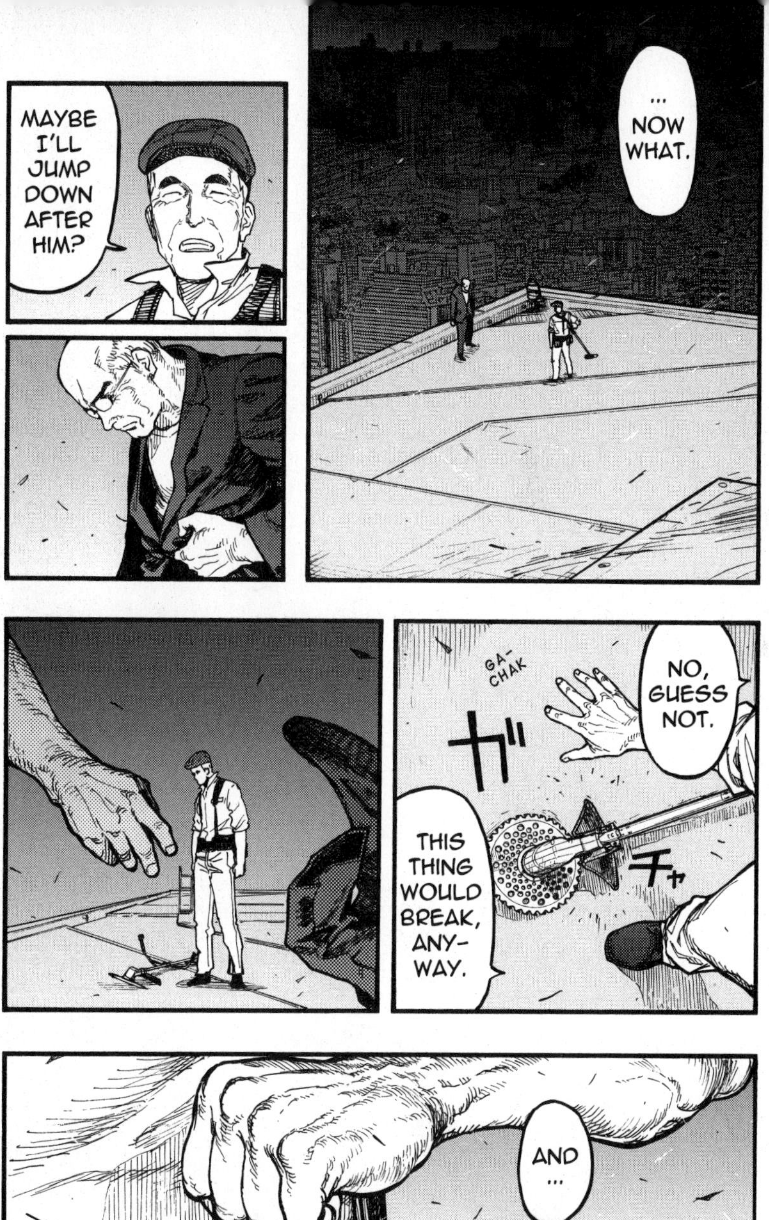
... NOW WHAT.
MAYBE I'LL JUMP DOWN AFTER HIM?
GA-CHAK
ガ
チャ
NO, GUESS NOT.
THIS THING WOULD BREAK, ANY-WAY.
AND ...

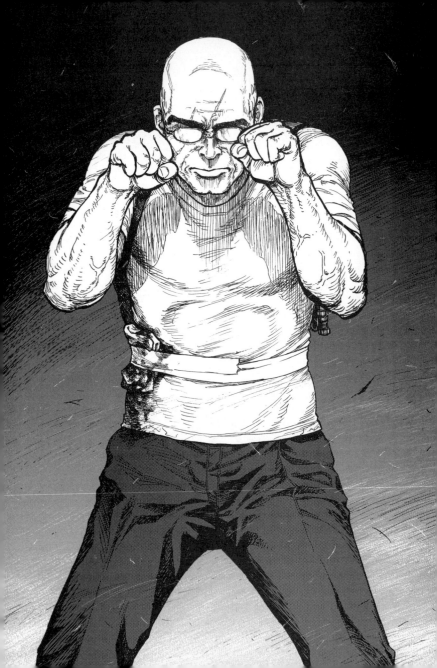

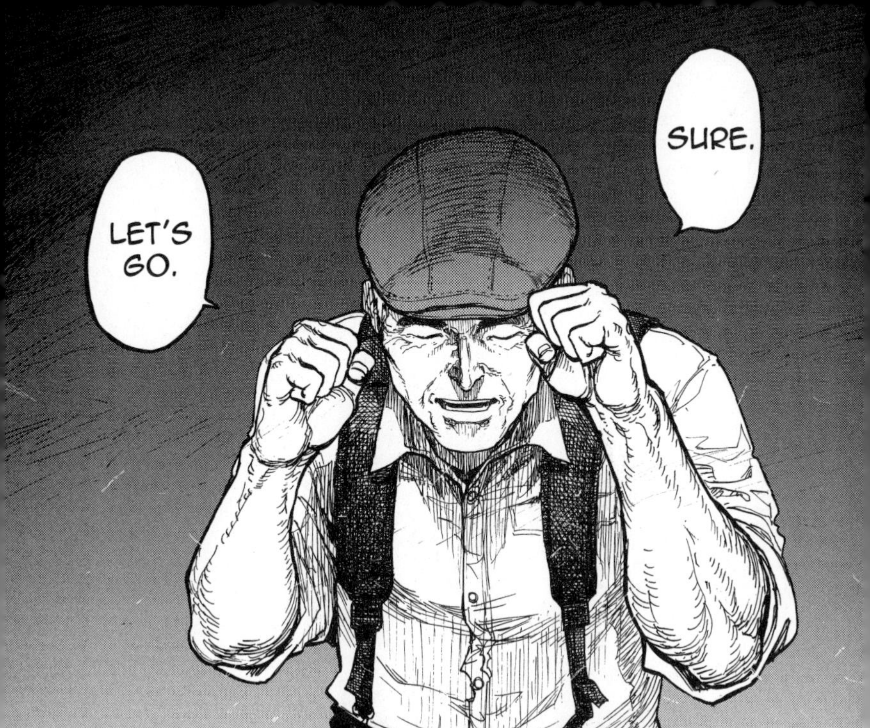
SURE.
LET'S GO.
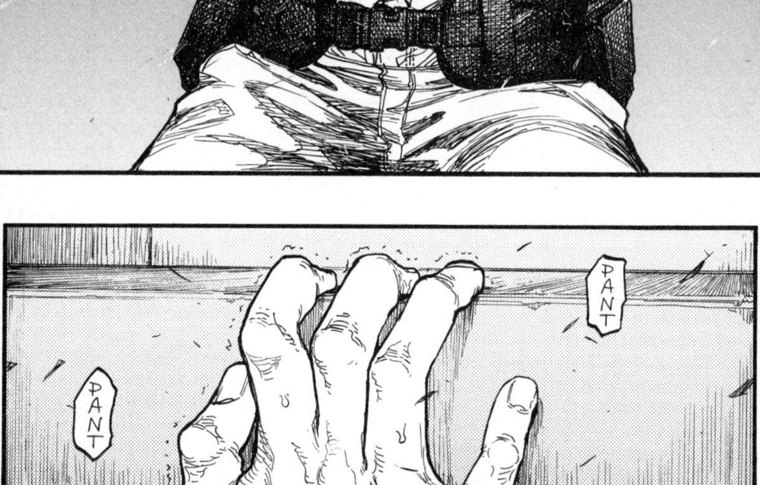
PANT
PANT

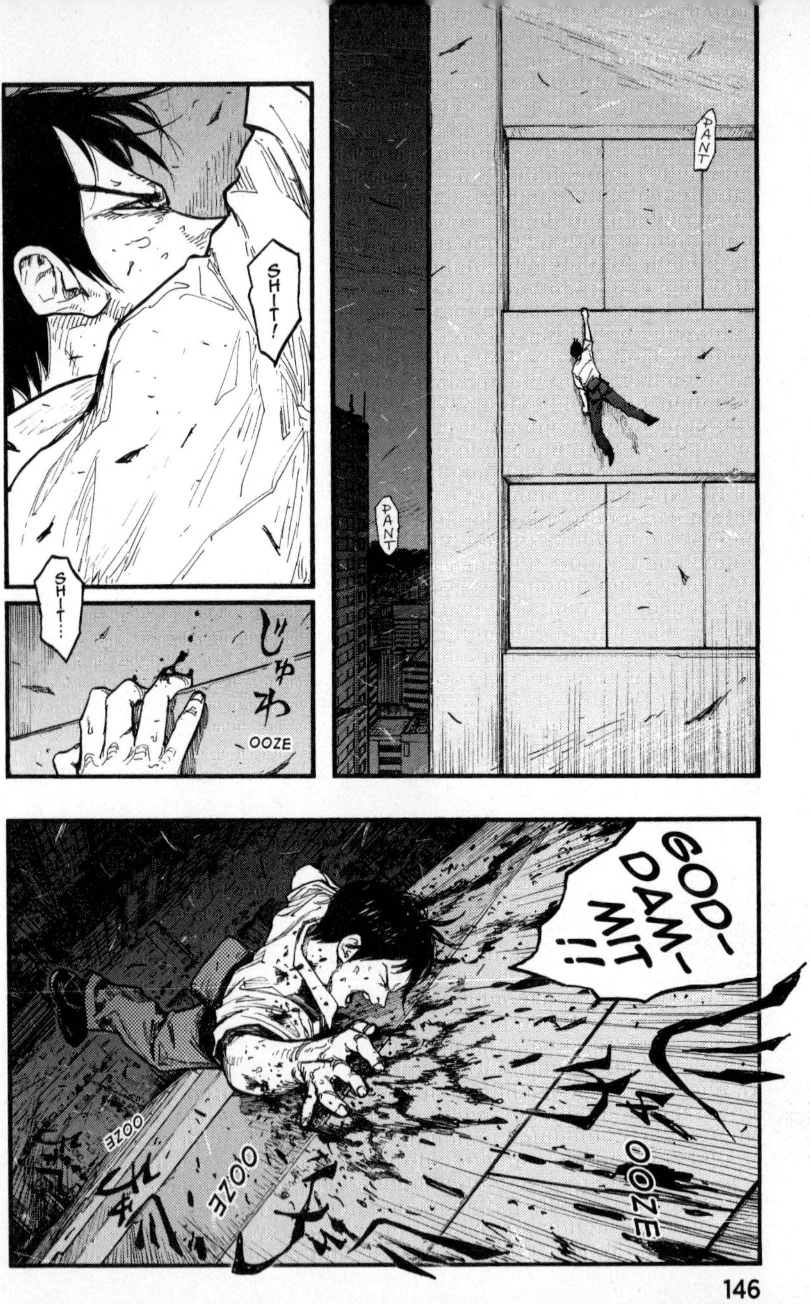
PANT
PANT
SHIT!
SHIT...
じゅわ
OOZE
GOD-DAM-MIT!!
OOZE
OOZE
OOZE

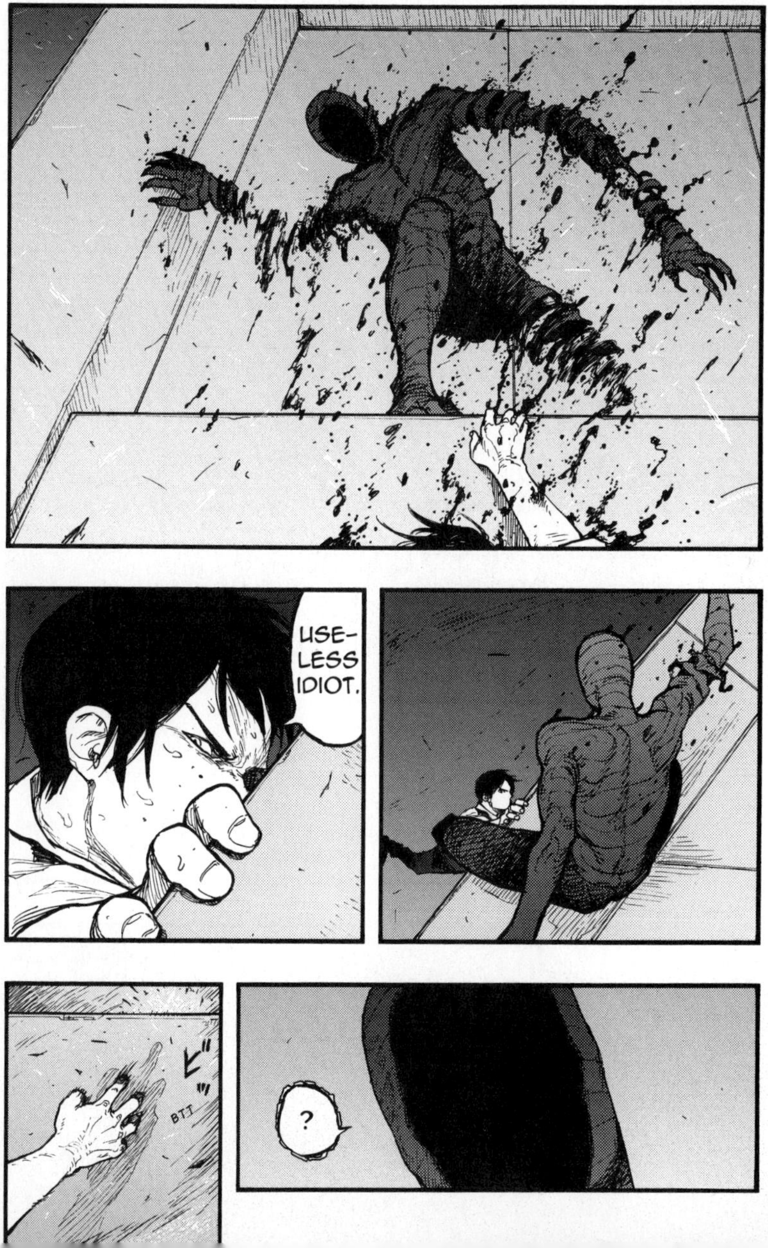
USE-
LESS
IDIOT.
ビッ
BTT
?

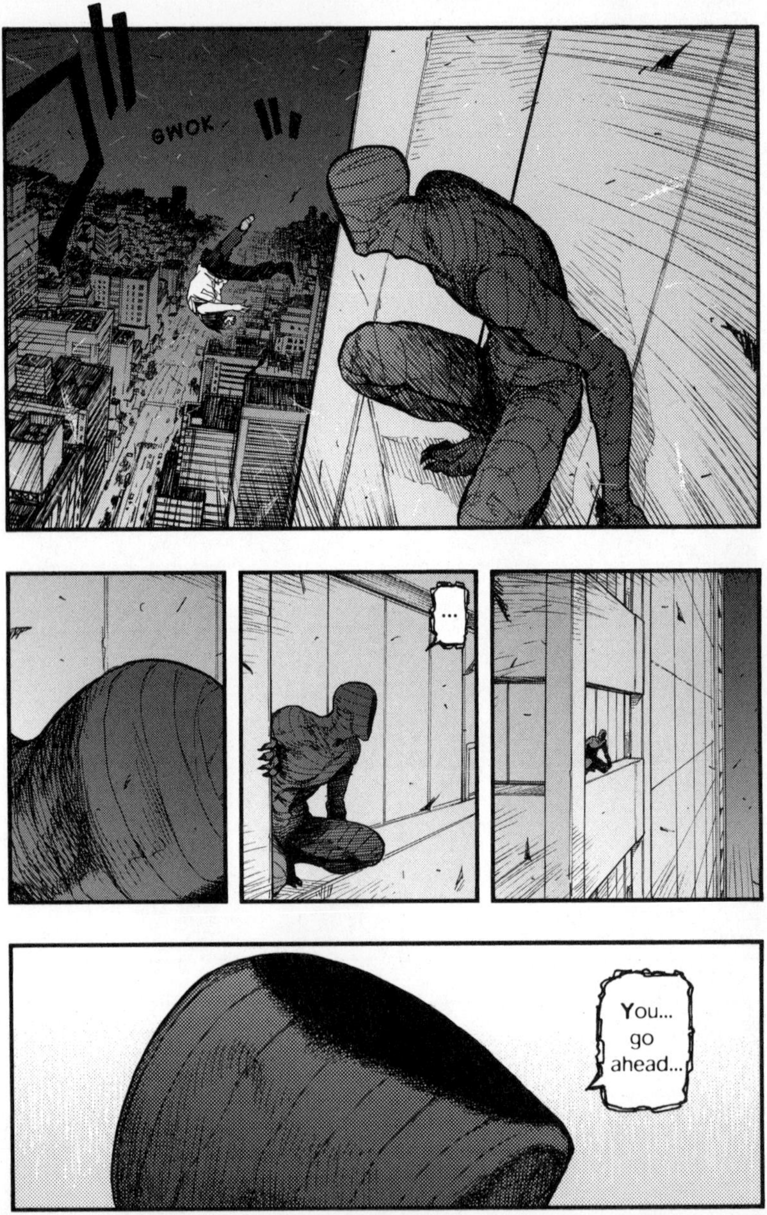
GWOK
...
You... go ahead...

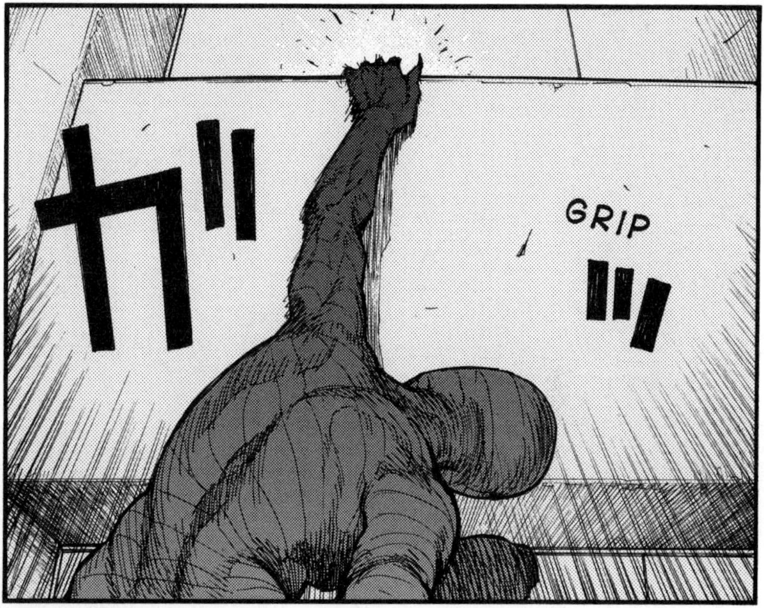
ガ
GRIP
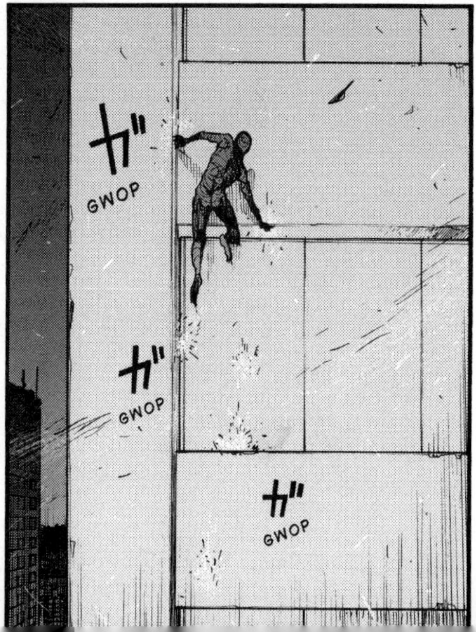
ガ
GWOP
ガ
GWOP
ガ
GWOP
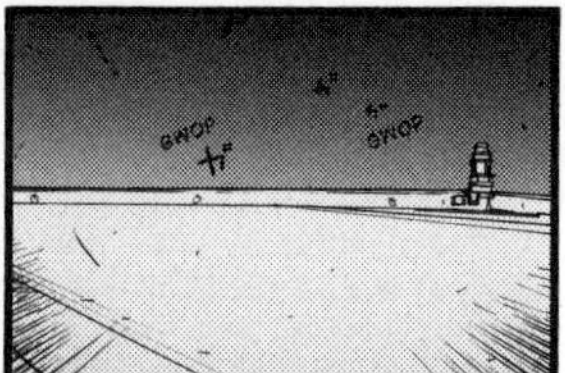
GWOP
GWOP
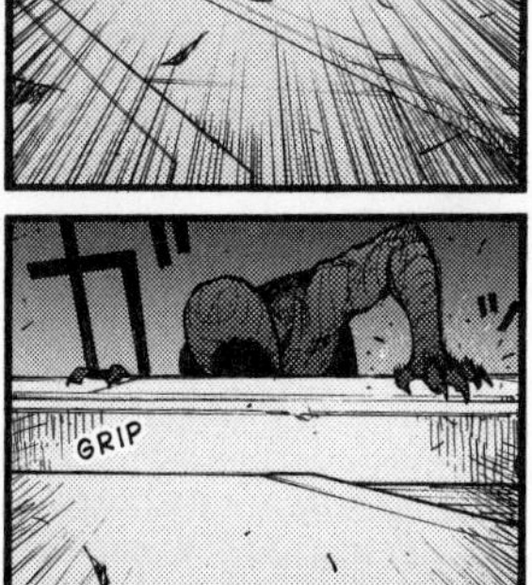
ガ
GRIP

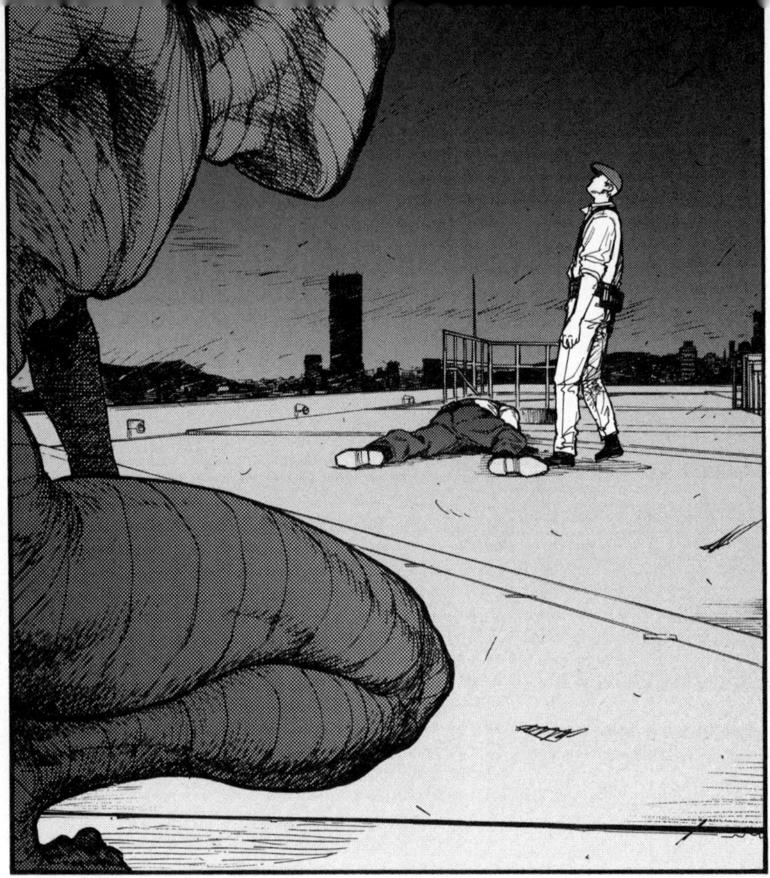

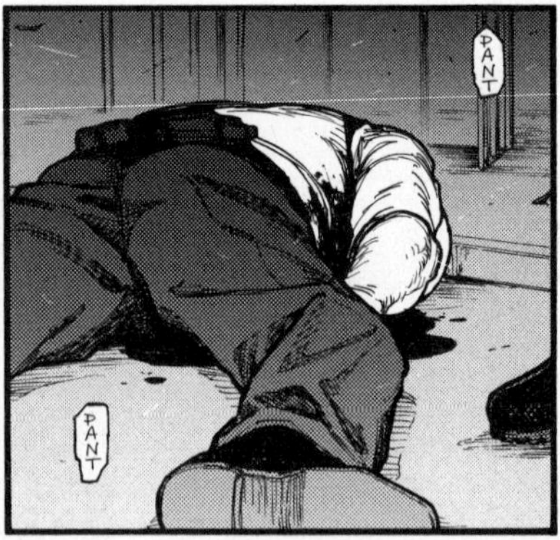
PANT
PANT

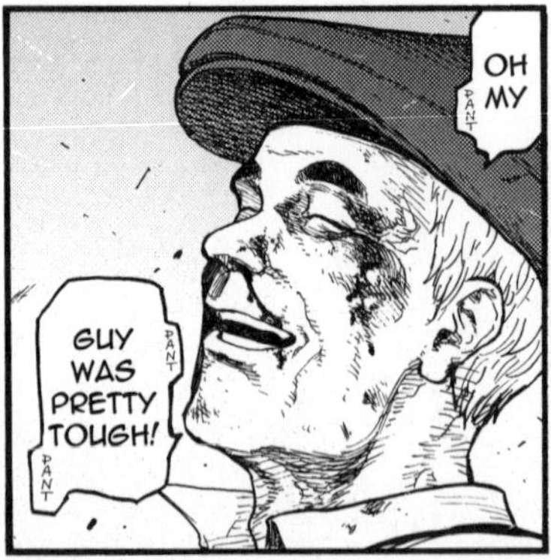
OH MY
PANT
GUY WAS PRETTY TOUGH!
PANT
PANT

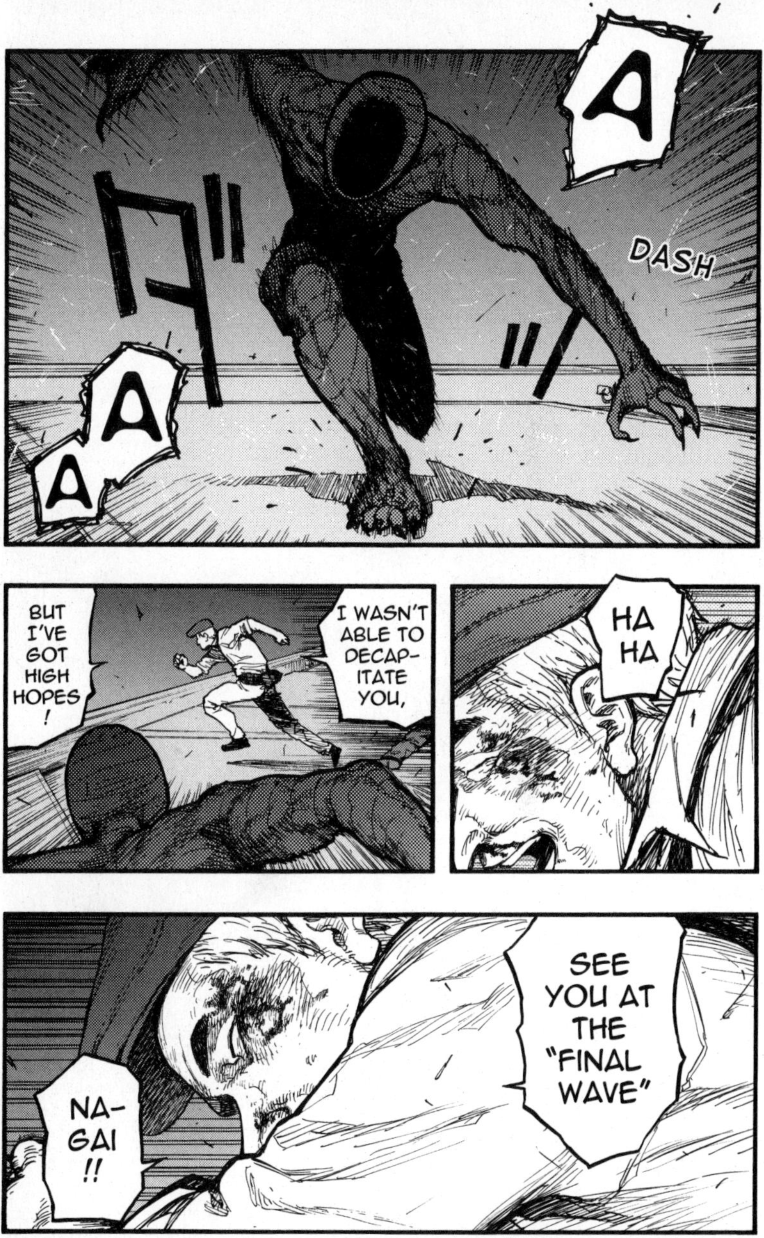
A
DASH
A A
HA HA
I WASN'T ABLE TO DECAP-ITATE YOU,
BUT I'VE GOT HIGH HOPES!
SEE YOU AT THE "FINAL WAVE"
NA-GAI!!

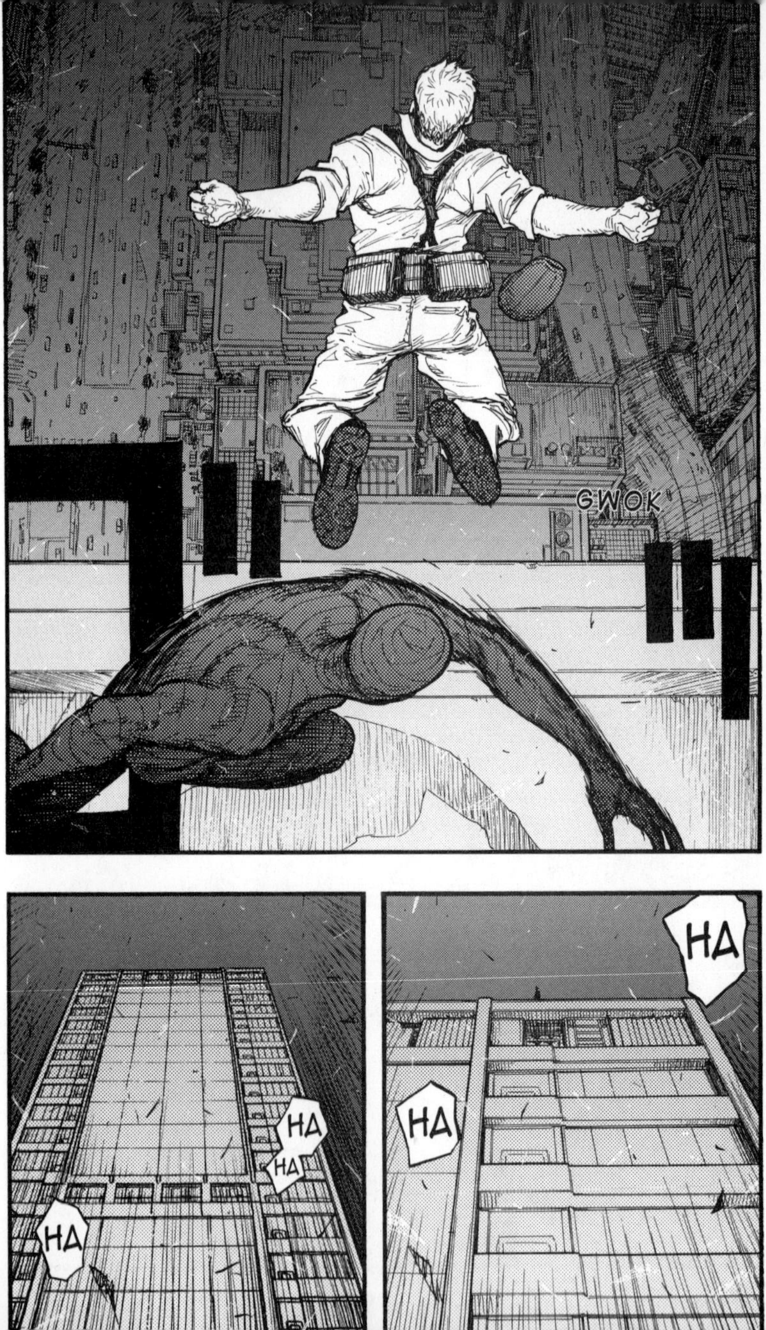
GWOK
HA
HA
HA
HA
HA

File:42 End

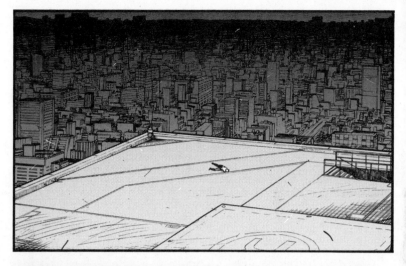

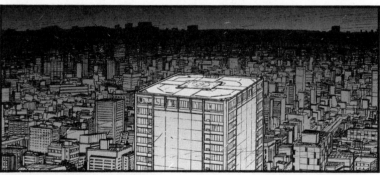

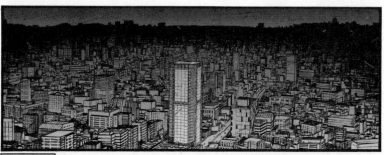

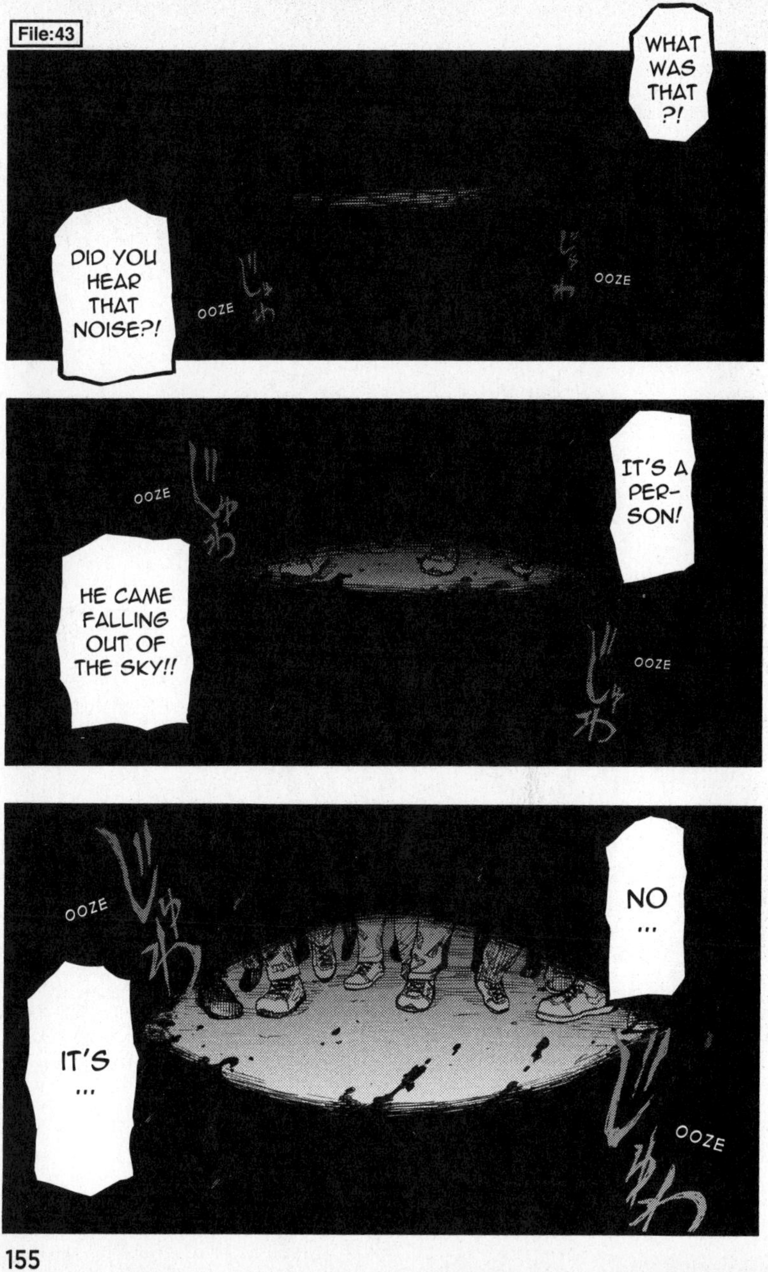
WHAT WAS THAT?!
OOZE
OOZE
DID YOU HEAR THAT NOISE?!
IT'S A PER-SON!
OOZE
HE CAME FALLING OUT OF THE SKY!!
OOZE
NO...
OOZE
OOZE
IT'S...

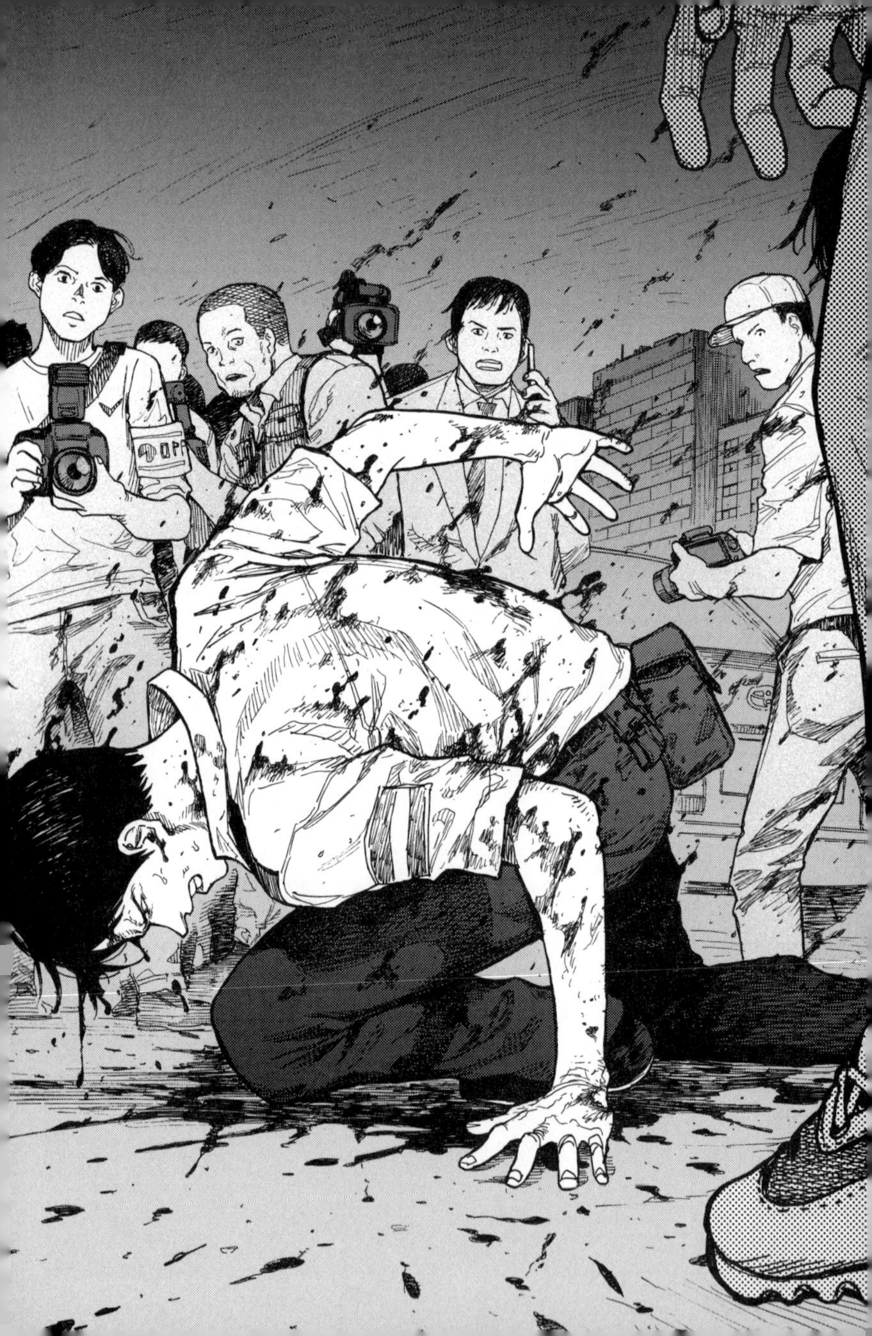

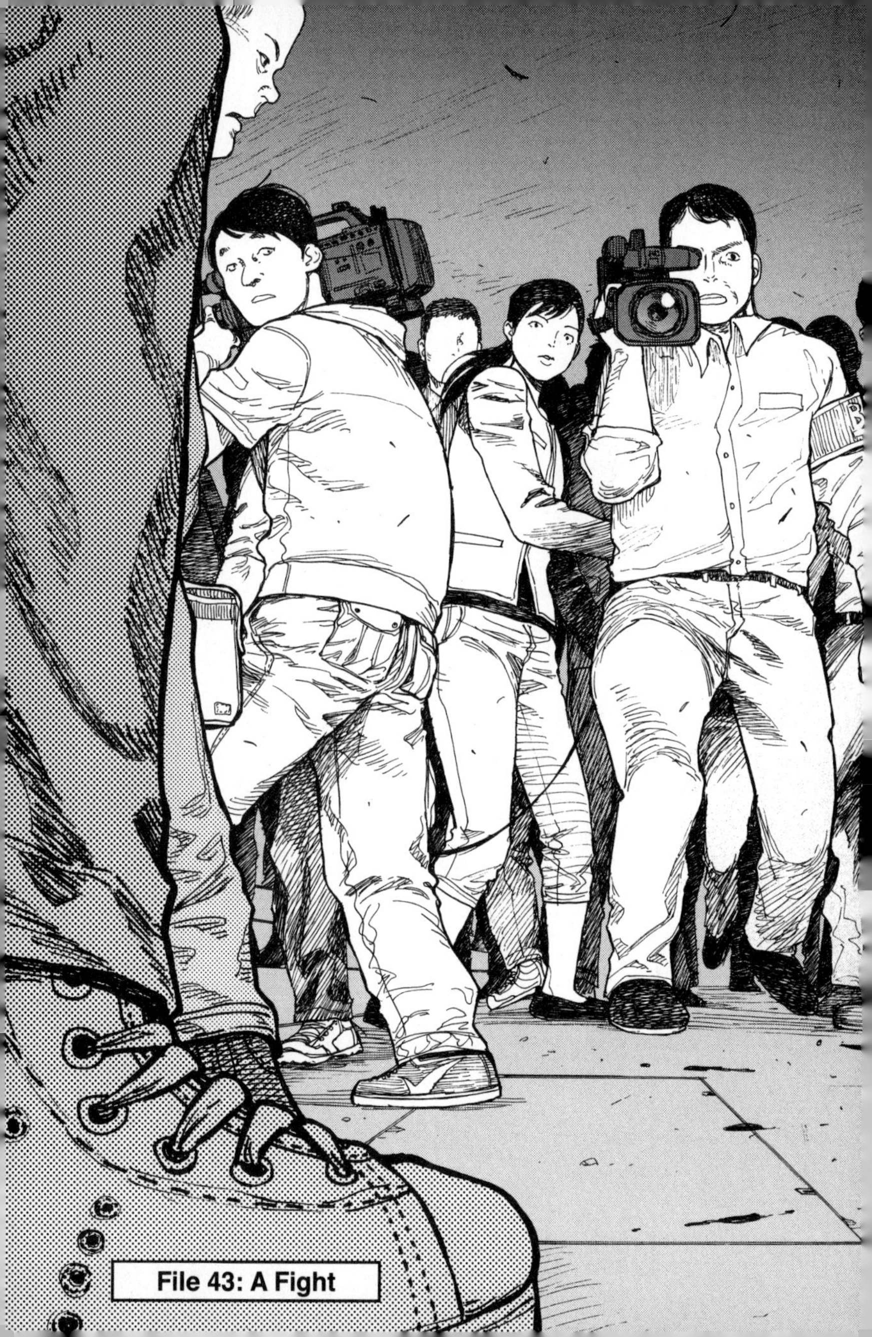
File 43: A Fight

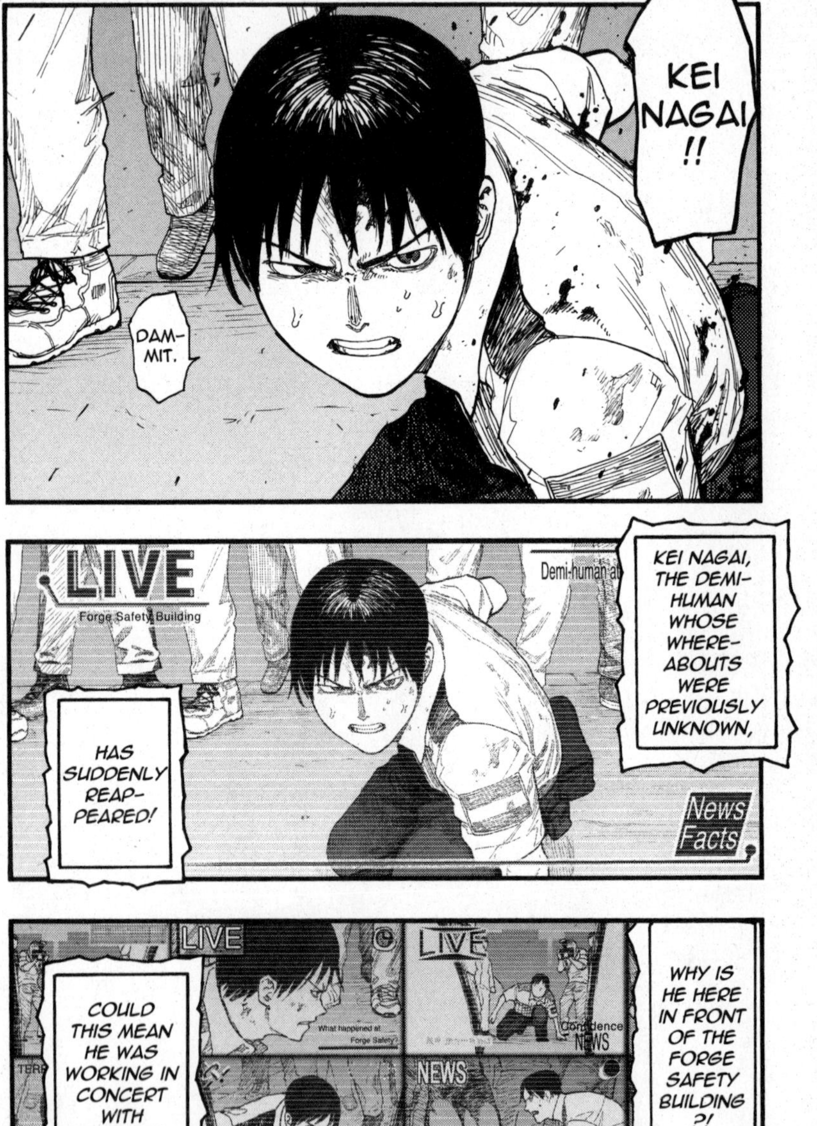
KEI NAGAI!!
DAM-MIT.
LIVE
Forge Safety Building
Demi-human at
KEI NAGAI, THE DEMI-HUMAN WHOSE WHERE-ABOUTS WERE PREVIOUSLY UNKNOWN,
HAS SUDDENLY REAP-PEARED!
News Facts
LIVE
LIVE
What happened at Forge Safety?
Confidence NEWS
NEWS
First, a demi-human attack. And now...
WHY IS HE HERE IN FRONT OF THE FORGE SAFETY BUILDING?!
COULD THIS MEAN HE WAS WORKING IN CONCERT WITH SATO?!

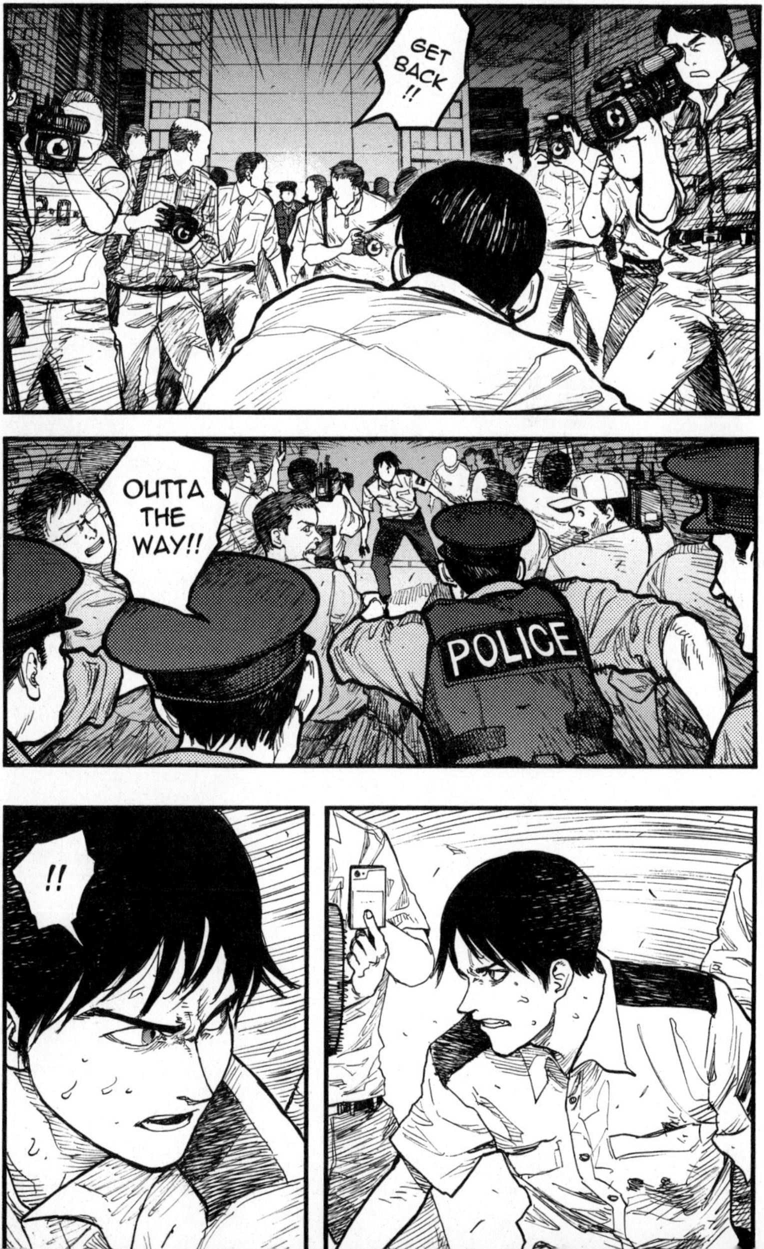
GET BACK !!
OUTTA THE WAY!!
!!

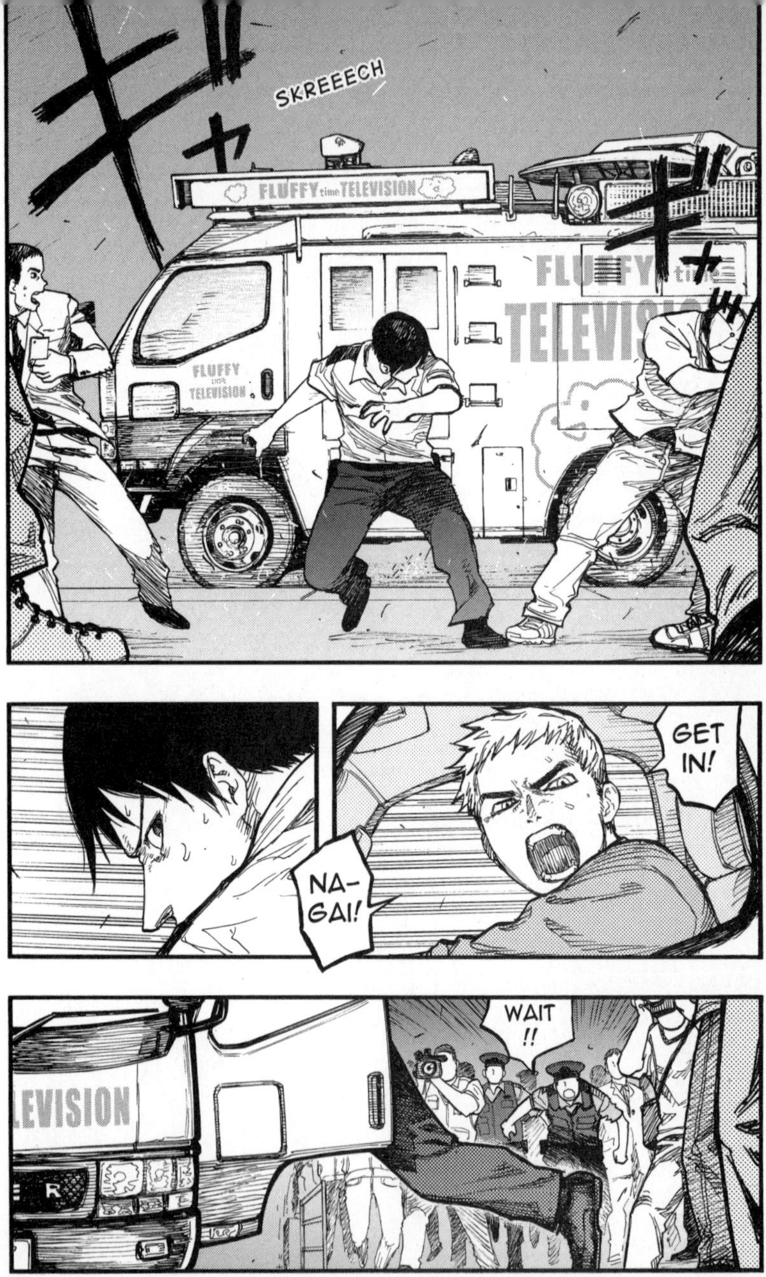
SKREEECH
FLUFFY time TELEVISION
GET IN!
NA-GAI!
WAIT !!

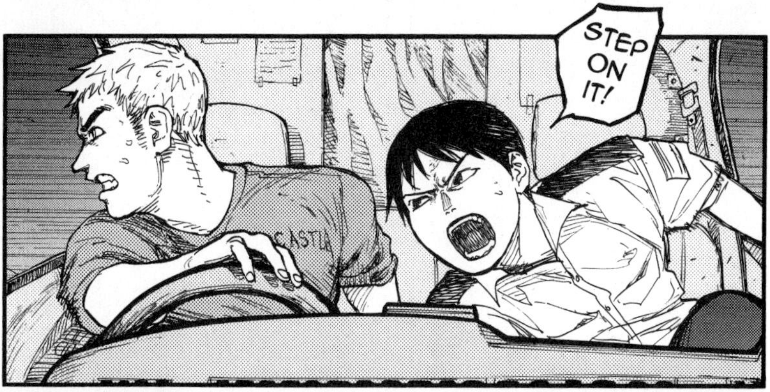
STEP ON IT!
CASTI
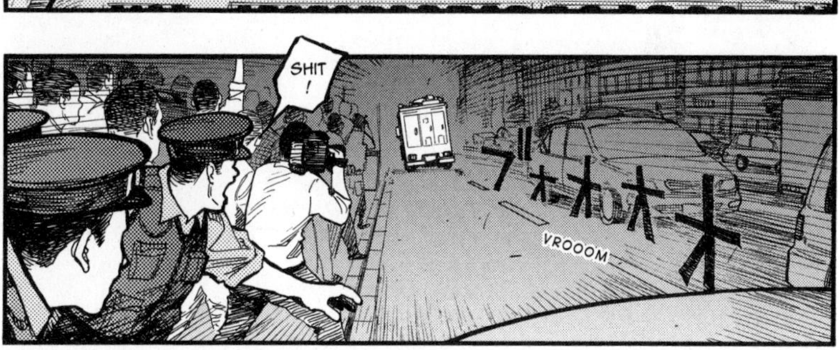
SHIT!
VROOOM
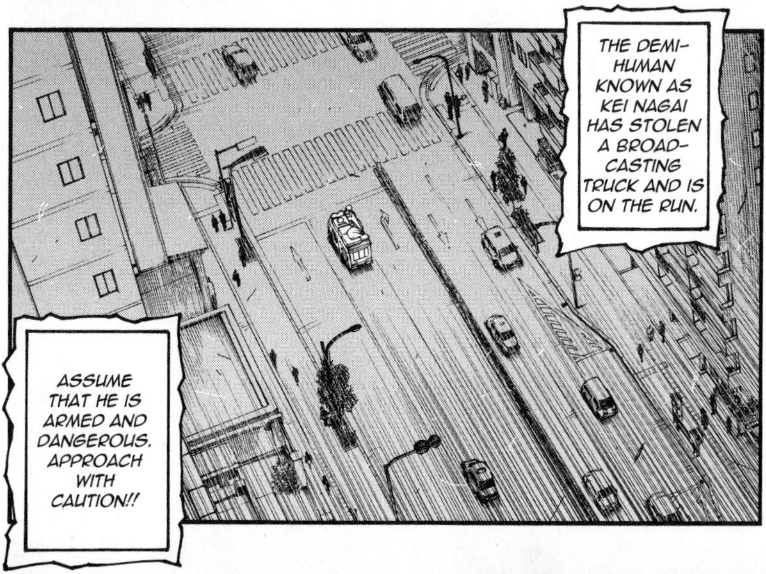
THE DEMI-HUMAN KNOWN AS KEI NAGAI HAS STOLEN A BROAD-CASTING TRUCK AND IS ON THE RUN.
ASSUME THAT HE IS ARMED AND DANGEROUS. APPROACH WITH CAUTION!!

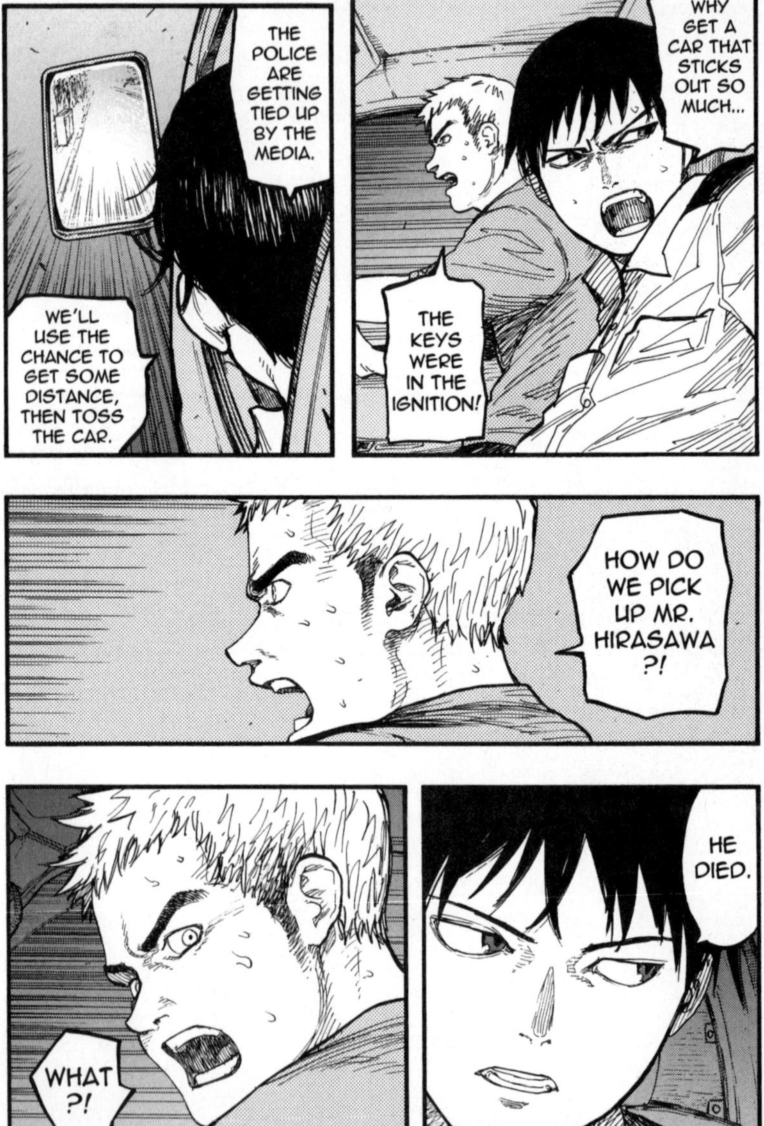
WHY GET A CAR THAT STICKS OUT SO MUCH...
THE KEYS WERE IN THE IGNITION!
THE POLICE ARE GETTING TIED UP BY THE MEDIA.
WE'LL USE THE CHANCE TO GET SOME DISTANCE, THEN TOSS THE CAR.
HOW DO WE PICK UP MR. HIRASAWA ?!
HE DIED.
WHAT ?!

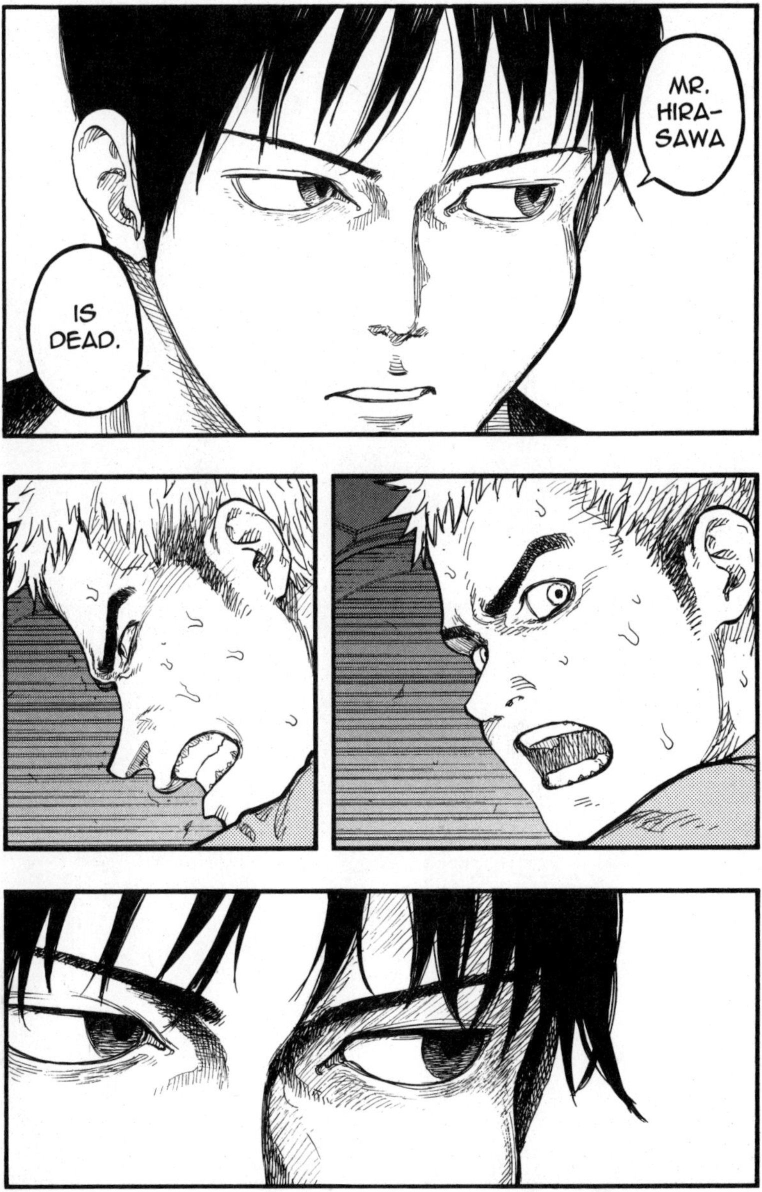
MR. HIRA-SAWA
IS DEAD.

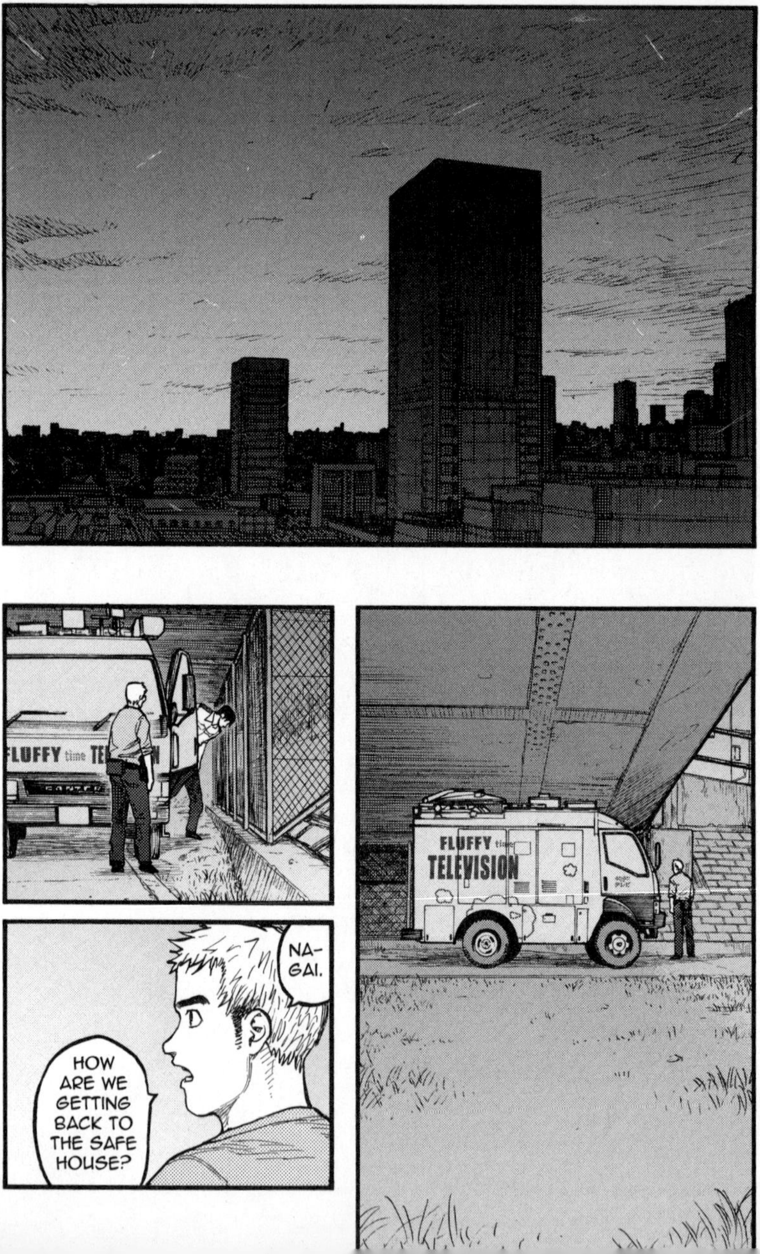
FLUFFY time
TELEVISION
FLUFFY time
NA-GAI.
HOW ARE WE GETTING BACK TO THE SAFE HOUSE?

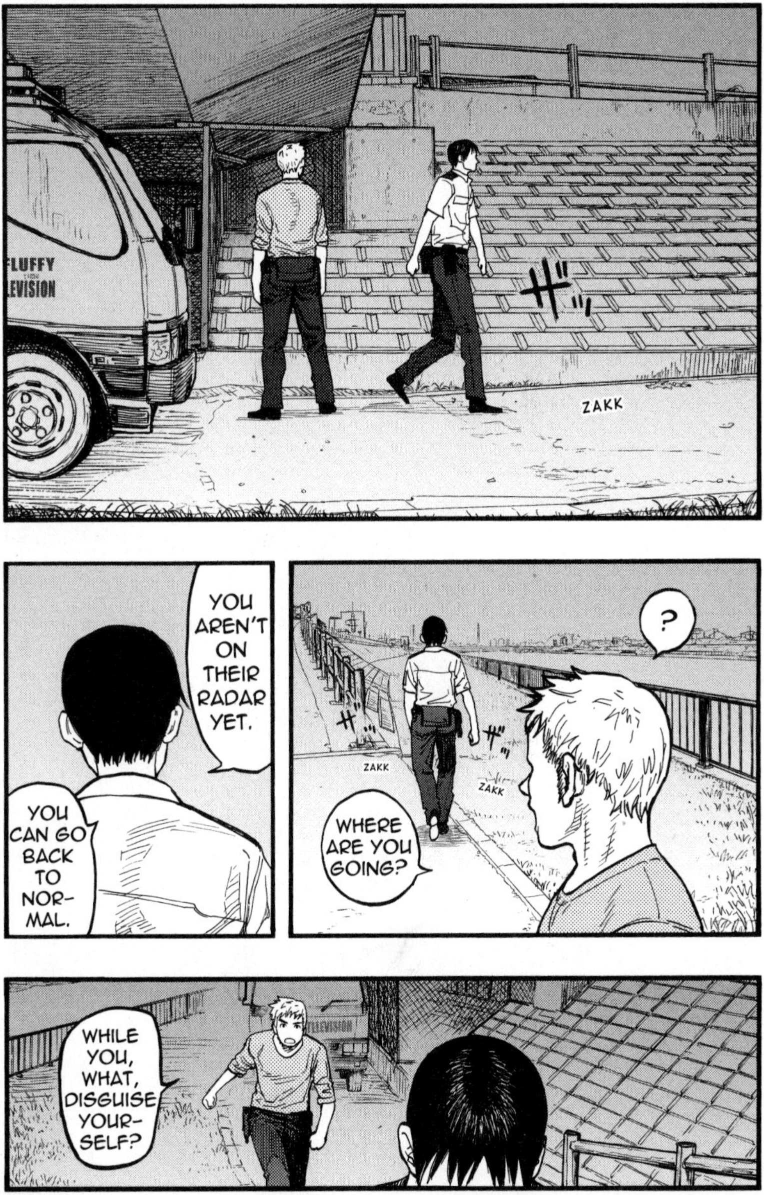
ZAKK
?
ZAKK
ZAKK
WHERE ARE YOU GOING?
YOU AREN'T ON THEIR RADAR YET.
YOU CAN GO BACK TO NOR-MAL.
WHILE YOU, WHAT, DISGUISE YOUR-SELF?

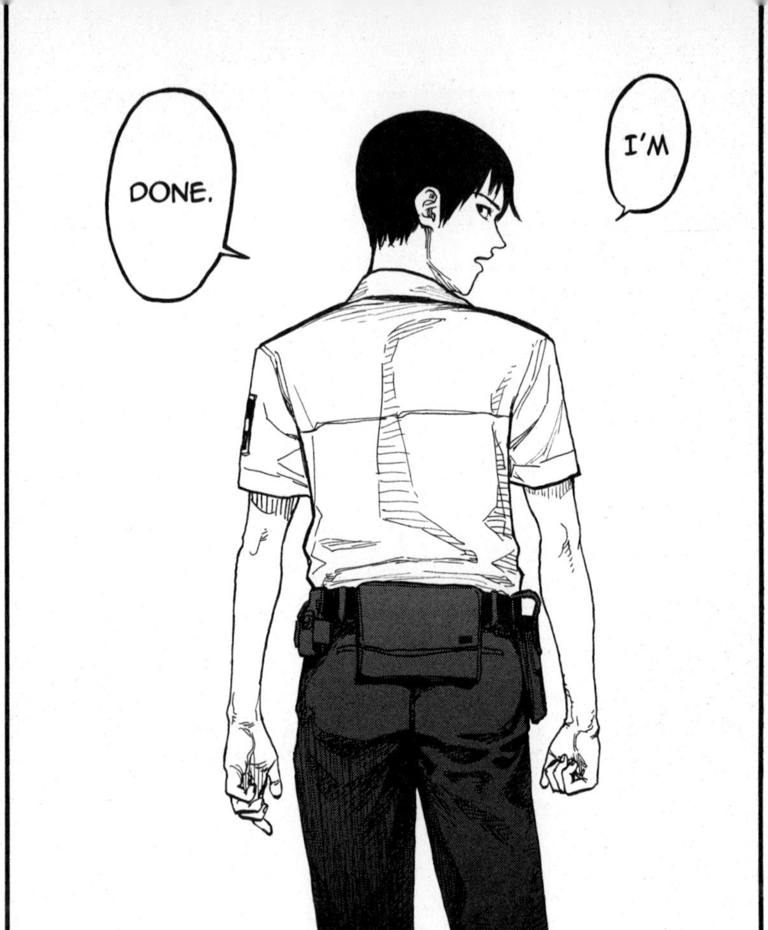
I'M
DONE.
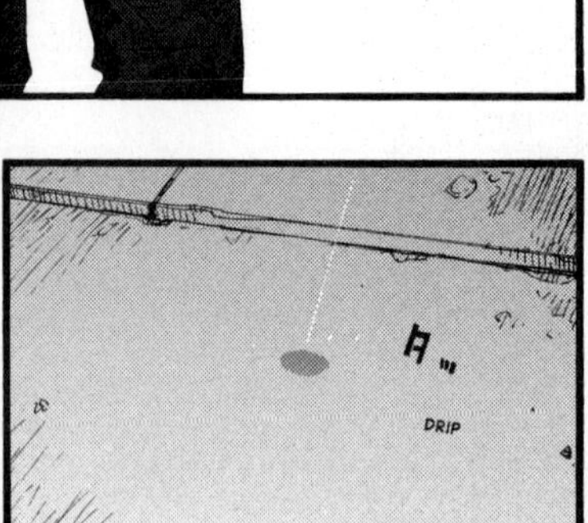
DRIP
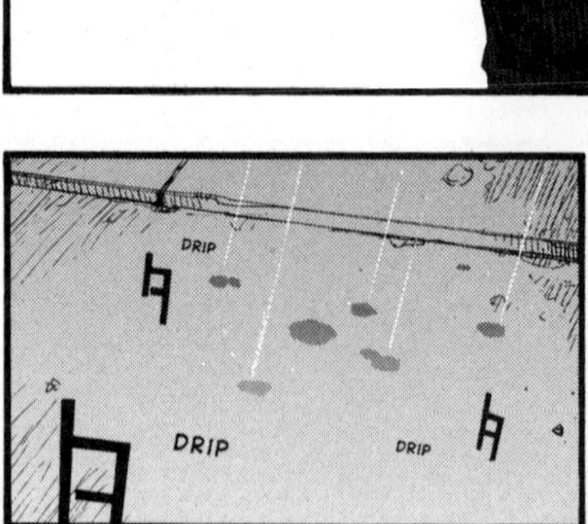
DRIP
DRIP
DRIP

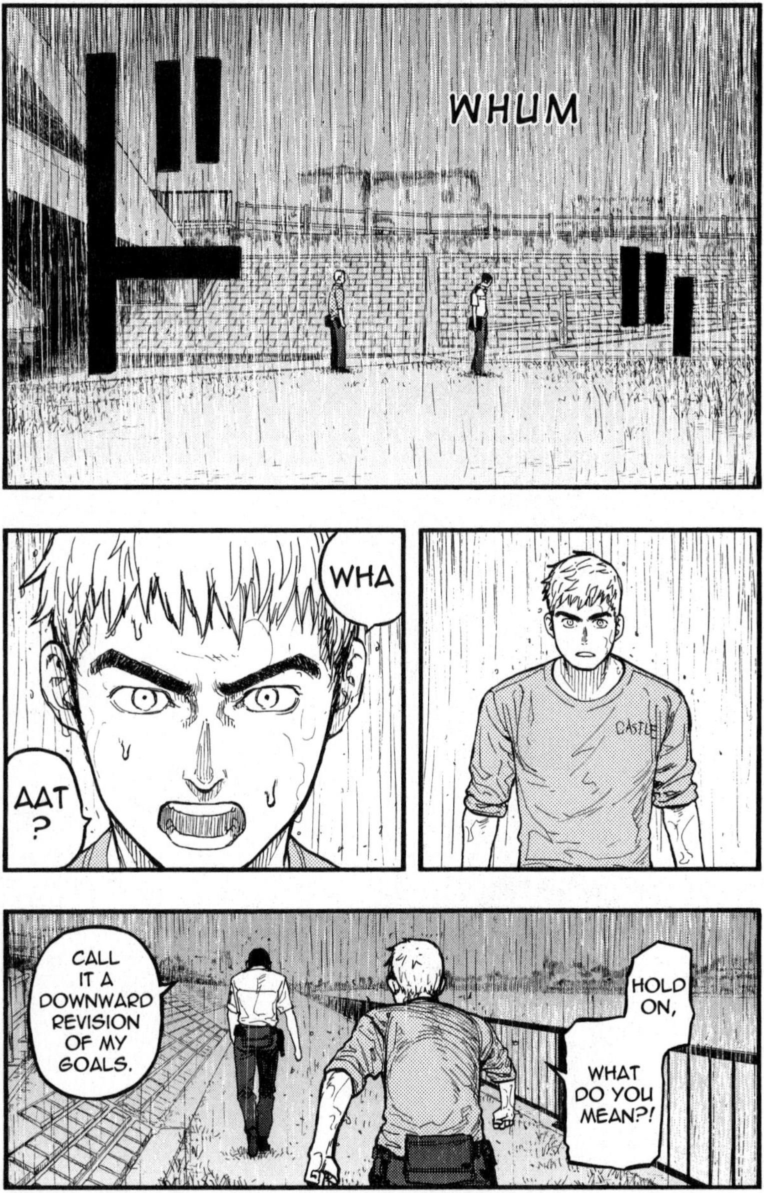
WHUM
CASTLE
WHA
AAT?
HOLD ON,
WHAT DO YOU MEAN?!
CALL IT A DOWNWARD REVISION OF MY GOALS.

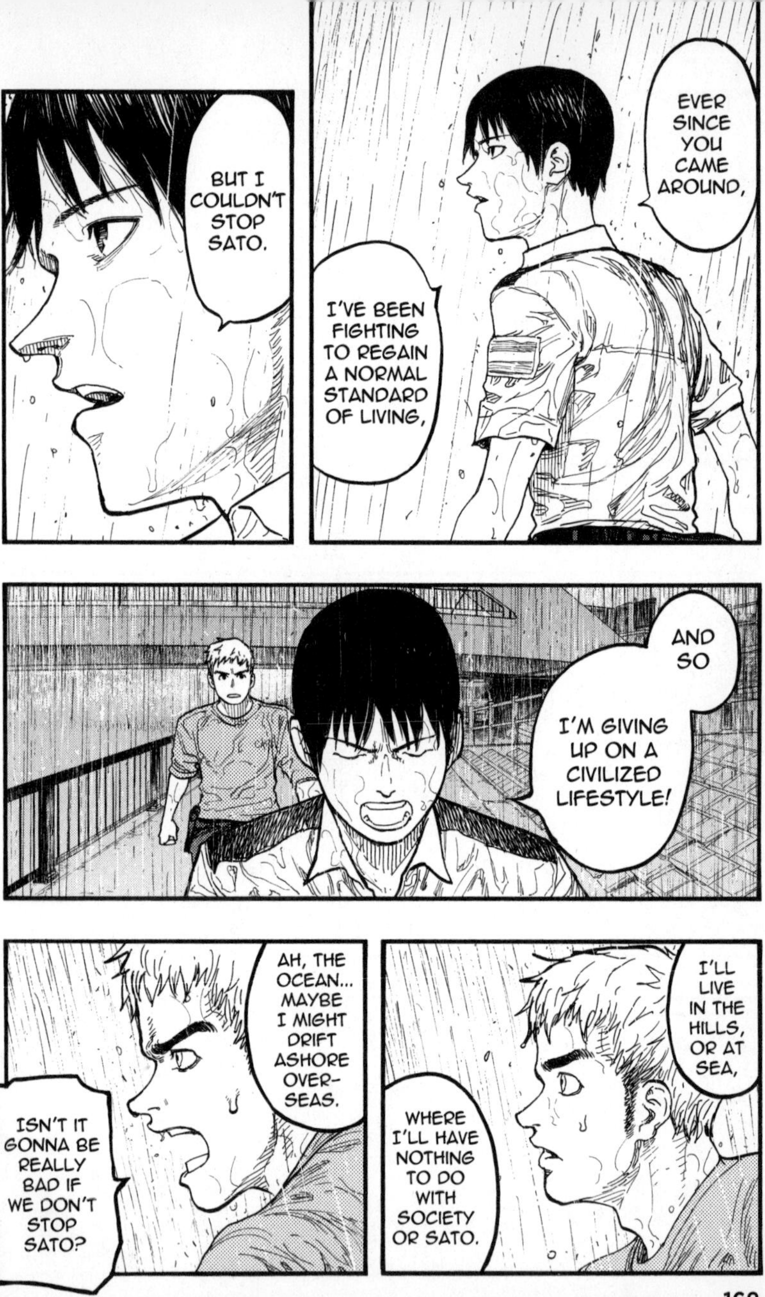
EVER SINCE YOU CAME AROUND,
I'VE BEEN FIGHTING TO REGAIN A NORMAL STANDARD OF LIVING,
BUT I COULDN'T STOP SATO.
AND SO
I'M GIVING UP ON A CIVILIZED LIFESTYLE!
I'LL LIVE IN THE HILLS, OR AT SEA,
WHERE I'LL HAVE NOTHING TO DO WITH SOCIETY OR SATO.
AH, THE OCEAN... MAYBE I MIGHT DRIFT ASHORE OVERSEAS.
ISN'T IT GONNA BE REALLY BAD IF WE DON'T STOP SATO?

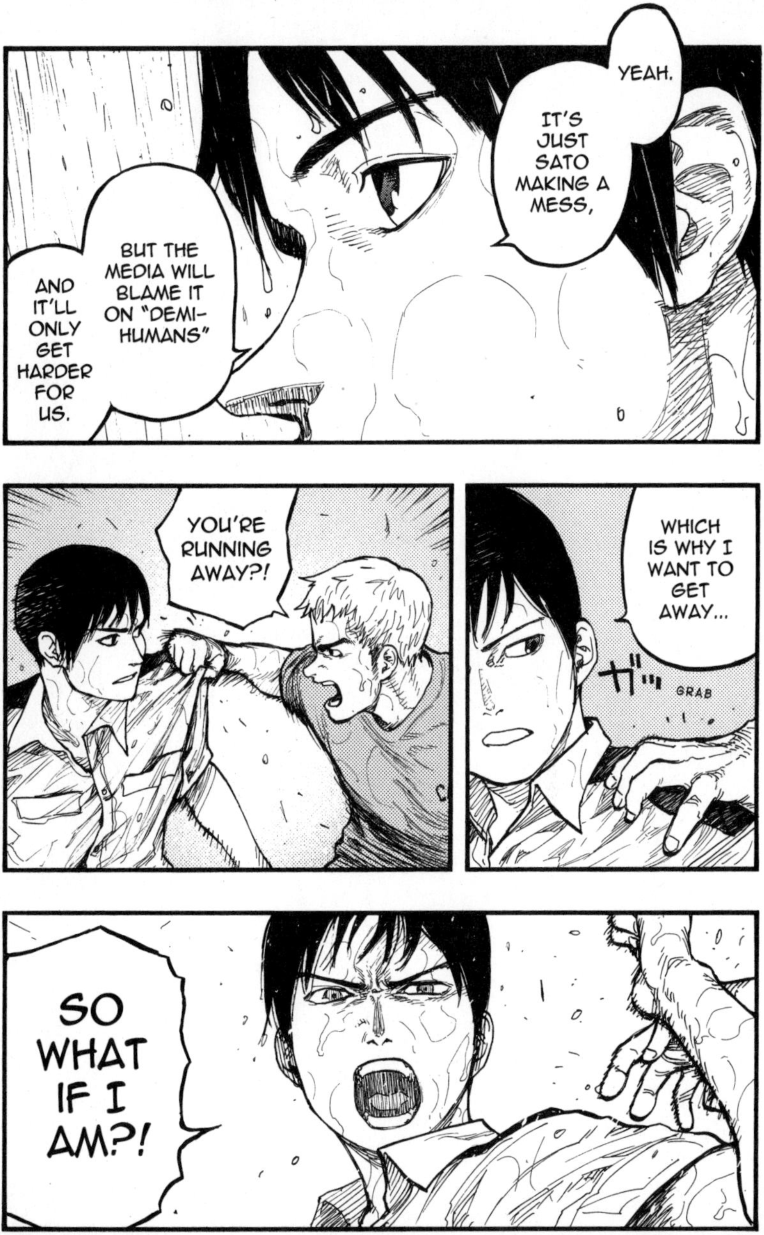
YEAH.
IT'S JUST SATO MAKING A MESS,
BUT THE MEDIA WILL BLAME IT ON "DEMI-HUMANS"
AND IT'LL ONLY GET HARDER FOR US.
WHICH IS WHY I WANT TO GET AWAY...
GRAB
YOU'RE RUNNING AWAY?!
SO WHAT IF I AM?!

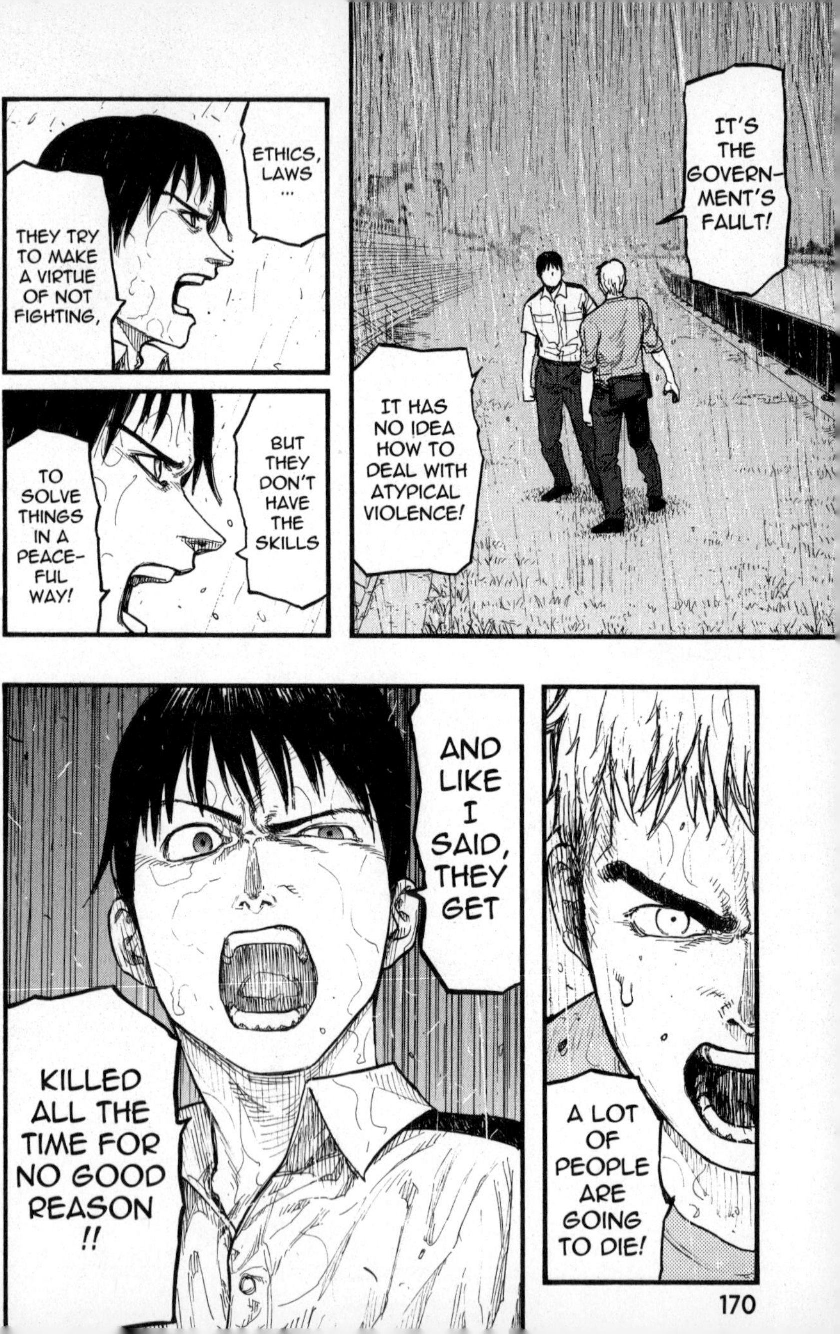
IT'S THE GOVERN-MENT'S FAULT!
IT HAS NO IDEA HOW TO DEAL WITH ATYPICAL VIOLENCE!
ETHICS, LAWS ...
THEY TRY TO MAKE A VIRTUE OF NOT FIGHTING,
BUT THEY DON'T HAVE THE SKILLS
TO SOLVE THINGS IN A PEACE-FUL WAY!
A LOT OF PEOPLE ARE GOING TO DIE!
AND LIKE I SAID, THEY GET
KILLED ALL THE TIME FOR NO GOOD REASON !!

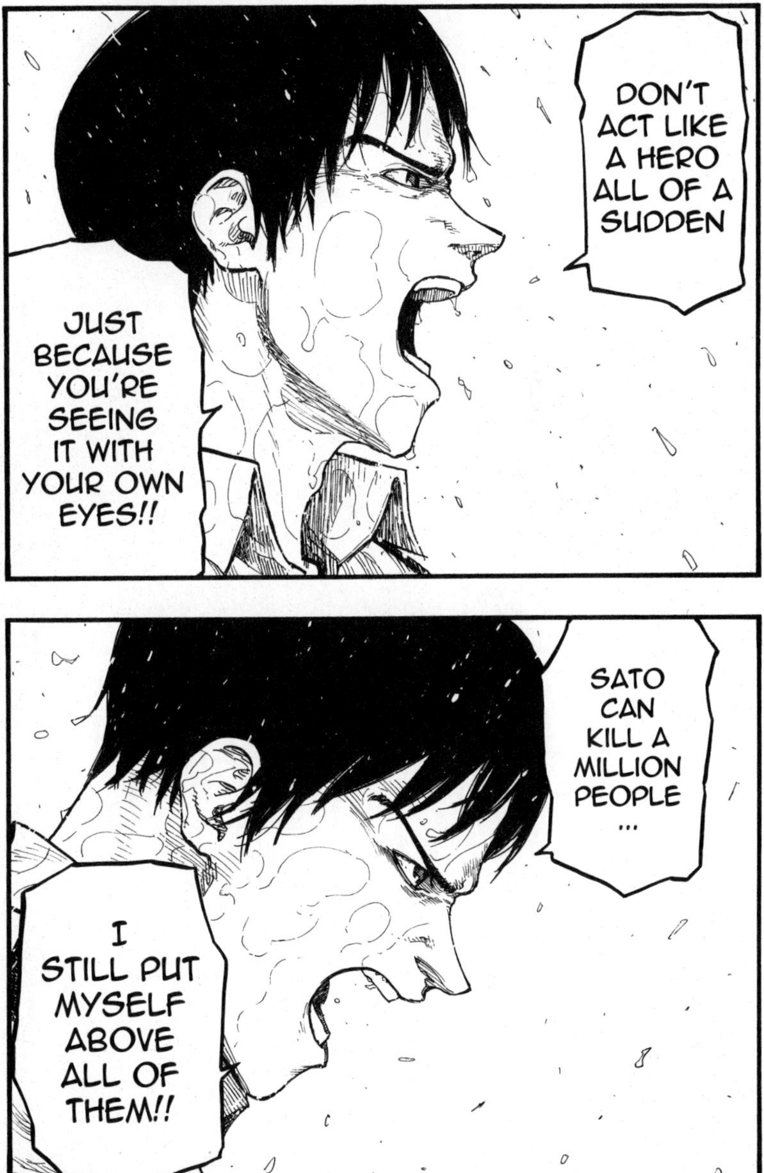
DON'T ACT LIKE A HERO ALL OF A SUDDEN
JUST BECAUSE YOU'RE SEEING IT WITH YOUR OWN EYES!!
SATO CAN KILL A MILLION PEOPLE ...
I STILL PUT MYSELF ABOVE ALL OF THEM!!

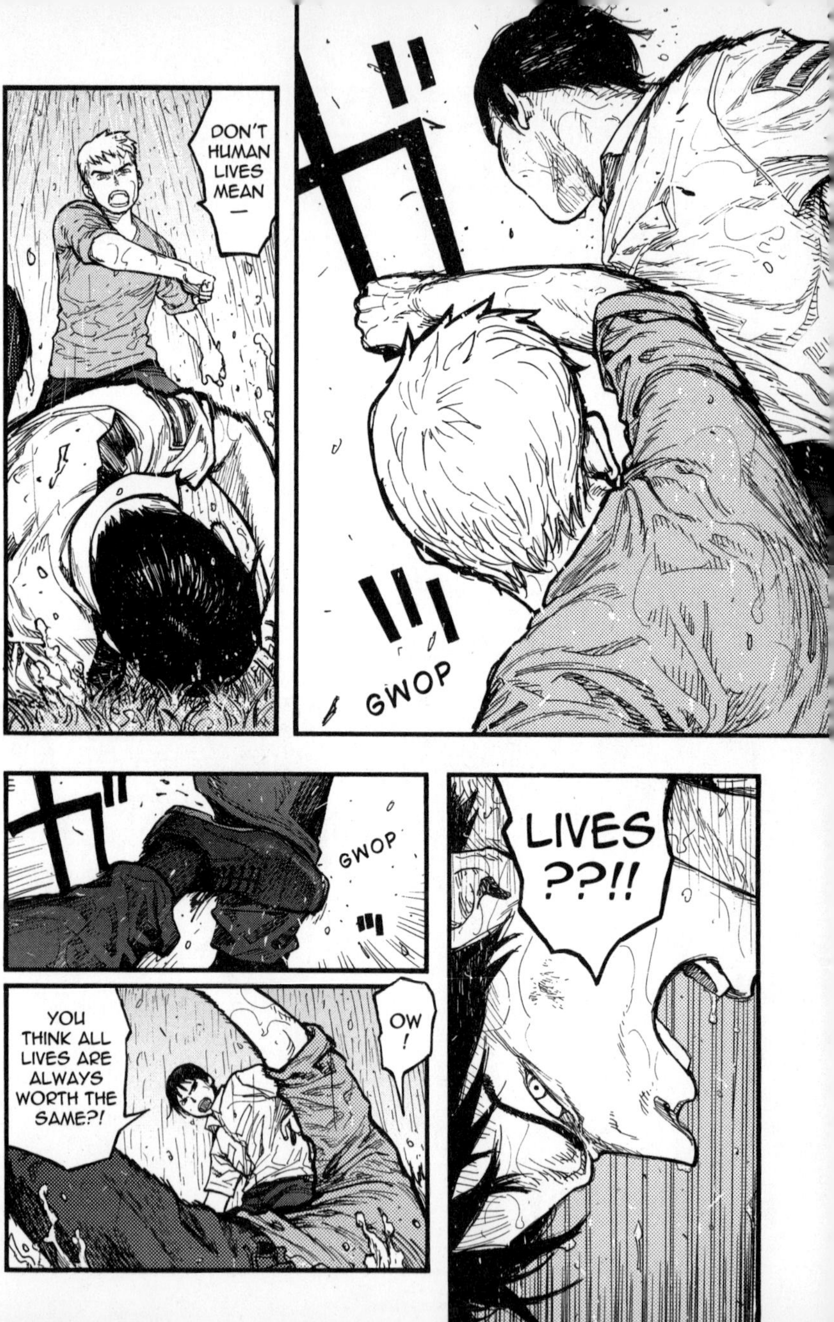
GWOP
DON'T HUMAN LIVES MEAN —
LIVES ??!!
GWOP
OW!
YOU THINK ALL LIVES ARE ALWAYS WORTH THE SAME?!

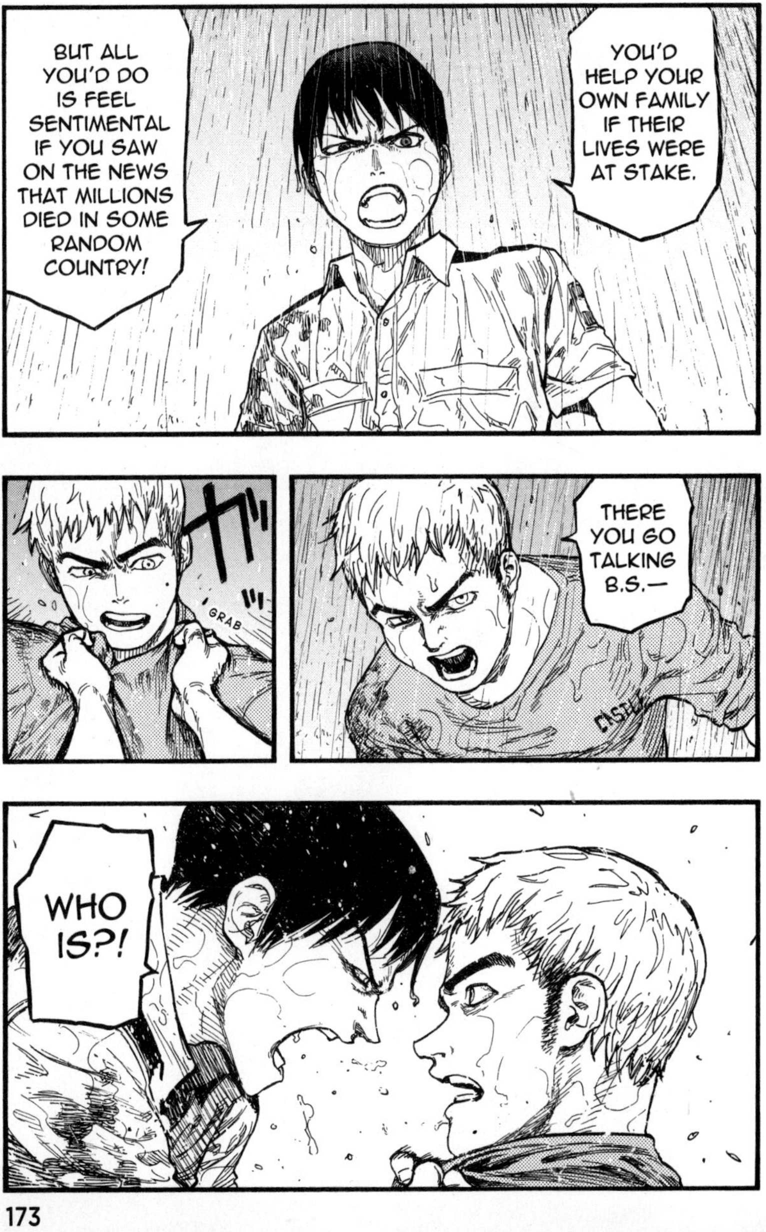
YOU'D HELP YOUR OWN FAMILY IF THEIR LIVES WERE AT STAKE.
BUT ALL YOU'D DO IS FEEL SENTIMENTAL IF YOU SAW ON THE NEWS THAT MILLIONS DIED IN SOME RANDOM COUNTRY!
THERE YOU GO TALKING B.S.—
GRAB
WHO IS?!

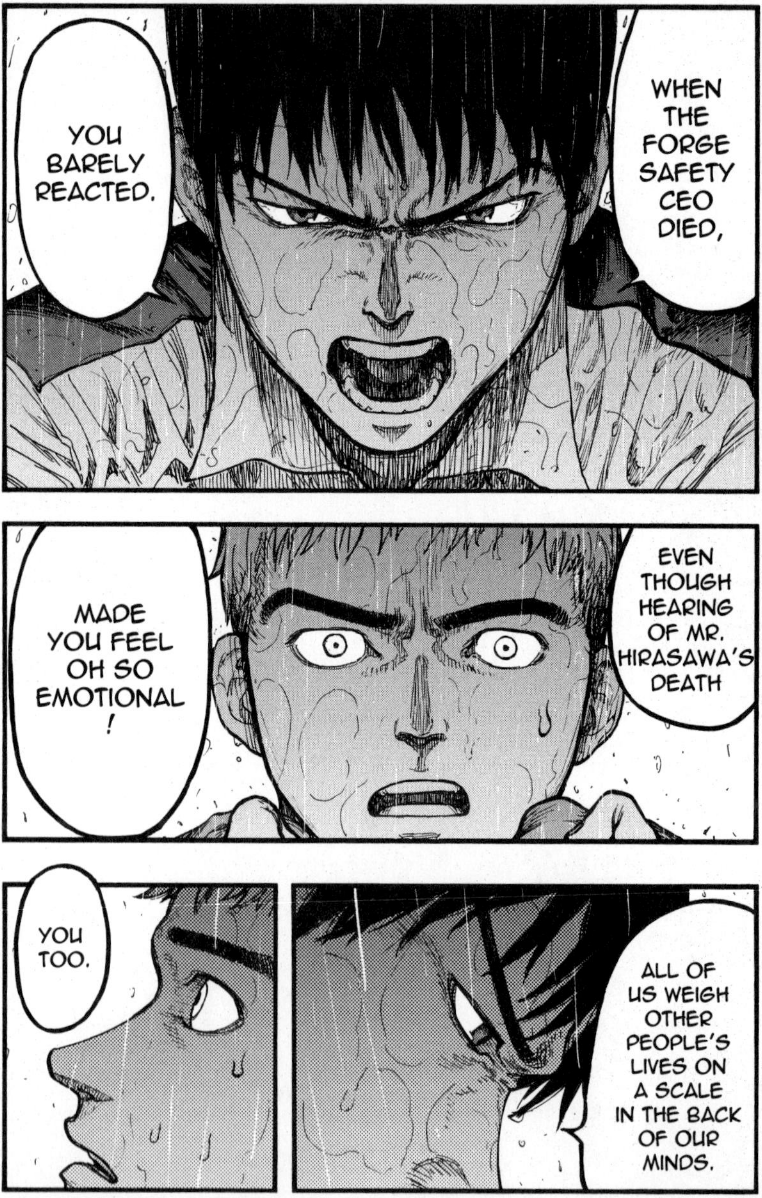
WHEN THE FORGE SAFETY CEO DIED,
YOU BARELY REACTED.
EVEN THOUGH HEARING OF MR. HIRASAWA'S DEATH
MADE YOU FEEL OH SO EMOTIONAL!
ALL OF US WEIGH OTHER PEOPLE'S LIVES ON A SCALE IN THE BACK OF OUR MINDS.
YOU TOO.

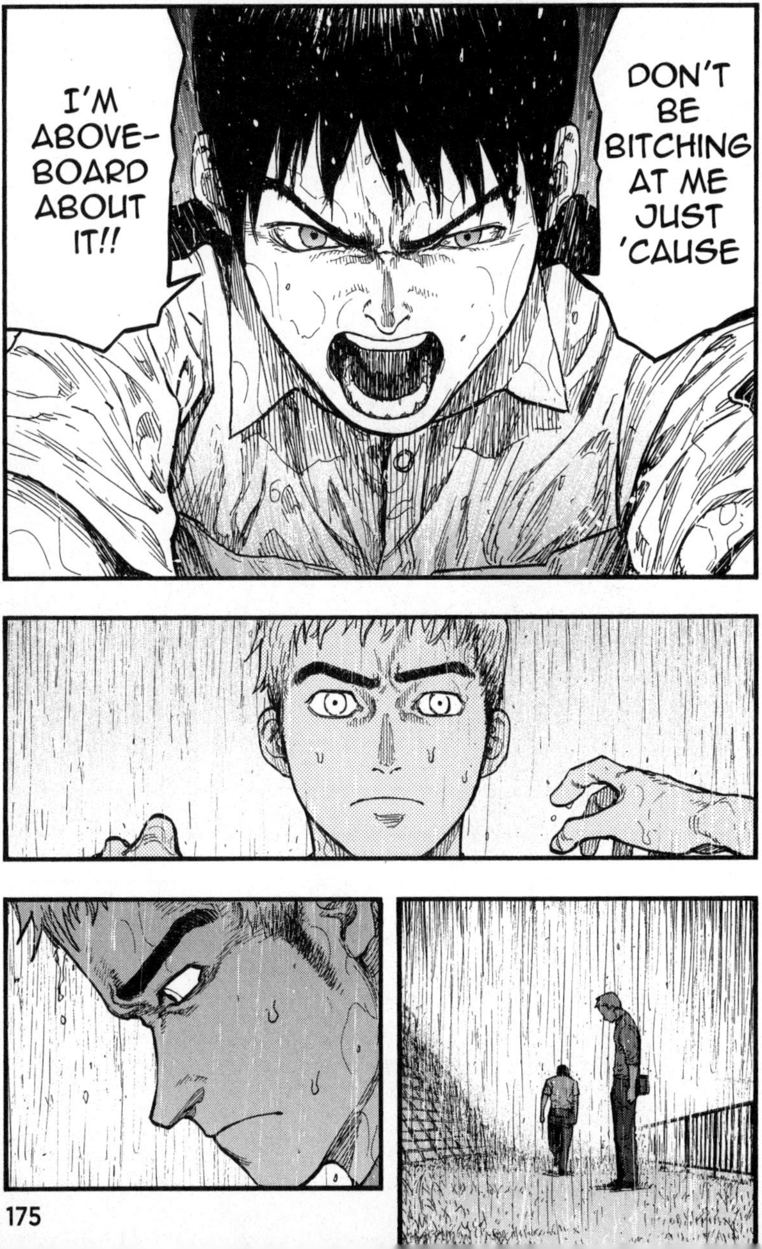
DON'T BE BITCHING AT ME JUST 'CAUSE
I'M ABOVE-BOARD ABOUT IT!!

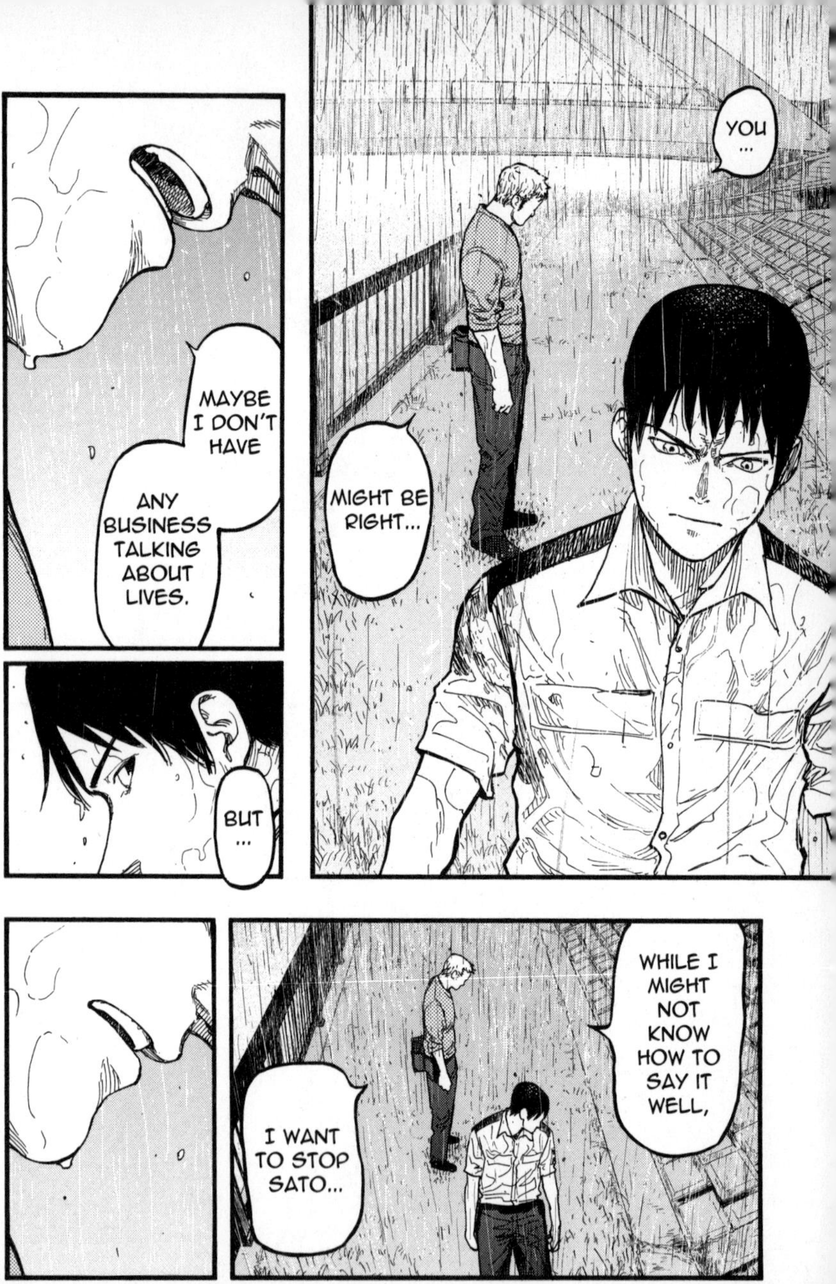
YOU ...
MIGHT BE RIGHT...
MAYBE I DON'T HAVE
ANY BUSINESS TALKING ABOUT LIVES.
BUT ...
WHILE I MIGHT NOT KNOW HOW TO SAY IT WELL,
I WANT TO STOP SATO...

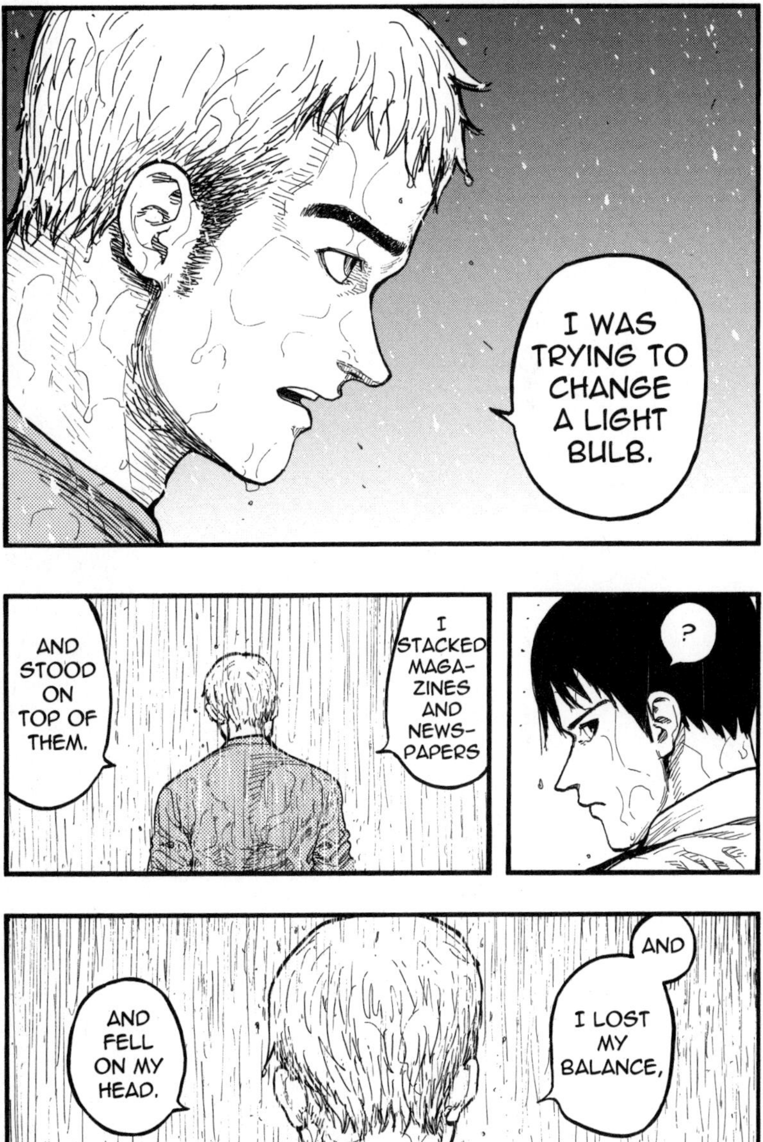
I WAS TRYING TO CHANGE A LIGHT BULB.
?
I STACKED MAGAZINES AND NEWSPAPERS
AND STOOD ON TOP OF THEM.
AND
I LOST MY BALANCE,
AND FELL ON MY HEAD.

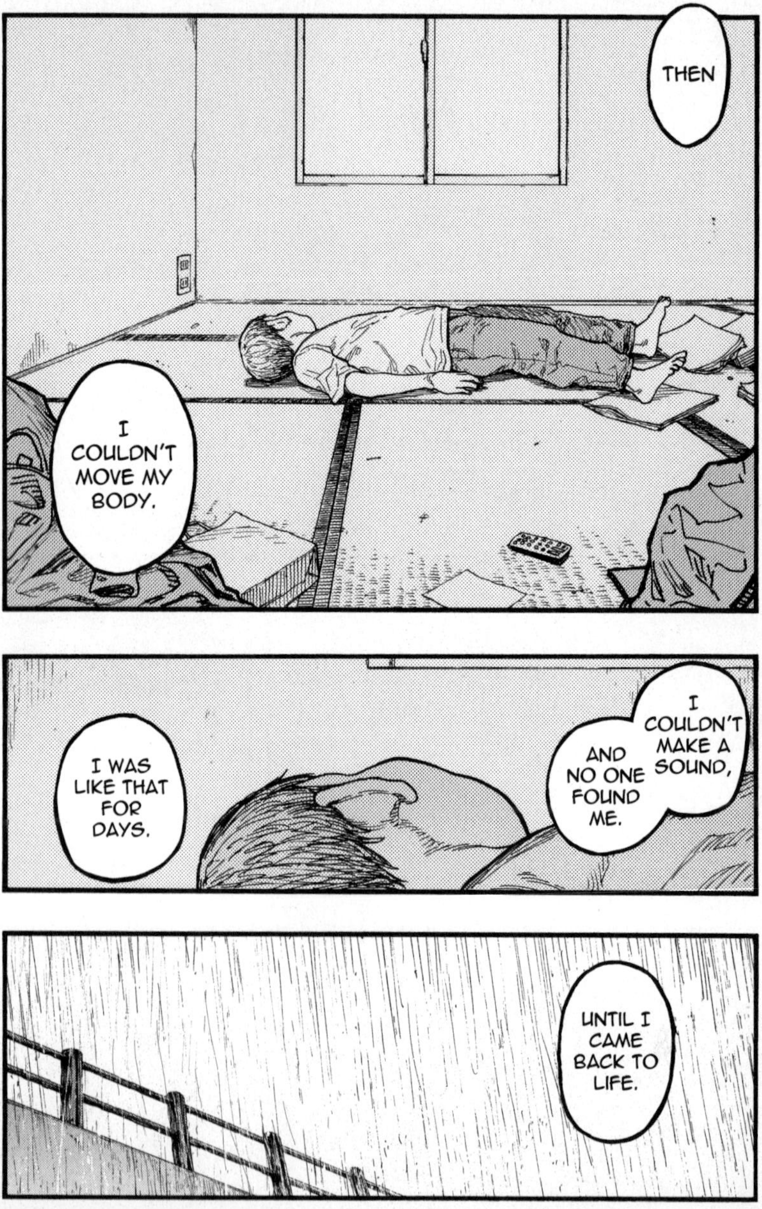
THEN
I COULDN'T MOVE MY BODY.
I COULDN'T MAKE A SOUND,
AND NO ONE FOUND ME.
I WAS LIKE THAT FOR DAYS.
UNTIL I CAME BACK TO LIFE.

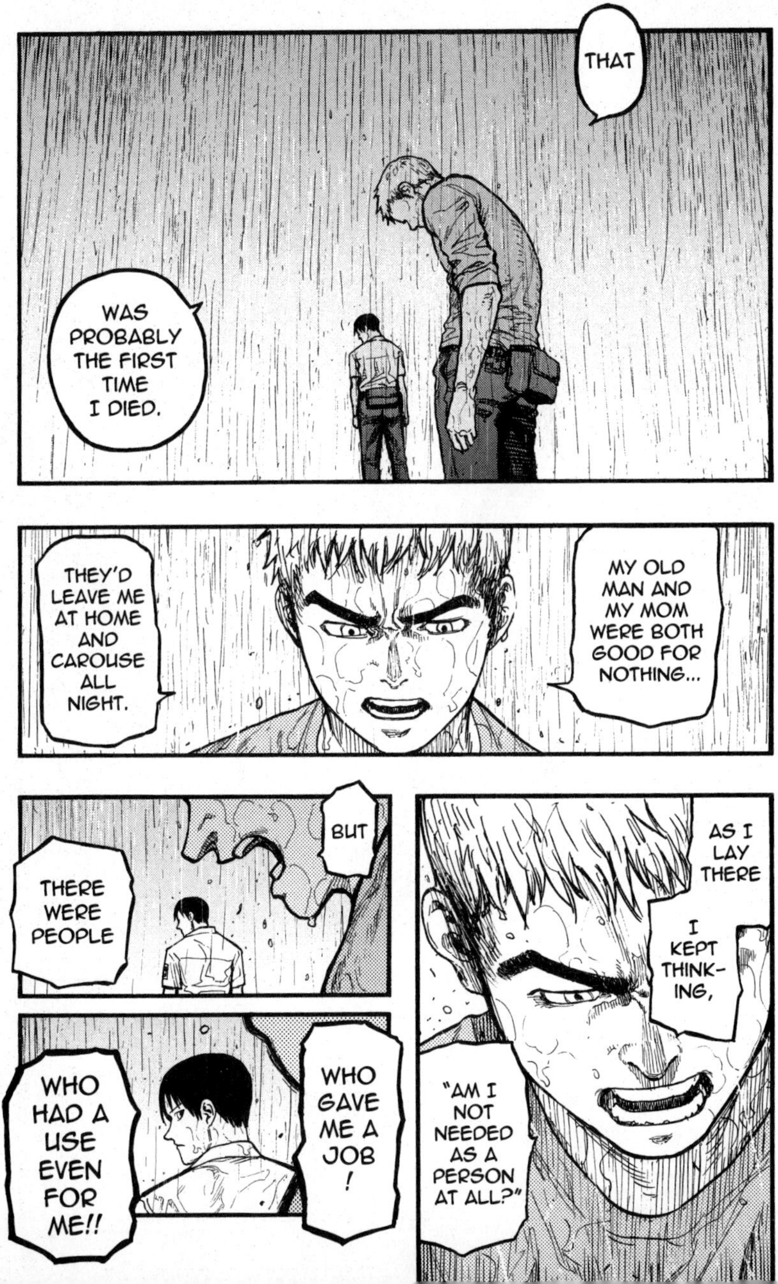
THAT
WAS PROBABLY THE FIRST TIME I DIED.
MY OLD MAN AND MY MOM WERE BOTH GOOD FOR NOTHING...
THEY'D LEAVE ME AT HOME AND CAROUSE ALL NIGHT.
AS I LAY THERE
I KEPT THINKING,
"AM I NOT NEEDED AS A PERSON AT ALL?"
BUT
THERE WERE PEOPLE
WHO GAVE ME A JOB!
WHO HAD A USE EVEN FOR ME!!

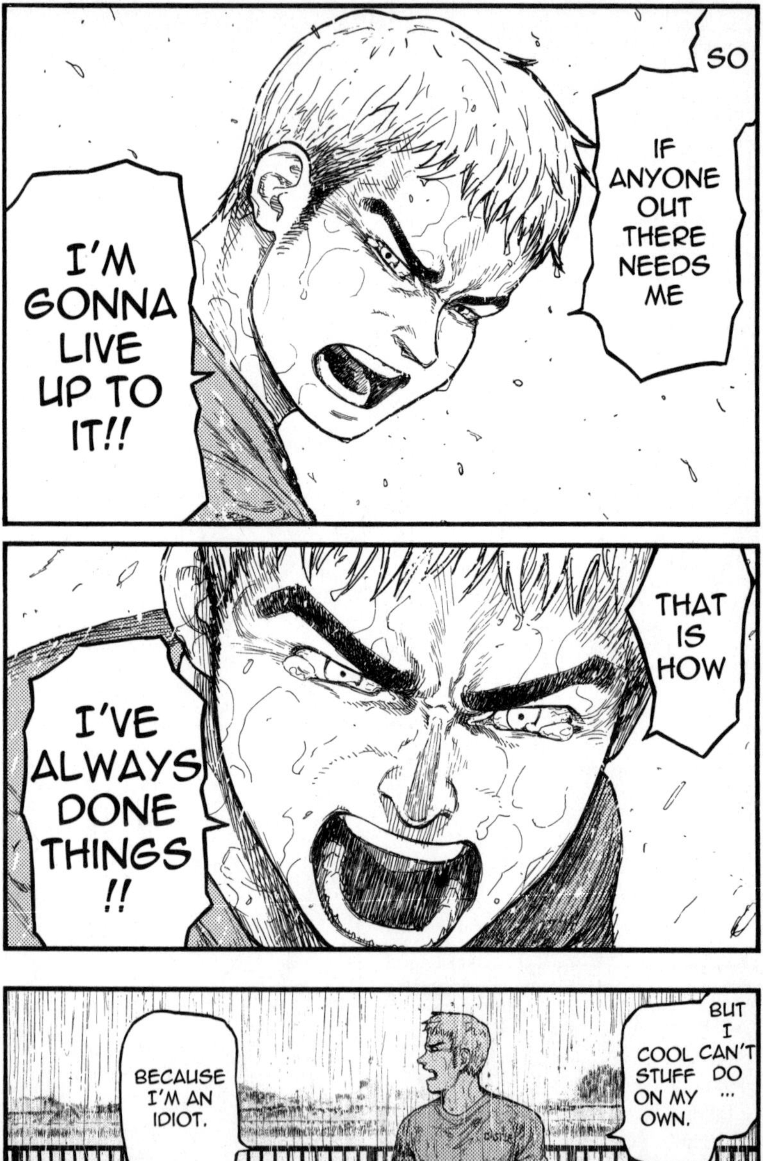
SO
IF ANYONE OUT THERE NEEDS ME
I'M GONNA LIVE UP TO IT!!
THAT IS HOW
I'VE ALWAYS DONE THINGS!!
BUT I CAN'T DO ... COOL STUFF ON MY OWN.
BECAUSE I'M AN IDIOT.

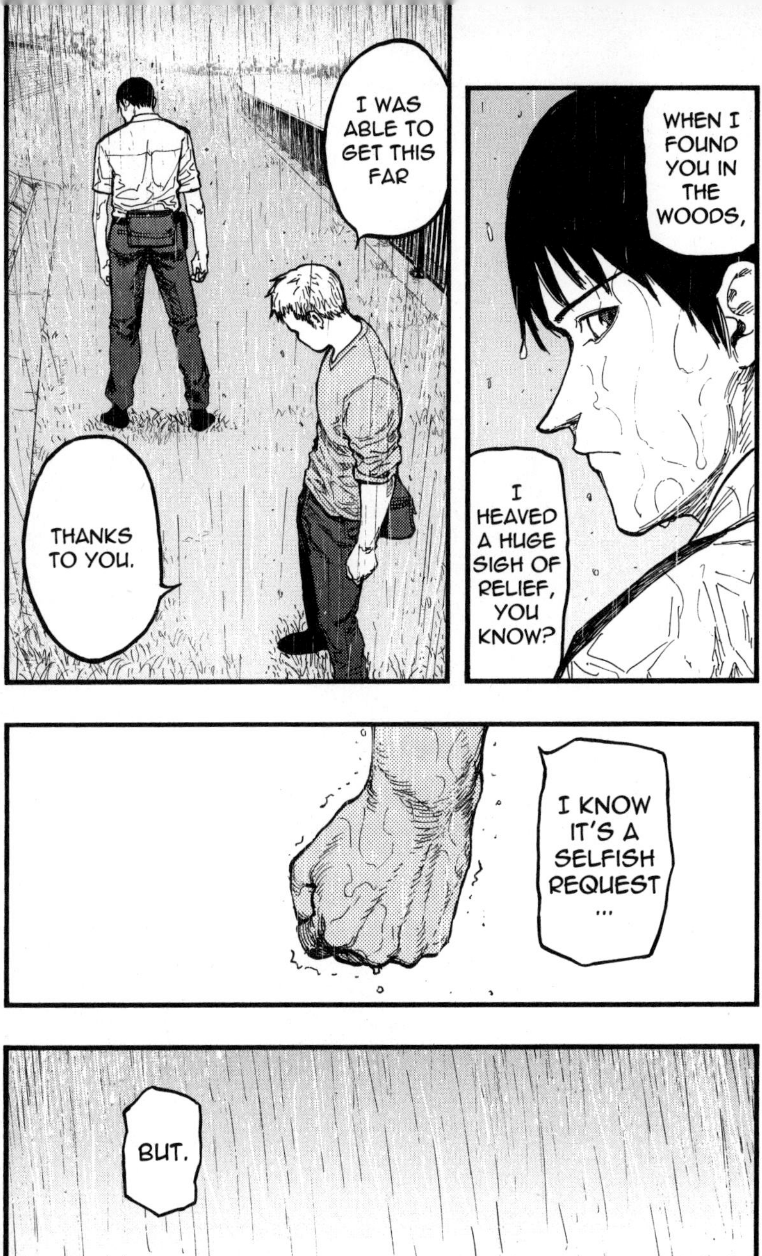
WHEN I FOUND YOU IN THE WOODS,
I HEAVED A HUGE SIGH OF RELIEF, YOU KNOW?
I WAS ABLE TO GET THIS FAR
THANKS TO YOU.
I KNOW IT'S A SELFISH REQUEST ...
BUT.

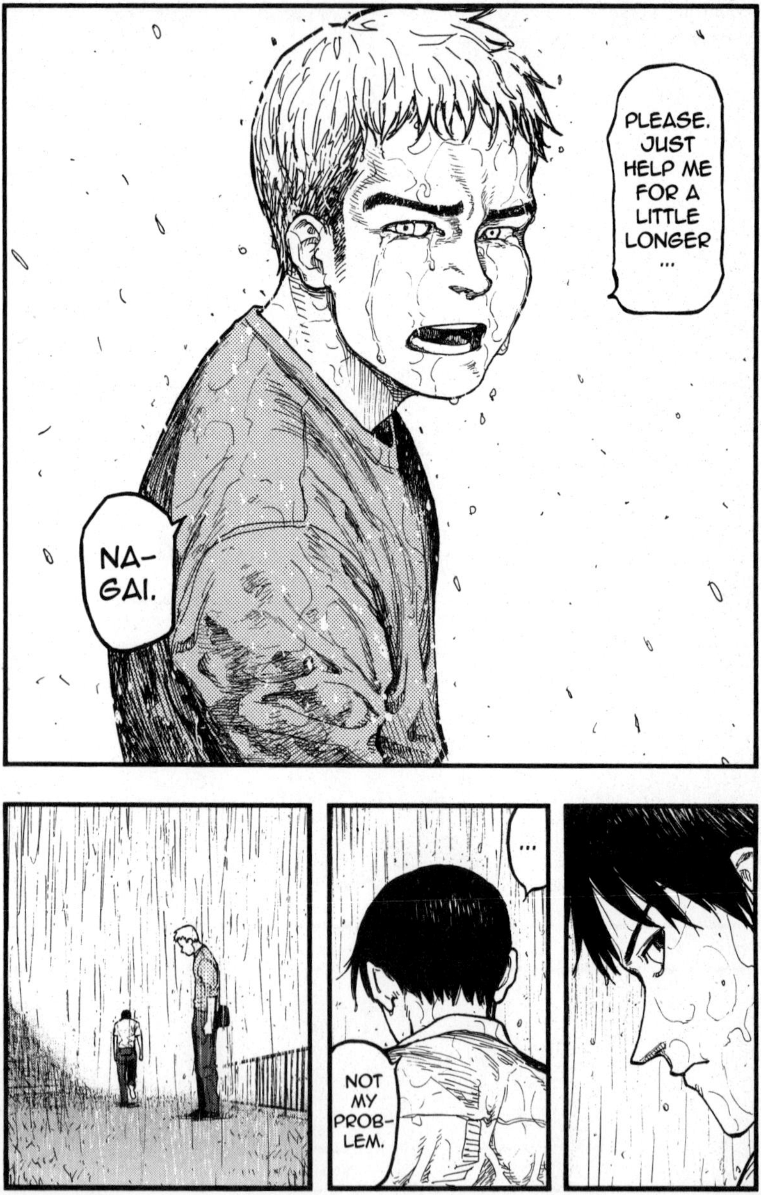
PLEASE. JUST HELP ME FOR A LITTLE LONGER ...
NA-GAI.
...
NOT MY PROB-LEM.

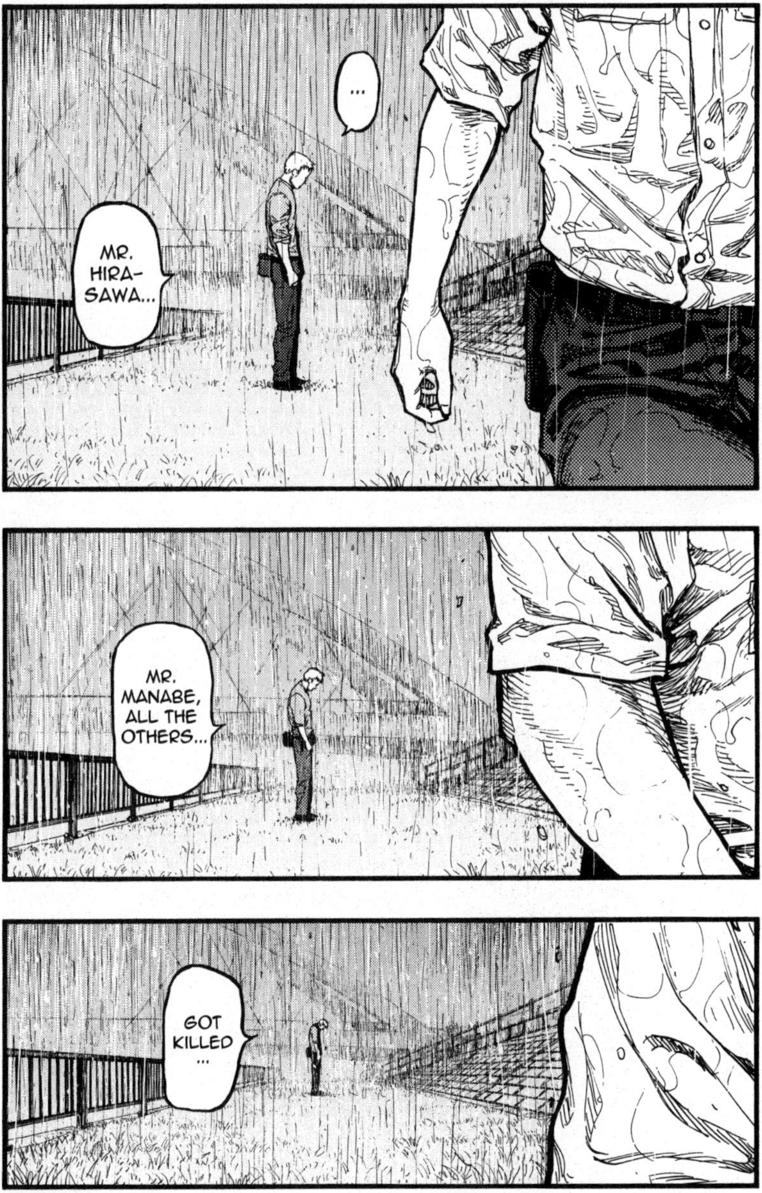
...
MR. HIRA-SAWA...
MR. MANABE, ALL THE OTHERS...
GOT KILLED ...

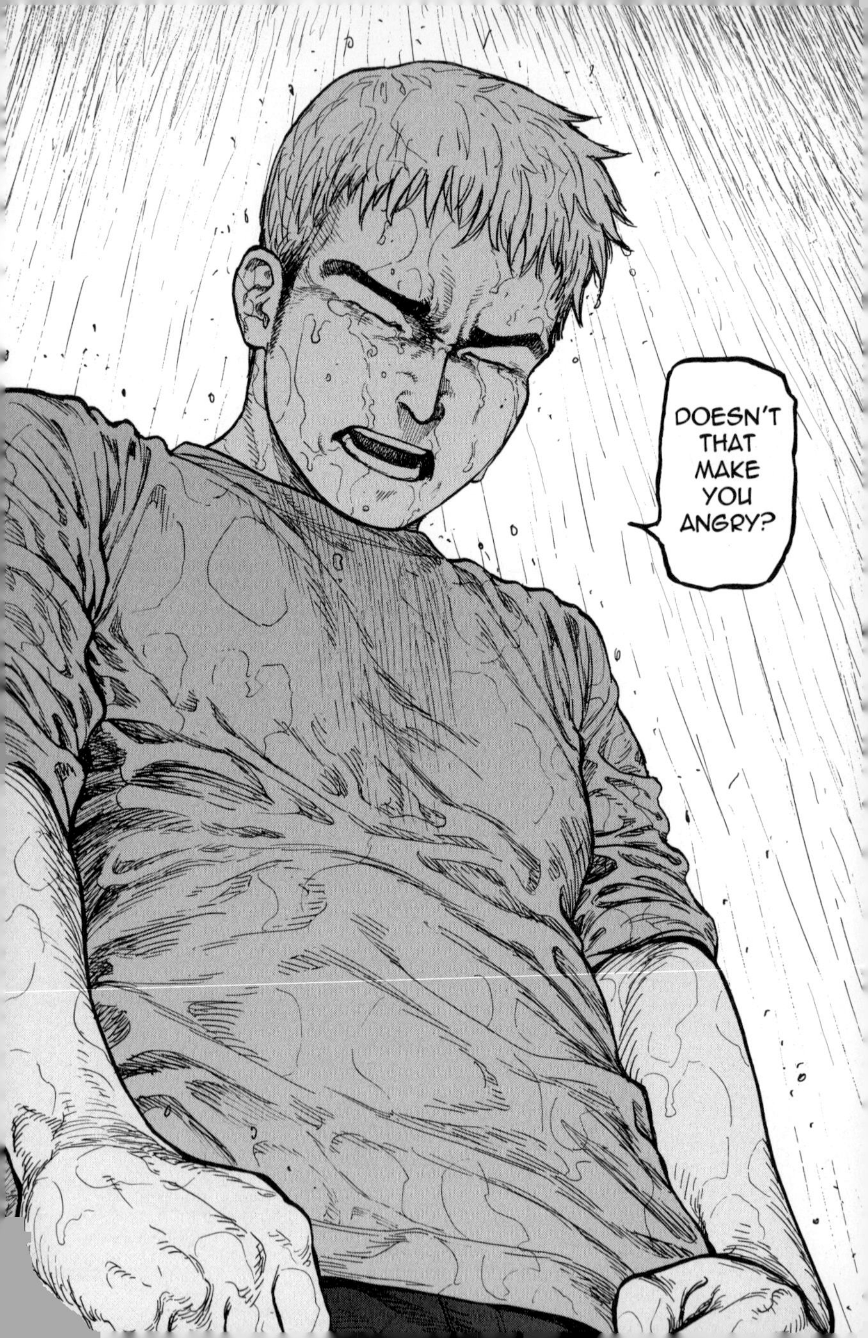
DOESN'T THAT MAKE YOU ANGRY?

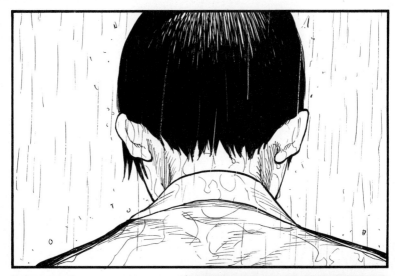

SHUT UP.

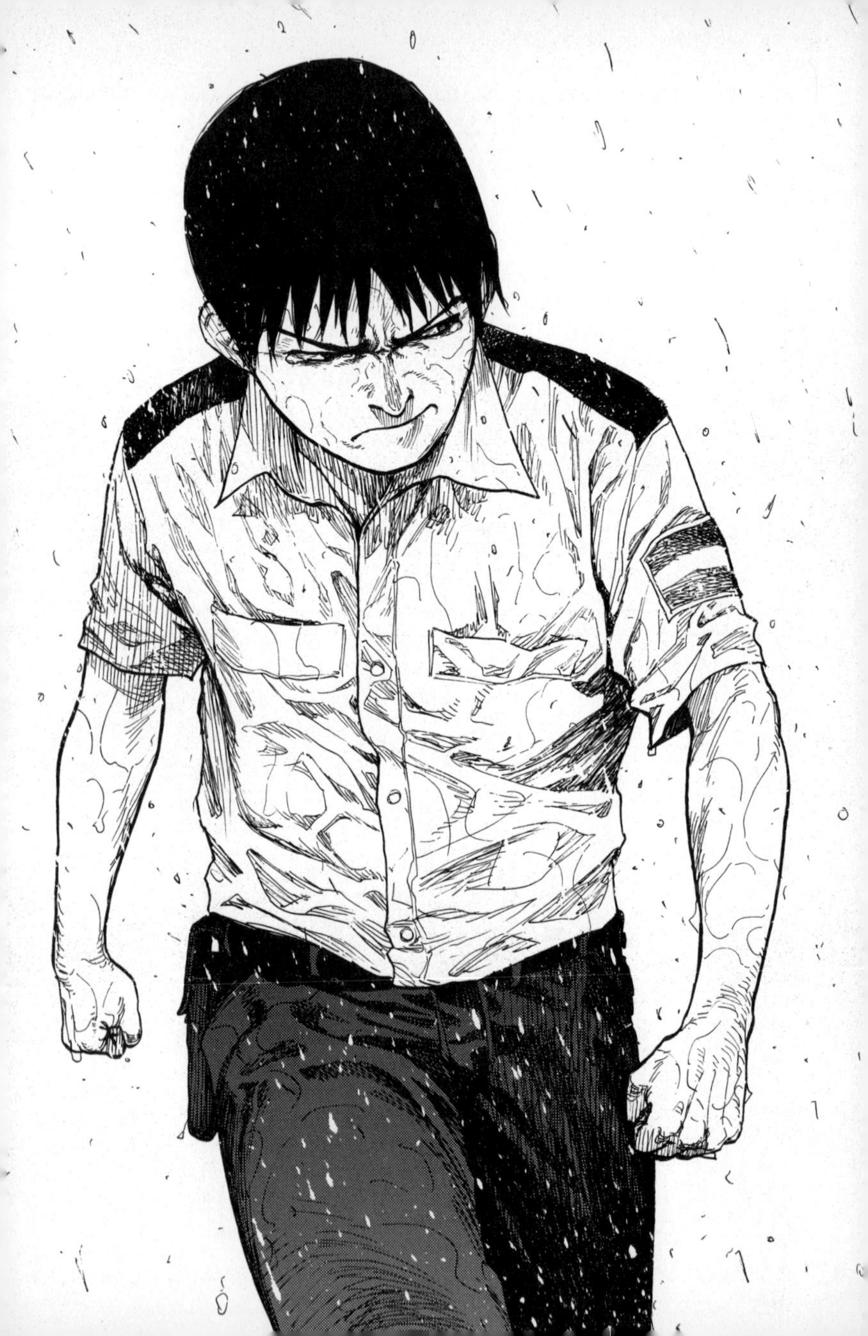

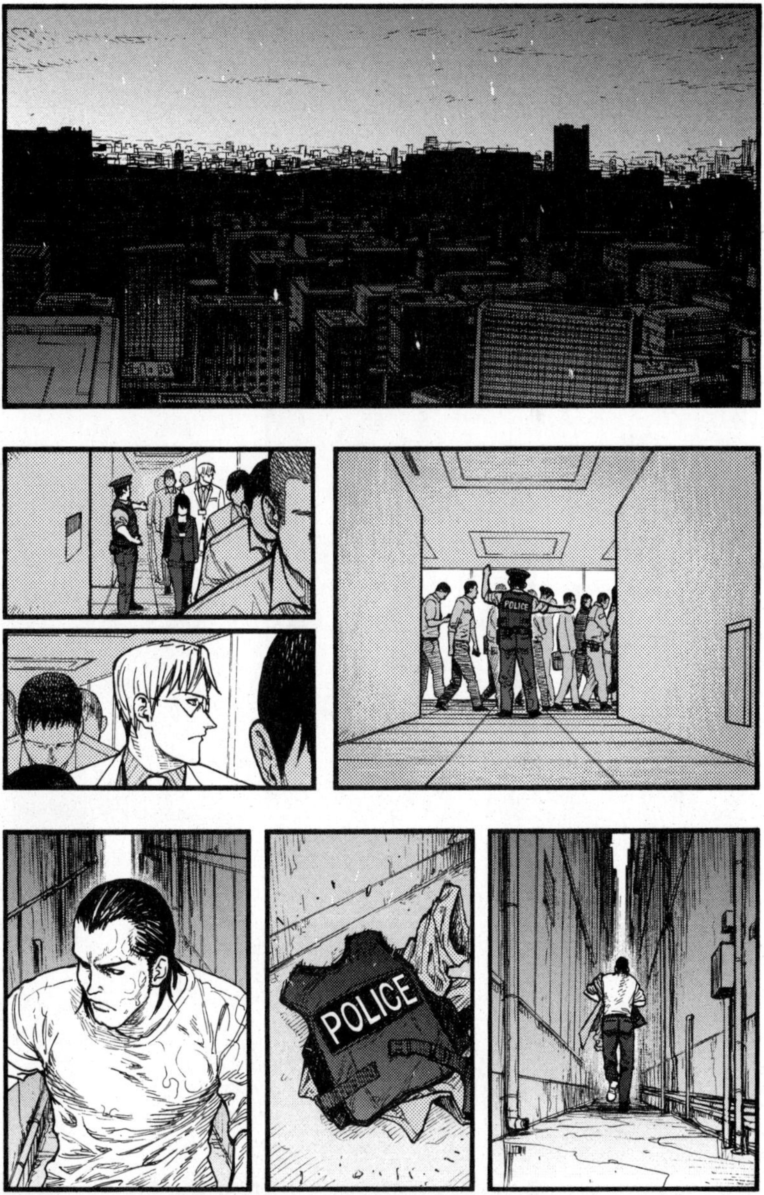
POLICE
POLICE

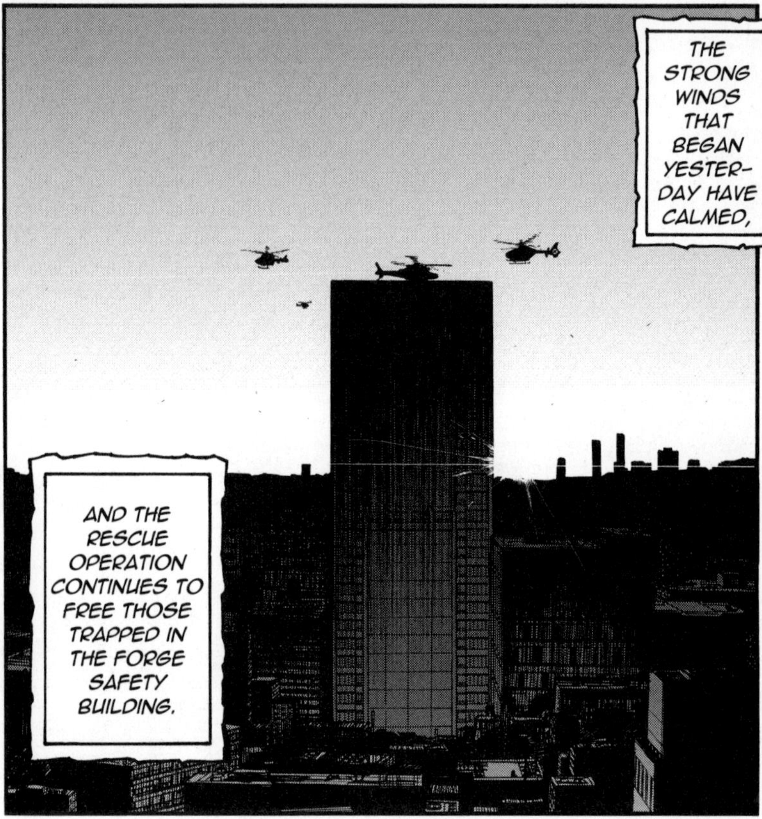
THE STRONG WINDS THAT BEGAN YESTER-DAY HAVE CALMED,
AND THE RESCUE OPERATION CONTINUES TO FREE THOSE TRAPPED IN THE FORGE SAFETY BUILDING.

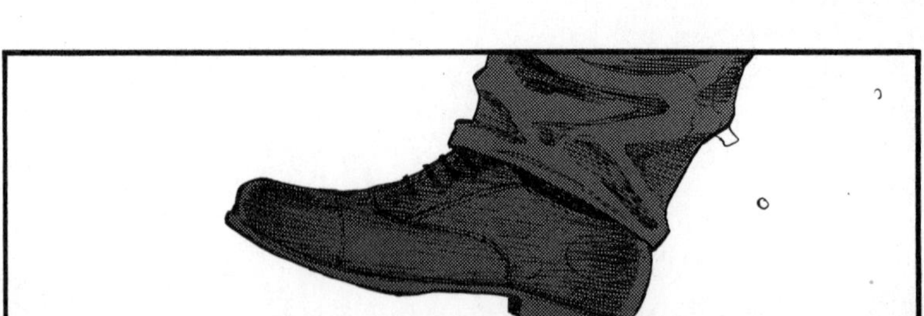

PHEW. TIME TO START A NEW LIFE.

NOT THAT I'M SURE IT COULD BE CALLED "A LIFE" ...

...

I PROBABLY WON'T EVER SEE ANYONE AGAIN.

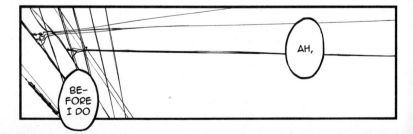

AH,

BE-FORE I DO

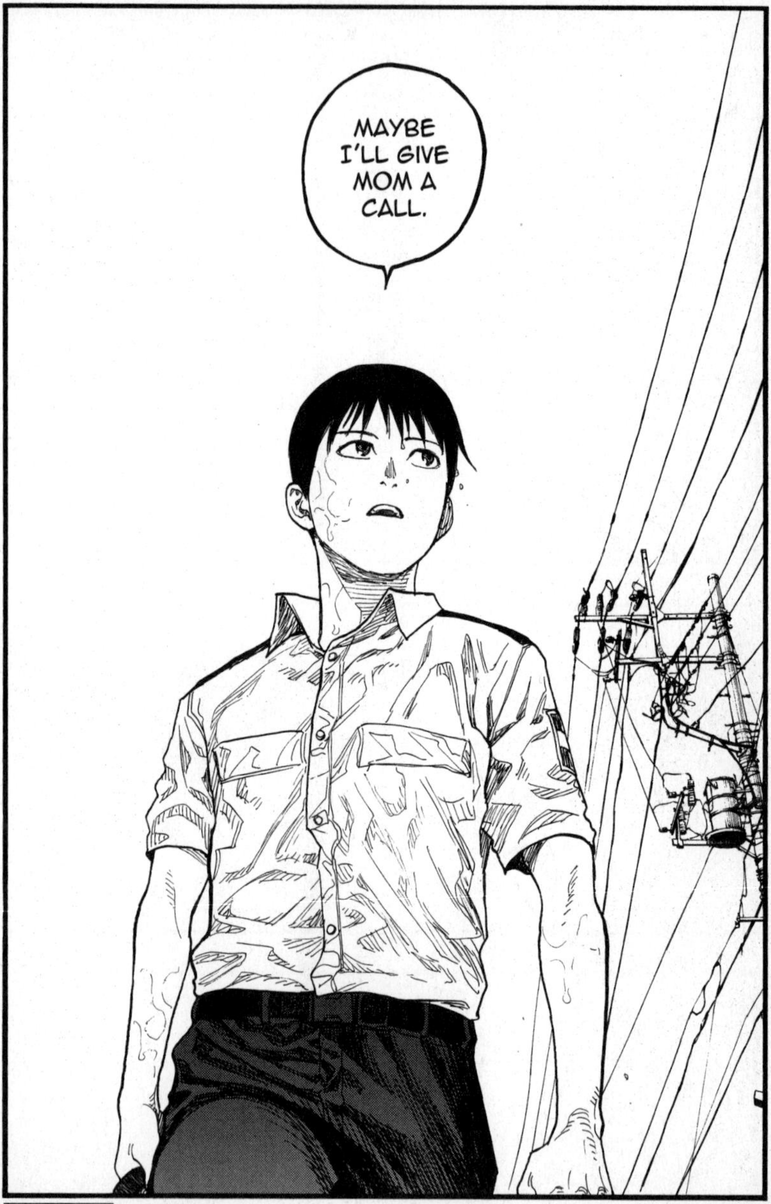
MAYBE I'LL GIVE MOM A CALL.

File:43 End

COMIC: GAMON SAKURAI

ASSISTANTS: CROUTON SANCHI (almost all tone range masking)

SAWANOSHOW (Line drawings

[File 39 "POLICE" logos: 62%] [File 39 police insignias: 54%] [File 39: p. 11, panel 3: fire extinguisher: 99%] [File 39: p. 20, panel 4: handcuffs: 90%]

[File 40 lights and AC: 78%] [File 40 fire extinguishers: 62%] [File 40: p. 41, panel 6: gun: 80%] [File 40: p. 47, panel 4: background: 99%] [File 40: p. 54, panel 2: background: 99%]

[File 41: p. 76, panels 2, 4, 5: cell: 99%] [File 41: p. 82, panels 1, 3: panic room: 88%] [File 41: p. 84, panel 1: lights and AC: 99%] [File 41: p. 86, panels 3, 4, 5: background: 90%]
[File 41: p. 87, panels 1, 2: background: 92%] [File 41: p. 90, panel 5: cell: 90%] [File 41: p. 91, panel 1: cell: 90%] [File 41: p. 93, panel 1, 2, 4: lights and AC: 100%]
[File 41: p. 94, panel 1: background: 100%] [File 41: p. 96, panel 4: "POLICE" logo: 100%] [File 41: p. 100, panel 3: lights and AC: 100%] [File 41: p. 101, panel 2: lights and AC: 100%]
[File 41: p. 104, panel 1: lights: 100%] [File 41: p. 106, panels 1, 3: mic, mouse: 99%] [File 41: p. 106, panel 2: lights: 100%] [File 41: p. 108, panels 3, 4: inside panel: 90%]
[File 41: p. 112, panel 4: inside panel: 82%]

[File 42: p. 117, panels 1, 2, 4: lawnmower: 90%] [File 42: p. 120, panel 4: lawnmower: 96%] [File 42: p. 121, panel 1: lights and AC: 100%]
[File 42: p. 128, panel 3: Forge Safety Bldg. except roof: 99%] [File 42: p. 130, panel 1: background except Forge Safety Bldg.: 90%]

[File 42: p. 138, panel 1: lawnmower: 71%] [File 42: p. 139, panel 1: lawnmower: 95%] [File 42: p. 143, panel 1: background except Forge Safety Bldg.: 95%]

[File 42: p. 143, panel 4: lawnmower: 95%] [File 42: p. 152, panel 3: Forge Safety Bldg.: 98%] [File 42: p. 153, panels 2, 3: Forge Safety Bldg. except roof: 98%]

[File 43: p. 162, panel 5: car: 95%] [File 43: p. 163, panels 2, 3: car: 99%] [File 43: p. 164, panel 1: Forge Safety Bldg.: 90%] [File 43: p. 164, panels 2, 3: background: 80%]
[File 43: p. 165, panels 1, 2: background: 90%] [File 43: p. 167, panels 1, 4: background: 94%] [File 43: p. 168, panel 3: background: 95%] [File 43: p. 170, panel 1: background: 95%]
[File 43: p. 176, panels 1, 4: background: 95%] [File 43: p. 180, panel 3: background: 95%] [File 43: p. 181, panel 2: background: 95%] [File 43: p. 185, panel 3: background: 95%]
[File 43: p. 188, panel 1: Forge Safety Bldg.: 80%])

KIMIYUKI MASAKI (Line drawings

[File 39: p. 5, panel 1: background: 95%] [File 39: p. 6, panels 2, 7: background: 98%] [File 39: p. 10, panel 1: gun: 100%] [File 39: p. 10, panel 4: background: 99%]
[File 39: p. 11, panel 1: gun: 90%] [File 39: p. 13, panel 4: background: 99%] [File 39: p. 19, panel 1: background: 99%] [File 39: p. 21, panels 2, 3: background: 91%]
[File 39: p. 22, panels 1, 2, 4, 5: background: 96%] [File 39: p. 23, panels 1, 2: background: 90%] [File 39: p. 24, panel 1: background: 92%]
[File 39: p. 25, panel 1: background: 96%] [File 39: p. 29, panel 1: background: 92%]

[File 40: p. 33, panel 5: gun: 80%] [File 40: p. 35, panel 1: background: 95%] [File 40: p. 36, panels 1, 4: gun: 94%] [File 40: p. 37, panel 1: background: 91%]
[File 40: p. 38, panels 1, 4: background: 97%] [File 40: p. 41, panel 3: background: 90%] [File 40: p. 42, panel 2: background: 85%] [File 40: p. 43, panel 3: gun: 95%]
[File 40: p. 44, panel 1: background: 80%] [File 40: p. 44, panel 3: gun: 90%] [File 40: p. 51, panel 1: background: 85%] [File 40: p. 52, panel 2: background: 42%]
[File 40: p. 54, panel 1: background: 99%] [File 40: p. 59, panel 1: background: 94%] [File 40: p. 68, panel 1: background: 95%] [File 40: p. 69, panels 1, 5: background: 92%]
[File 40: p. 72, panel 2: background: 95%]

[File 41: p. 77, panels 1, 2, 3: background: 99%] [File 41: p. 79, panel 1: background: 95%] [File 41: p. 80, panel 2: outside window: 98%] [File 41: p. 82, panel 2: gun: 95%]
[File 41: p. 84, panel 5: background: 97%] [File 41: p. 85, panel 4: outside window: 98%] [File 41: p. 92, panel 5: background: 100%] [File 41: p. 96, panels 1, 4: background: 99%]
[File 41: p. 98, panel 3: gun: 99%] [File 41: p. 100, panel 1: gun: 95%] [File 41: p. 102, panel 1: outside window: 99%] [File 41: p. 102, panels 2, 3: Kei's gun: 99%]
[File 41: p. 105, panel 1: gun: 99%] [File 41: p. 107, panel 1: gun: 100%]

[File 42: p. 124, panel 2: knife: 99%] [File 42: p. 125, panel 1: beer: 99%] [File 42: p. 126, panel 1: knife: 99%] [File 42: p. 128, panel 1: background: 95%]
[File 42: p. 137, panel 3: background except Forge Safety Bldg.: 93%] [File 42: p. 146, panel 1: background except Forge Safety Bldg.: 96%]
[File 42: p. 149, panel 2: background except Forge Safety Bldg.: 96%]

[File 43: p. 160, panel 1: broadcast truck: 85%] [File 43: p. 161, panel 3: inside panel: 96%] [File 43: p. 164, panels 2, 3: broadcast truck: 95%] [File 43: p. 165, panel 4: broadcast truck: 95%]
[File 43: p. 178, panels 1, 3: background: 81%] [File 43: p. 189, panels 1, 4: background: 96%] [File 43: p. 190, panel 1: background: 100%])

Ajin: Demi-Human, volume 9

Translation: Ko Ransom
Production: Risa Cho
           Hiroko Mizuno

© 2017 Gamon Sakurai. All rights reserved.
First published in Japan in 2016 by Kodansha, Ltd., Tokyo
Publication for this English edition arranged through Kodansha, Ltd., Tokyo

Published by Vertical, Inc., New York

Originally published in Japanese as *Ajin 9* by Kodansha, Ltd.
Ajin first serialized in *good! Afternoon*, Kodansha, Ltd., 2012·

This is a work of fiction.

ISBN: 978-1-945054-19-8

Manufactured in the United States of America

First Edition

Vertical, Inc.
451 Park Avenue South
7th Floor
New York, NY 10016
www.vertical-inc.com